MANAGERIAL ACCOUNTING

Dr. Risha Khandelwal

TAP

Toronto Academic Press

MANAGERIAL ACCOUNTING

Dr. Risha Khandelwal

Toronto Academic Press
4164 Lakeshore Road
Burlington ON L7L 1A4
Canada
www.tap-books.com

Email: orders@arclereducation.com

ISBN: 978-1-77956-277-7

ABOUT THE AUTHOR

Dr. Risha Khandelwal has expertise in finance and global business as an academician and researcher. She has been teaching and conducting research for more than six years. She has held positions at JECRC University in Jaipur and GL A University in Mathura. She received the UGC fellowship after passing the NET-JRF. She has written case studies, book chapters, and research papers that have been indexed by Google Scholar and SCOPUS. She is proficient in utilizing econometrics to analyze secondary data. She is currently a freelancer, helping academics with their research projects.

Table of Contents

List of Figures

PREFACE

Managerial accounting plays a crucial role in assisting managers in making informed decisions within an organization. It involves the process of identifying, measuring, analyzing, interpreting, and communicating financial information to aid in managerial decision-making. Unlike financial accounting, which focuses on external reporting, managerial accounting primarily serves internal users, such as managers and executives.

The field of managerial accounting has evolved significantly over the years, adapting to the changing business environment. It now encompasses various techniques and tools that enable managers to effectively plan, control, and evaluate the performance of their organizations. This book aims to provide a comprehensive understanding of these techniques and their applications.

One of the primary reasons individuals from different fields will benefit from this book is the integration of managerial accounting with other functional areas of business. For instance, individuals working in finance will gain insights into how managerial accounting techniques can aid in financial planning, budgeting, and performance evaluation. By understanding these concepts, finance professionals can enhance their ability to contribute to the overall success of an organization.

Similarly, individuals in marketing can leverage managerial accounting to analyze the profitability of different products, customer segments, and marketing campaigns. This knowledge will enable marketers to make data-driven decisions, ensuring the allocation of resources to the most profitable initiatives. Additionally, understanding managerial accounting will allow marketing professionals to collaborate effectively with finance teams, aligning their strategies with the financial objectives of the organization.

Operations professionals can also benefit greatly from understanding managerial accounting. By utilizing techniques such as cost-volume-profit analysis and variance analysis, operations managers can optimize resource allocation, improve efficiency, and control costs. This knowledge will enable them to make informed decisions regarding production levels, pricing, and process improvements, ultimately enhancing the overall operational performance.

Furthermore, individuals aspiring to become managers or entrepreneurs will find this book invaluable. It will equip them with the necessary skills to evaluate financial performance, develop budgets, and make strategic decisions based on financial data. Understanding managerial accounting will enable these individuals to effectively communicate with stakeholders, including investors, lenders, and board members, by presenting financial information in a clear and concise manner.

Beyond specific fields, this book will also benefit individuals seeking a holistic understanding of business operations. By comprehending managerial accounting concepts, readers will gain insights into the financial implications of various business decisions. This knowledge will facilitate a broader perspective on how different functional areas of a business interact and contribute to its overall success.

—Author

CHAPTER 1

Introduction to Managerial Accounting

LEARNING OBJECTIVES

After studying this chapter, you will be able to:

- Define managerial accounting;
- Understand the scope of managerial accounting;
- Differentiate between managerial accounting and financial accounting;
- Understand the role of managerial accounting in decision-making.

INTRODUCTORY EXAMPLE

As an example, let's examine a manufacturing company. This company produces solar panels, which are in high demand in the market. The management group has to choose between continuing to produce solar panels or focusing on creating a new product line.

To make an informed choice, the management group needs to assess the solar panel production department's financial performance. They have to find out if the department is profitable enough to cover its overhead and contribute to the overall success of the company. This is where managerial accounting comes in.

By looking through the financial statements of the solar panel production department, the management team can get additional insight into its performance. They are able to evaluate the department's revenue, costs, and profitability. They are able to identify any inefficiencies or areas in need of development. Making a decision regarding the production department's future requires consideration of this information.

Managerial accounting helps managers assess the overall financial performance of the company as well as the performance of individual departments. Managers can assess the company's overall profitability, liquidity, and solvency by carefully reviewing its financial accounts. They are able to identify any areas that need attention that involve financial risk or areas of concern.

Furthermore, managerial accounting provides managers with the means to foresee and project future events. Managers can forecast future financial performance with confidence by looking at past financial data and market trends. As a result, they are able to anticipate potential challenges and opportunities and modify their approach appropriately.

In summary, organizational decision-making depends on managerial accounting. It provides managers with the tools and information they need to evaluate the financial performance of their departments or divisions as well as the company as a whole. By looking at financial statements, managers can assess revenue, expenses, profitability, and identify areas for improvement. They are also able to evaluate the company's overall financial health and project its financial future. Ultimately, management accounting provides managers with the information they need to make decisions that will boost the success and profitability of the company.

UNIT INTRODUCTION

Managerial accounting refers to the process of collecting, analyzing, and interpreting financial information for internal use by managers in an organization. Its main objective is to provide accurate and timely information to support the processes of controlling, planning, and making decisions. Giving managers reliable and accurate information they can use to boost organizational performance and accomplish strategic goals is the main objective of managerial accounting. This includes budget preparation, performance reports, and financial analysis. Developing methods for cost allocation is a component of managerial accounting, in addition to recognizing and evaluating fixed and variable costs. All things considered, managerial accounting plays a critical role in supporting managers in an organization's smart decision-making and effective resource management (Skousen & Walther, 2012).

1.1. DEFINITION OF MANAGERIAL ACCOUNTING

The goal of managerial accounting, a subfield of accounting, is to support internal decision-making processes by giving managers and executives access to information. In order to assist managers in planning, directing, and assessing the success of their company, managerial accounting entails the analysis and interpretation of financial data. This covers performance evaluation, cost analysis, and budgeting. Managers need managerial accounting data to successfully allocate resources, establish objectives, and assess the performance of their business strategies (Edmonds, 2017).

Quick Fact

According to a survey by the Institute of Management Accountants, 82% of businesses use managerial accounting to help them make important business decisions. This statistic highlights how widely accepted and important the discipline is.

1.2. THE SCOPE OF MANAGERIAL ACCOUNTING

Learning Objectives

- To understand the scope of managerial accounting in cost analysis, budgeting, performance evaluation, and decision making.

A variety of tasks are included in the field of managerial accounting with the goal of providing managers within an organization with information. These responsibilities include obtaining, evaluating, interpreting, and disseminating non-financial and financial information. The main objective of managerial accounting is to support managers in making well-informed decisions that will benefit the company as a whole (Brewer, Garrison, & Noreen, 2022).

1. Cost Analysis: This involves determining the expenses related to producing goods or rendering services. Through cost analysis, managers can find areas where expenses can be reduced or eliminated, increasing an organization's profitability.
2. Budgeting: This involves creating an organization's financial plan, which includes projecting future earnings and outlays. By developing reasonable budgets, managers can effectively distribute resources and monitor performance in relation to these objectives.
3. Performance Evaluation: Comparing actual outcomes with anticipated or planned results is required for this. Managers can find areas of success and areas that need improvement by examining these variances. The organization can then use this information to set new goals and make necessary adjustments.
4. Decision Making: Frequently, managers must make decisions based on a thorough examination of both financial and non-financial data. By providing relevant information, managerial accounting enables managers to make informed decisions that align with the organization's goals and objectives.

All things considered; managerial accounting is extremely important in helping managers make decisions. By providing accurate and timely information, it helps managers drive the organization towards success (Garrison et al., 2010).

Did You Understand?

1. What is the definition of managerial accounting?
2. What are the main aspects of managerial accounting and how do they help managers make decisions?

Answer 1: Managerial accounting is a branch of accounting that focuses on providing information to internal users, such as managers and executives, to aid in decision-making processes. It involves analyzing and interpreting financial data to help managers make informed decisions about planning, controlling, and evaluating the performance of their business. This includes budgeting, cost analysis, and performance measurement. The information provided by managerial accounting is crucial for managers to effectively allocate resources, set goals, and evaluate the success of their business strategies.

Answer 2: The main aspects of managerial accounting are cost analysis, budgeting, performance evaluation, and decision making. Cost analysis involves determining expenses related to producing goods or rendering services, which helps managers identify areas where expenses can be reduced.

Budgeting involves creating a financial plan for the organization, allowing managers to allocate resources efficiently and track performance against goals.

Performance evaluation compares actual outcomes with anticipated results, helping managers identify areas of success and areas for improvement. Decision making often requires a thorough examination of financial and non-financial data, and managerial accounting provides relevant information to support informed decision making.

1.3. DIFFERENCES BETWEEN MANAGERIAL ACCOUNTING AND FINANCIAL ACCOUNTING

Learning Objectives

- The main objective of this section is to differentiate between managerial accounting and financial accounting in terms of systems, valuation, a focus on reporting, timing, aggregation, and efficiency.

Within an organization, there are two distinct accounting branches that serve different purposes: managerial accounting and financial accounting. Although they both entail the measurement, analysis, and reporting of financial information, their target audiences and areas of emphasis are different (Figure 1.1).

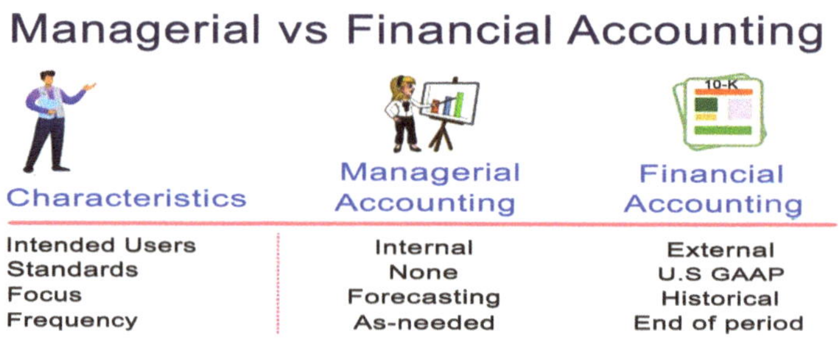

Figure 1.1. Difference between managerial and financial accounting.

Source: Difference between Managerial and Financial Accounting – Universal CPA Review (2022).

The following categories show how financial and managerial accounting differ from one another.

1. Systems: The main goal of managerial accounting is to support managers in making wise business decisions by offering internal information. In order to support planning, controlling, and decision-making processes, financial data must be gathered, analyzed, and interpreted. The information generated by

managerial accounting is not intended for external reporting, but rather for internal use by managers to evaluate performance, set goals, and allocate resources efficiently.

Conversely, the primary focus of financial accounting is to provide external financial information to various stakeholders, including creditors, investors, and regulatory bodies. To guarantee consistency and comparability of financial statements, it adheres to particular rules and guidelines, such as International Financial Reporting Standards (IFRS) or Generally Accepted Accounting Principles (GAAP). An organization's assets, liabilities, revenues, and expenses are all included in the financial performance and position report that financial accounting is meant to provide (Richardson, 2002).

Systems-wise, managerial accounting usually makes use of cost accounting systems, which concentrate on the distribution and management of expenses inside a company. These systems support managers in monitoring and evaluating expenses related to specific tasks, products, or departments. Managers can decide wisely about pricing, production, and resource allocation by knowing the cost behavior and cost drivers.

Financial accounting, on the other hand, follows accrual accounting systems, which record transactions when they occur, regardless of when the cash is received or paid. By ensuring that income and expenses are recorded in the time that they are earned or incurred, this system improves the accuracy of the financial performance of an organization.

2. Evaluation: According to Edmonds, (2017), valuation is one significant area in which these two branches differ. The process of determining how much an asset, liability, or business entity is worth is called valuation. Historical cost—that is, the initial expense incurred in acquiring an asset or incurring a liability—is the standard foundation for valuation in financial accounting. Because this method is based on verifiable transactions, it guarantees objectivity and dependability in financial reporting (Richardson, 2002).

However, managerial accounting gives greater flexibility to the methods used for valuation. In order to make well-informed decisions, managers are free to use alternative valuation techniques like market value or replacement cost. Managers can evaluate the current value of assets and liabilities, which may differ from their historical cost, thanks to this flexibility. By considering the current market conditions and economic factors, managers can make more accurate assessments of the value of their organization's resources.

Moreover, future-oriented valuation is a key component of managerial accounting. To project the future value of the organization's assets, liabilities, and overall financial performance, managers employ forecasting techniques and projections. This forward-looking approach helps managers in making strategic decisions, such as capital budgeting and investment analysis (Richardson, 2002).

The following categories show how financial and managerial accounting differ from one another (Brewer, Garrison, & Noreen, 2022).

3. A Focus on Reporting: There are also notable differences between the reporting focus of financial accounting and managerial accounting. Reports on managerial accounting are tailored to satisfy the unique requirements of internal

stakeholders. These reports are frequently more in-depth and contain non-financial data like staff performance, customer feedback, and production statistics. These reports are meant to support managers in their decision-making regarding the day-to-day operations of the company.

Financial accounting reports, on the other hand, have standardized formats that are prescribed by accounting standards. These reports are primarily concerned with providing a summary of the company's financial performance and position. The information presented in financial accounting reports is essential for external stakeholders to assess the company's financial health and make investment or lending decisions (Garrison et al., 2010).

4. Timing: When it comes to timing, management accounting places a strong emphasis on using current or real-time data to assist in decision-making. It offers current information that is important for making decisions about business, both now and in the future.

In contrast, financial accounting uses past data to create financial statements. These statements are prepared at the end of a reporting period, such as a month, quarter, or year, and provide a summary of a company's financial performance during that period.

5. Aggregation: When it comes to aggregation, managerial accounting concentrates on giving specific details about certain goods, departments, or projects within a company. It breaks down the financial data into smaller components to assist in decision-making at a more granular level. To calculate profitability, it might, for instance, offer cost details for every department or product line.

Contrarily, financial accounting gathers all of the financial information of an organization. It gathers information from all projects, departments, and products to provide a comprehensive picture of the company's financial situation and performance. This aggregated data is used by external users to evaluate the company's overall financial performance and health (Richardson, 2002).

6. Efficiency: In terms of efficiency, both managerial and financial accounting play crucial roles in ensuring the smooth functioning of an organization. However, managerial accounting is usually thought to be more effective at providing accurate and timely information for decision-making. Because it is customized to meet the specific needs of internal users, it can provide more precise and up-to-date information. This gives managers the ability to respond quickly to changing conditions and make well-informed decisions.

Keyword

Financial Statements – These are important documents that provide a snapshot of a company's financial health. They include the balance sheet, income statement, and cash flow statement.

Contrarily, financial accounting could be thought of as less effective in terms of timeliness and detail. Financial accounting reports may take longer to prepare and may not include the level of detail needed for daily decision-making because of the requirement for accuracy and compliance with GAAP. However, its focus on providing reliable and standardized information is essential for external stakeholders, such as investors and lenders, who rely on this information to assess the company's financial health and make investment decisions (Brewer, Garrison, & Noreen, 2022).

Did You Understand?

1. What are the main differences between managerial accounting and financial accounting?
2. How does managerial accounting differ from financial accounting in terms of valuation and reporting?

Answer 1: Managerial accounting focuses on providing internal information to assist managers in decision-making, while financial accounting provides external financial information to stakeholders. Managerial accounting uses cost accounting systems to track and analyze costs, while financial accounting follows accrual accounting systems to ensure accurate financial reporting. Managerial accounting allows for more flexibility in valuation methods, while financial accounting relies on historical cost. Managerial accounting reports are tailored to meet the specific needs of internal stakeholders, while financial accounting reports follow standardized formats. Managerial accounting emphasizes the use of real-time data, while financial accounting relies on historical data. Managerial accounting provides detailed information on individual products or departments, while financial accounting aggregates the financial data of the entire organization.

Answer 2: Managerial accounting allows for more flexibility in valuation methods, such as using market value or replacement cost, while financial accounting relies on historical cost. This flexibility enables managers to assess the current value of assets and liabilities. Managerial accounting also focuses on future-oriented valuation, using forecasting techniques and projections to estimate the future value of assets and liabilities. In terms of reporting, managerial accounting reports are tailored to meet the specific needs of internal stakeholders and include non-monetary information. Financial accounting reports follow standardized formats and provide a summary of the company's financial performance and position. Managerial accounting emphasizes the use of real-time data for decision-making, while financial accounting relies on historical data.

1.4. THE ROLE OF MANAGERIAL ACCOUNTING IN STRATEGIC DECISION MAKING

Learning Objectives

The main objective of this section is understanding the following roles of managerial accounting in strategic decision making:

- Analyzing business performance;
- Identifying long-term goals;
- Analyzing expenditure and controlling expenses;
- Providing managers with accurate and timely financial data;
- Assessing the financial viability of potential strategic decisions;
- Monitoring and controlling the implementation of strategic decisions;
- Providing non-financial information;
- Offering financial insights on trends.

Managerial accounting plays a crucial role in the process of strategic decision making within an organization. By providing relevant financial information, it assists managers in making informed decisions that align with the organization's goals and objectives.

1.4.1. Analyzing Business Performance

In order to determine the general health and success of a business, business performance analysis evaluates a variety of key performance indicators (KPIs). These key performance indicators (KPIs) can be financial metrics such as revenue, profit margins, and return on investment (ROI) or operational metrics such as market share, employee productivity, and customer satisfaction. By looking at these KPIs, businesses can find areas for improvement, gain a comprehensive understanding of their strengths and weaknesses, and make well-informed decisions to support growth and profitability.

One of the key benefits of business performance analysis is its ability to provide a clear picture of a company's financial health. Financial KPIs like revenue and profit margins help organizations assess their financial health and identify any potential problems. For example, if a company's profit margins are consistently declining, pricing or cost management issues may need to be addressed. By spotting these issues early on, businesses can take corrective action to improve their financial performance and ensure long-term success. Analyzing operational KPIs is equally important for strategic decision-making as financial metrics. One important indicator of how well a company is meeting customer expectations is customer satisfaction. Through consistent monitoring and evaluation of customer satisfaction metrics, companies can pinpoint their strengths and areas for development. This information can then be used to develop strategies to enhance customer experience, increase customer loyalty, and ultimately drive revenue growth (Skousen & Walther, 2012).

Keyword

Profit Margins – These refer to the percentage of profit a company makes on each sale. It is a measure of how efficiently a company is managing its costs and pricing its products or services.

Another operational measure that has a big influence on how well a business performs is employee productivity. Businesses can find possible process bottlenecks or inefficiencies by examining employee productivity levels. Businesses that want to increase productivity, optimize workflow, and streamline operations should consider using this analysis. In addition, businesses can inspire their staff and foster a positive work environment, which will boost productivity and overall business success, by keeping an eye on and rewarding high-performing employees.

Market share analysis is yet another crucial aspect of business performance analysis. Businesses can assess opportunities for expansion as well as understand their place in the market by analyzing market share. For instance, a business may need to make investments in marketing and sales tactics to raise brand awareness and market penetration if its market share is small in comparison to that of its rivals. Conversely, a business with a high market share might need to concentrate on client retention and loyalty initiatives in order to hold onto its position (Brewer, Garrison, & Noreen, 2022).

1.4.2. Identifying Long-Term Goals

Managerial accounting is essential for giving managers in an organization relevant financial information. Making decisions based on this information is crucial if you want to eventually help achieve your long-term objectives. Making strategic decisions requires weighing the possible effects of various options and analyzing a variety of factors. By utilizing managerial accounting techniques, managers can assess the financial implications of their decisions and align them with the organization's long-term goals.

Financial statements are one tool that managerial accounting uses to help with long-term goal identification. These financial statements give a thorough picture of the assets, liabilities, and equity of an organization. Managers can identify areas that need improvement and obtain important insights into the organization's financial health by examining these statements. Managers can look into the underlying causes and take proactive measures to address a problem, such as if a company's income statement shows declining profits (Figure 1.2).

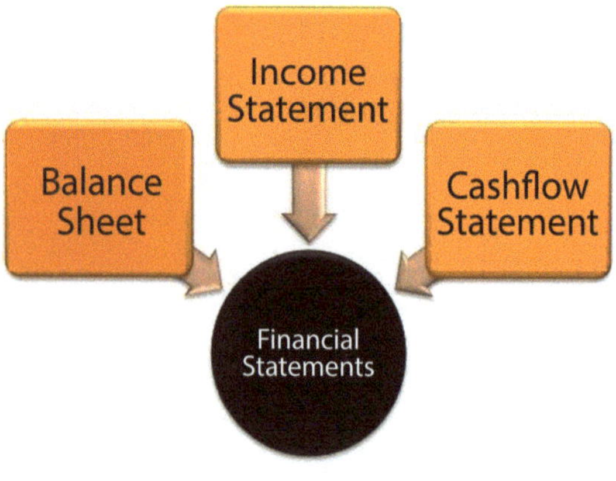

Figure 1.2. Examples of financial statements.

Source: Colibri (2023).

Furthermore, managerial accounting involves the use of cost analysis techniques. Managers can identify the most economical strategy for accomplishing their long-term objectives with the aid of cost analysis. Managers can minimize expenses and maximize profitability by making well-informed decisions based on the costs associated with various options. For example, managers can use cost analysis to assess each product's potential profitability and identify which ones fit with the organization's long-term goals if the company is thinking about growing its product line.

Another essential component of managerial accounting that helps with long-term goal identification is budgeting. A budget is a financial plan that outlines an organization's anticipated income and expenses for a given time frame. Managers can effectively allocate resources and prioritize initiatives that lead to long-term goals by developing a budget. For example, if a company's long-term goal is to increase market share, managers can allocate a larger portion of the budget to marketing and sales activities.

In addition to financial statements, cost analysis, and budgeting, managerial accounting also involves forecasting. Using past data and present trends, forecasting enables managers to project future financial results. Managers can find opportunities and risks that could affect the organization's long-term objectives by examining this data. Managers can use forecasting techniques, for example, to anticipate changes in consumer demand and modify their strategies if a company operates in a highly competitive market.

1.4.3. Analyzing Expenditure and Controlling Expenses

Analyzing expenses in-depth means looking closely at what a company spends. Finding areas where costs can be optimized or decreased is made easier with the help of this analysis. By closely examining expenses, managers can make well-informed decisions and obtain insights into cost drivers that will increase profitability (Garrison et al., 2010). Effective cost control is a prerequisite for efficient financial management. It means monitoring and controlling spending to ensure that it aligns with the organization's strategic objectives. By implementing cost control measures, managers can prevent overspending and identify areas where costs can be decreased without compromising output or quality.

Accurate financial data is essential for making strategic decisions. Managers need to evaluate options' financial implications before making decisions. Through cost analysis and control, managers can make strategic decisions that align with the organization's goals.

To analyze spending effectively, managers must first categorize expenses into different categories. Thanks to this classification, they are able to identify expenses such as direct labor and material costs that are directly related to the production of goods or services. Like overhead, indirect costs must also be considered. By categorizing expenses, managers can comprehend the cost structure of the company and make informed decisions (Garrison et al., 2010).

Managers can analyze costs using a variety of tools and techniques after they have been classified. For example, cost-volume-profit (CVP) analysis can be used to find the breakeven point, or the amount of sales needed to cover all costs. By understanding the breakeven point, managers can assess the financial implications of different sales volumes and determine the profitability of specific products or services.

An additional helpful tool for expenditure analysis is variance analysis. It ascertains the reasons behind any discrepancies between projected and actual expenses. By using this analysis to determine the reasons behind cost variations and put corrective measures in place, managers can effectively control expenses.

Managers must take the initiative to control spending. One doable tactic is to set up a budgeting system. Budgets serve as financial road maps for managers, assisting them in allocating resources and monitoring expenses. By establishing clear financial targets and regularly comparing actual performance against budgeted figures, managers can spot areas of concern and take appropriate action to control expenses.

Putting cost-cutting measures into practice is another method of managing spending. This entails figuring out how to reduce or eliminate wasteful expenditures. For instance, managers can lower purchasing costs by negotiating better deals with suppliers or lower utility costs by putting energy-saving measures in place. By constantly seeking cost-saving opportunities, managers can improve the organization's financial performance (Brewer, Garrison, & Noreen, 2022).

1.4.4. Providing Managers with Accurate and Timely Financial Data

One of the main objectives of managerial accounting is to provide managers with accurate financial data. This entails gathering and examining financial data from multiple sources, including:

- Cost reports;
- Budgets;
- The company's financial statements.

By ensuring the accuracy of this data, managers can rely on it to make informed decisions. For instance, accurate financial data is essential in determining the costs and revenues related to a given product line if a manager wishes to ascertain the profitability of that particular product line.

Keyword

Financial Viability – It is a crucial aspect of any business. It refers to the ability of a company or organization to sustain its operations and generate profits over the long term.

Timeliness is another essential element of managerial accounting. Managers need to get financial information as soon as possible so they can make informed decisions. In today's dynamic business environment, delays in acquiring financial data can hinder decision-making and adversely impact an organization's overall performance. Therefore, it is the duty of managerial accountants to ensure that financial data is collected, processed, and reported on time. This can be achieved by utilizing advanced accounting software and systems that automate the collection and processing of financial data.

Managerial accounting not only offers precise and timely financial data, but also pertinent financial data for decision-making. Managers need information that is specific to their needs and goals. For example, a marketing manager may require financial data regarding the expenses and income of the different campaigns in order to evaluate each campaign's effectiveness. Managerial accounting provides managers with the relevant financial information they require to make choices that align with the company's overarching business plan.

Managerial accounting assists managers with the interpretation and analysis of financial data in addition to delivering precise and timely financial data. The organization's financial performance might not be fully understood from financial data alone. Managers need to look through this data to find trends, patterns, and potential areas for improvement. By comparing the financial performance of different departments, managers can identify areas where savings or new sources of revenue can be generated. By interpreting financial data to make well-informed decisions, managers can positively impact the company's overall success.

1.4.5. Assessing the Financial Viability of Potential Strategic Decisions

Managers need to consider the possible financial ramifications of their strategic decisions. This means analyzing the benefits and drawbacks of each option to determine whether the prospective gains outweigh the initial outlay. The techniques and tools required to carry out this analysis successfully are provided by managerial accounting.

One such tool is the cost-volume-profit (CVP) analysis. Using CVP analysis, managers can gain a better understanding of how changes in costs, volume, and selling prices will impact the company's profitability. Managers can find the breakeven point—the amount of sales required to cover all costs—by using this analysis. This data is crucial for assessing the financial viability of prospective strategic choices. If a decision requires a significant increase in sales to cover costs, managers are able to evaluate whether it is realistic and feasible.

Analyzing relevant costs is a crucial component of determining financial viability. In managerial accounting, costs are classified as relevant or irrelevant. While irrelevant costs won't change regardless of the outcome, relevant costs will change in response to a decision. By focusing on relevant costs, managers can make more accurate assessments of the financial impact of a decision. This facilitates their ability to make decisions that align with the strategic objectives of the company.

In addition to relevant cost analysis and CVP analysis, managerial accounting provides tools for budgeting and forecasting. Setting financial objectives and allocating resources to meet them are both parts of budgeting. By creating a budget, managers can assess a strategic decision's financial viability and ensure that it is in line with the organization's overall financial objectives. Conversely, forecasting is the process of estimating future economic results using historical data and market trends. This enables managers to foresee potential risks and opportunities related to their strategic decisions.

Facts Sheet

According to a report by the Association for Financial Professionals, 75% of organizations consider budgeting and forecasting as the most important managerial accounting functions. This highlights the integral role that these activities play in planning and decision-making processes.

Furthermore, managerial accounting provides performance measurement tools that help assess the financial impact of strategic decisions. The company's performance is monitored and evaluated using key performance indicators (KPIs) in relation to predefined objectives. Managers can ascertain whether strategic choices lead to the intended financial outcomes by monitoring key performance indicators (KPIs). This data is essential for making changes and making sure the business stays on course to meet its financial goals.

1.4.6. Monitoring and Controlling the Implementation of Strategic Decisions

One of the key areas that managerial accounting is crucial is the monitoring and control of the strategic decision-making process. These decisions are made by the top management and have an impact on the distribution of resources, the establishment of goals, and the creation of plans of action.

Monitoring the decision-making process's development and making sure the intended results are being realized are important aspects of monitoring the implementation of strategic decisions. This requires the application of a number of managerial accounting techniques, such as variance analysis, budgeting, and performance measurement. Budgeting includes creating a financial plan that outlines the expected revenue, outlays, and costs associated with implementing the strategic decision. Variance analysis is used to identify any differences between the actual and budgeted financial results, and any necessary corrective action is then implemented. In order to determine whether a strategic decision was effective, performance measurement entails comparing the organization's performance to predefined goals and benchmarks (Brewer, Garrison, & Noreen, 2022).

To ensure that strategic decisions are implemented appropriately and that the intended results are achieved, corrective action is required. Tools from managerial accounting, such as profitability analysis, cost-volume-profit analysis, and cost analysis, must be used for this. Cost analysis involves cost allocation and identification in order to determine the organization's cost structure and pinpoint inefficient areas. Determining price, production levels, and sales strategies all benefit from an understanding of the relationship between costs, volume, and profit. The application of cost-volume-profit analysis is used to achieve this. Analyzing profitability entails comparing the profitability of various goods, services, or company divisions in order to pinpoint problem areas and choose how best to deploy resources.

1.4.7. Providing Non-Financial Information

The provision of non-financial information is one of the primary characteristics of managerial accounting. A vast array of data that is not directly tied to monetary values but is nevertheless highly relevant for decision-making is included in the category of non-financial information. This includes information about:

- Customer satisfaction;
- Employee productivity;
- Market trends;
- Environmental impact, among others.

By analyzing and presenting this non-financial information, managerial accounting assists managers in making well-informed decisions that align with the organization's strategic goals.

Non-financial data offers a comprehensive picture of the organization's performance, making it especially important for strategic decision-making. Financial data does not always give the whole picture, even though it can reveal information about the organization's profitability and financial health. This void is filled by non-financial data, which provides a more comprehensive view of the organization's activities.

For example, consider a manufacturing company that is experiencing a decline in sales. If the business only looks at financial data, it can conclude that cutting expenses is the best course of action. But by taking into account non-financial data, like market research and customer feedback, the business might find that the drop in sales is actually the result of a drop in product quality. The strategic choice in this instance would be to enhance product quality as opposed to concentrating only on cost cutting.

Monitoring the success of strategic decisions and identifying areas for improvement are two more uses for non-financial data. Managers can spot trends, patterns, and problem areas by examining non-financial data that may not be obvious from looking at financial data alone. To assess the effectiveness of a new customer service initiative, for example, a retail company might monitor customer satisfaction scores. If the scores show a significant improvement, it indicates that the strategic decision to enhance customer service has been effective. However, if the scores drop or stay the same, it indicates that the strategic choice needs to be reevaluated and adjusted.

Non-financial data also helps assess the organization's environmental and social impact. In today's business landscape, organizations are increasingly expected to operate responsibly and sustainably. Managers can evaluate the performance of the company in relation to non-financial metrics like waste management, community involvement, and carbon emissions. This information is crucial for making strategic decisions that align with sustainability goals and meet the expectations of stakeholders (Edmonds, 2017).

1.4.8. Offering Financial Insights on Trends

One of the primary functions of managerial accounting is to provide financial information that helps managers identify trends and patterns within the organization. Managers can identify areas that need attention or improvement and obtain a deeper understanding of the company's performance by analyzing financial data. Managers can determine which goods and services are performing well and which are not, for example, by looking at sales data. This information can then be used to allocate resources effectively and make informed decisions about product development, marketing strategies, or cost-cutting measures.

Moreover, forecasting and budgeting heavily rely on managerial accounting. Managers can forecast future trends and create accurate financial projections by examining past financial data. Planning for upcoming investments, like expanding operations or introducing new products, is especially crucial. Managers can make well-informed decisions about resource allocation and guarantee that the company's financial resources are being used optimally by utilizing the financial insights offered by managerial accounting.

Cost analysis is a key component of managerial accounting. Managers can find inefficiencies in the organization and put cost-cutting measures in place by examining the expenses related to different activities and processes. Managers may find, for instance, that some manufacturing processes are excessively costly and can be streamlined or outsourced to cut costs by performing a thorough cost analysis. Managers can use this information to make well-informed decisions about strategies for cutting costs and raise the company's overall profitability.

Managerial accounting helps with evaluations of performance in addition to financial insights. Managers can determine what needs to be improved and evaluate how well their decisions are working by comparing actual performance to predefined goals and targets. Managers can ensure that the organization is on track to meet its goals by making necessary adjustments and taking corrective action through this evaluation process (Skousen & Walther, 2012).

Quick Fact

A study conducted by the American Accounting Association found that organizations using performance evaluation systems based on managerial accounting principles experienced a 15% increase in productivity compared to those without such systems. This underscores the importance of using managerial accounting techniques to evaluate and improve organizational performance.

Did You Understand?

Question: How does managerial accounting support strategic planning?

Answer: Managerial accounting supports strategic planning by providing managers with relevant financial information and analysis. This information helps in identifying opportunities and threats, evaluating the feasibility of strategic initiatives, and assessing the financial impact of different options. By understanding the costs and benefits associated with various strategic choices, managers can make informed decisions that maximize the organization's profitability and long-term success. Managerial accounting also aids in resource allocation, as it helps managers determine the optimal allocation of resources to different strategic initiatives.

A CASE STUDY

ZARA: ON MANAGERIAL ACCOUNTING

- Introduction:

This case study focuses on Zara, a renowned fashion retailer known for its fast-fashion business model. Zara's success can be attributed to its effective use of managerial accounting techniques, which allow the company to make informed decisions and maintain a competitive advantage in the industry. This study will explore how Zara utilizes managerial accounting to drive its business operations and achieve its strategic objectives.

- Key Concepts of Managerial Accounting:

Managerial accounting involves the collection, analysis, and interpretation of financial information to assist managers in making informed decisions. It differs from financial accounting, which primarily focuses on reporting financial information to external stakeholders. Managerial accounting provides internal stakeholders, such as managers and executives, with the necessary information to guide the organization's day-to-day operations and long-term planning.

- Zara's Use of Managerial Accounting:

Zara's success lies in its ability to quickly respond to changing fashion trends and deliver new products to its stores within a short period. To achieve this, Zara relies on its efficient supply chain management, which is supported by its use of managerial accounting techniques.

- **Cost Management:** Zara effectively manages its costs by closely monitoring its production processes. The company keeps a tight control over its inventory levels, ensuring that it produces only what is needed. This reduces the risk of excess inventory and minimizes storage costs. Zara also adopts a just-in-time manufacturing approach, where it produces goods based on customer demand, further reducing inventory costs.
- **Budgeting and Planning:** Zara utilizes budgeting and planning techniques to set targets and allocate resources effectively. The company sets sales and production targets based on market demand and its own strategic objectives. By closely monitoring its budget performance, Zara can identify and address any deviations from its plans promptly.
- **Performance Measurement:** Zara uses performance measurement tools, such as key performance indicators (KPIs), to evaluate its operational and financial performance. These KPIs include metrics like sales growth, inventory turnover, and return on investment. By regularly monitoring these indicators, Zara can identify areas for improvement and take corrective actions accordingly.

- **Decision-Making:** Zara's use of managerial accounting techniques enables the company to make data-driven decisions. For example, when deciding whether to introduce a new product line, Zara conducts a cost-benefit analysis to assess its potential profitability. This analysis considers factors such as production costs, expected sales, and market trends, allowing Zara to make informed decisions that align with its overall business strategy.
- Conclusion:

Zara's success can be attributed to its effective use of managerial accounting techniques. By closely managing costs, setting targets through budgeting and planning, measuring performance, and making data-driven decisions, Zara maintains a competitive advantage in the fast-fashion industry. This case study highlights the importance of managerial accounting in driving business success and provides valuable insights for other organizations aiming to achieve similar results.

SUMMARY

Chapter 1 introduces managerial accounting as a crucial branch of accounting that collects, analyzes, and interprets financial information for internal use by managers in an organization. It focuses on providing accurate and reliable data to aid in decision-making, planning, and controlling activities. Key aspects of managerial accounting include cost analysis, budgeting, and performance evaluation. By analyzing these variances, managers can identify areas of success and areas for improvement, enabling them to make adjustments and set new goals.

Managerial accounting is often considered more efficient in terms of providing timely and relevant information for decision-making. It is a vital tool in strategic decision making, providing managers with financial information to make informed decisions that align with the organization's goals and objectives. It involves analyzing business performance, identifying long-term goals, and controlling expenses. Business performance analysis involves evaluating key performance indicators (KPIs) such as revenue, profit margins, and return on investment (ROI). Operational KPIs like customer satisfaction, employee productivity, and market share also play a crucial role in identifying areas for improvement.

Managerial accounting is also essential for understanding and controlling expenses within an organization. It categorizes costs into direct and indirect costs using tools like cost-volume-profit (CVP) analysis and variance analysis. A proactive approach to expense control involves implementing budgeting systems and cost reduction strategies. Accurate and timely financial data is essential for managers to make informed decisions.

Managerial accounting is also crucial for organizations to evaluate their social and environmental impact, make strategic decisions, and identify trends. It helps managers allocate resources effectively, make informed decisions about product development, marketing strategies, and cost-cutting measures. Cost analysis helps identify inefficiencies and implement cost-saving measures, while performance evaluation assesses the effectiveness of decision-making and areas for improvement.

MULTIPLE CHOICE QUESTIONS

1. **What is the primary purpose of managerial accounting?**
   a. To provide financial information to external stakeholders
   b. To assist managers in decision-making and resource management
   c. To prepare budgets and performance reports
   d. To identify and evaluate costs
2. **Which of the following is NOT a function of managerial accounting?**
   a. Preparing budgets
   b. Identifying and evaluating costs

c. Providing financial information to external stakeholders
d. Analyzing and interpreting financial data

3. **What is the difference between managerial accounting and financial accounting?**
   a. Managerial accounting focuses on internal use by managers, while financial accounting is for external reporting.
   b. Managerial accounting focuses on historical data, while financial accounting focuses on future projections.
   c. Managerial accounting uses cost accounting systems, while financial accounting uses accrual accounting systems.
   d. Managerial accounting provides detailed information, while financial accounting provides summarized information.
4. **What is one benefit of business performance analysis?**
   a. Assessing financial stability
   b. Evaluating market share
   c. Monitoring employee productivity
   d. All of the above
5. **How does managerial accounting assist in identifying long-term goals?**
   a. By analyzing financial statements
   b. Through cost analysis techniques
   c. By creating budgets
   d. All of the above
6. **What is the purpose of analyzing expenditures in an organization?**
   a. To identify areas where expenses can be reduced or optimized
   b. To increase profitability by making informed decisions
   c. To understand the cost structure of the organization
   d. All of the above
7. **How can managers control expenses effectively?**
   a. By implementing cost control measures
   b. By monitoring and managing costs
   c. By preventing overspending
   d. All of the above
8. **Why is accurate financial information important for strategic decision-making?**
   a. It helps evaluate the financial implications of various alternatives
   b. It provides insights into cost drivers
   c. It aligns decisions with the organization's goals
   d. All of the above

9. What is the purpose of categorizing costs in managerial accounting?

a. To identify expenses directly related to production

b. To understand the cost structure of the organization

c. To make informed decisions based on cost analysis

d. All of the above

10. How does managerial accounting assist in monitoring and controlling the implementation of strategic decisions?

a. By tracking progress and comparing actual results with budgeted amounts

b. By using cost analysis and profitability analysis

c. By evaluating performance against predetermined goals

d. All of the above

Answers to Multiple Choice Questions

1. (b); 2. (c); 3. (a); 4. (d); 5. (d); 6. (d); 7. (d); 8. (d); 9. (d); 10. (d)

REFERENCES

1. Brewer, P. C., Garrison, R. H., & Noreen, E. W., (2022). Introduction to Managerial Accounting. McGraw-Hill.
2. Colibri, A., (2023). *Understanding Financial Statements: A Bright and Beautiful Beginner's Guide*. Colibri Digital Marketing. https://colibridigitalmarketing.com/understanding-financial-statements/ (accessed on 04 April 2024).
3. *Difference Between Managerial and Financial Accounting,* (2022). Universal CPA Review. https://www.universalcpareview.com/ask-joey/difference-between-managerial-and-financial-accounting/ (accessed on 04 April 2024).
4. Edmonds, T. P., (2017). Fundamental Managerial Accounting Concepts.4-20
5. Garrison, R. H., Noreen, E. W., Brewer, P. C., & McGowan, A., (2010). Managerial accounting. Issues in Accounting Education, 25(4), 792–793.
6. Richardson, A. J., (2002). Professional dominance: The relationship between financial accounting and managerial accounting, 1926–1986. Accounting Historians Journal, 29(2), 91–121.
7. Skousen, C. J., & Walther, L. M., (2012). Introduction to Managerial Accounting. 30-48.

CHAPTER 2

Cost Concepts and Behavior

LEARNING OBJECTIVES

After studying this chapter, you will be able to:

- Types of costs;
- Cost behavior and its impact on decision-making;
- Cost-volume-profit (CVP) analysis.

INTRODUCTORY EXAMPLE

Cost concepts and behavior are important aspects to consider when managing a business. Understanding how costs behave can help businesses make informed decisions and improve their financial performance.

Let's consider a hypothetical example of a manufacturing company called KenTech Inc. KenTech Inc. produces a product called Widget, which is sold for $10 per unit. The company incurs various costs in the production process, such as materials, labor, and overhead expenses.

The cost of materials for each Widget is $2. This cost remains constant regardless of the number of units produced. This type of cost is known as a variable cost because it varies in direct proportion to the level of production.

The labor cost per Widget is $4. However, the labor cost is not directly tied to the number of units produced. Instead, the labor cost is fixed and remains the same regardless of the production level. This type of cost is known as a fixed cost.

Lastly, the overhead expenses for KenTech Inc. amount to $20,000 per month. These expenses include rent, utilities, and administrative costs. Unlike the material and labor costs, overhead expenses are not directly tied to the number of units produced. Instead, they remain the same regardless of the production level. Therefore, overhead expenses are considered fixed costs.

By understanding the different types of costs and their behavior, KenTech Inc. can make better decisions regarding their pricing strategy and production levels. For example, if the company wants to increase its profitability, it can analyze the variable costs and find ways to reduce them. On the other hand, if the company wants to expand its production, it can evaluate the fixed costs and determine the level of production that would be most cost-effective.

In conclusion, understanding cost concepts and behavior is crucial for businesses to effectively manage their finances. By analyzing different types of costs and their behavior, businesses can make informed decisions that can lead to improved financial performance.

UNIT INTRODUCTION

The cost of a product or service is an important factor to consider when making a purchase decision. It refers to the amount of money that needs to be paid in order to obtain the desired item.

There are various factors that can contribute to the cost of a product or service. These include;

- The cost of raw materials;
- Production expenses;
- Overhead costs;
- Any additional charges such as shipping or taxes.

It is important for businesses to carefully calculate these costs in order to determine a suitable price for their products or services.

In addition to the cost of production, businesses may also consider other factors when determining the price of their products. These factors include:

- Market demand;
- Competition;
- Desired profit margins.

By taking these factors into account, businesses can set a price that is competitive yet profitable (Hoque, 2005).

It is also worth noting that the cost of a product or service can vary depending on the quality or level of customization. Higher quality products or services often come with a higher price tag, as they require more expensive materials or skilled labor. Similarly, customized products or services may have a higher cost due to the additional time and effort required to meet specific customer requirements.

When considering the cost of a product or service, it is important for consumers to weigh the price against the perceived value. While a lower price may be appealing, it does not always guarantee the best value. Consumers should consider factors such as durability, reliability, and customer support when determining the true value of a product or service.

Overall, cost plays a significant role in the decision-making process for both businesses and consumers. By carefully considering the factors that contribute to the cost of a product or service, businesses can set a competitive yet profitable price. Similarly, consumers can make informed purchase decisions by evaluating the price against the perceived value (Hoque, 2005).

2.1. TYPES OF COSTS

Learning Objectives

After studying this section, you will have a clear understanding of various types of costs, including:

- Fixed costs;
- Variable costs;
- Semi-variable costs;
- Direct costs;
- Indirect costs;
- Opportunity costs;
- Sunk costs.

There are several types of costs that businesses incur in their operations. Understanding these costs is essential for effective financial management. Here are some common types of costs:

2.1.1. Fixed Costs

According to Hoque, (2005), fixed costs are expenses that do not change with the level of production or sales. These costs remain constant regardless of the company's output. Examples of fixed costs include rent, insurance premiums, salaries of permanent employees, and property taxes (Figure 2.1).

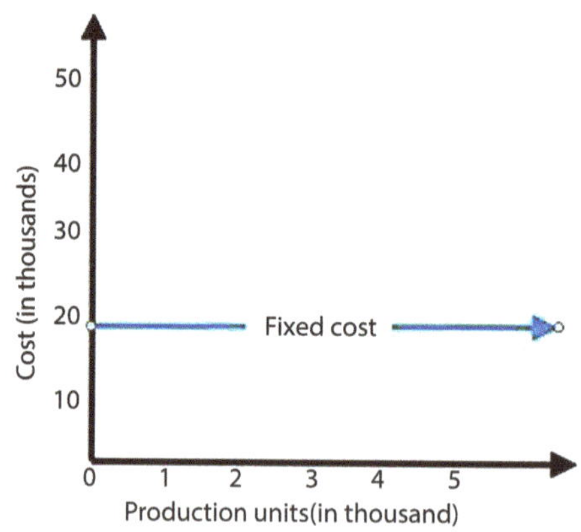

Figure 2.1. *An illustration of fixed cost.*

Source: S (2023).

To illustrate fixed costs, let's consider a manufacturing company called XYZ Corp. This company produces widgets and has the following fixed costs:

- **Rent:** $2,000 per month.
- **Salaries:** $5,000 per month.
- **Insurance:** $1,500 per month.

Regardless of how many widgets XYZ Corp produces or sells, these fixed costs remain the same. Even if the company doesn't produce any widgets in a given month, it still has to pay $2,000 for rent, $5,000 for salaries, and $1,500 for insurance.

To calculate the total fixed costs for XYZ Corp, we can use the following formula:

Total Fixed Costs = Rent + Salaries + Insurance

= $2,000 + $5,000 + $1,500

= $8,500

Therefore, XYZ Corp's total fixed costs amount to $8,500 per month.

Understanding fixed costs is crucial for businesses as it helps in determining the break-even point and setting prices. By identifying and analyzing fixed costs, companies can make informed decisions about their operations and financial strategies (Hoque, 2005).

2.1.2. Variable Costs

Variable costs are expenses that fluctuate in direct proportion to the level of production or sales. These costs vary as the volume of output changes. As production increases, variable costs increase, and as production decreases, variable costs decrease (Kioko & Marlowe, 2023) (Figure 2.2).

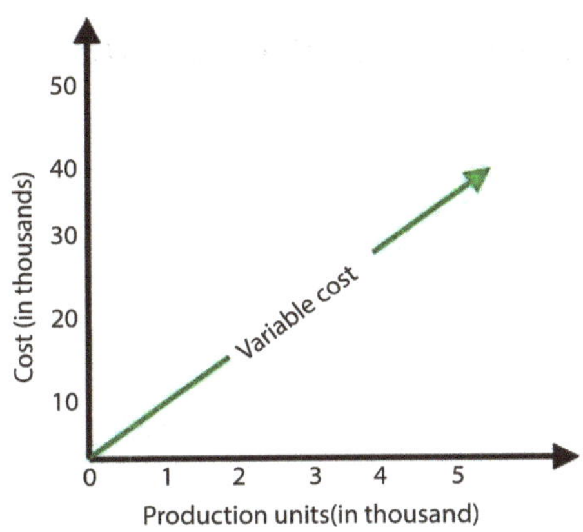

Figure 2.2. *An illustration of variable cost.*

Source: S (2023).

To illustrate variable costs, let's consider a manufacturing company that produces bicycles. The variable costs associated with producing each bicycle include the cost of raw materials, labor wages, and electricity. As the company increases its production, these costs will also increase.

Remember

The law of diminishing returns states that as production increases, the marginal cost of each additional unit produced will eventually exceed the marginal revenue.

Formula for calculating variable costs:

Variable Costs = Cost of Raw Materials + Labor Wages + Electricity

For instance, let's assume that the cost of raw materials for each bicycle is $50, labor wages are $20, and electricity costs amount to $10. If the company produces 100 bicycles, the variable costs can be calculated as follows:

Variable Costs = $50 (Cost of Raw Materials) + $20 (Labor Wages) + $10 (Electricity) = $80 per bicycle

If the company decides to increase its production to 200 bicycles, the variable costs will also double:

Variable Costs = $50 (Cost of Raw Materials) + $20 (Labor Wages) + $10 (Electricity) = $80 per bicycle

Total Variable Costs = $80 per bicycle × 200 bicycles = $16,000

Variable costs are an important consideration for businesses, as they directly impact profitability. By closely monitoring and managing these costs, businesses can make informed decisions regarding pricing, production levels, and overall financial performance.

2.1.3. Semi-Variable Costs

Semi-variable costs, also known as mixed costs, are expenses that consist of both fixed and variable components. These costs are not solely dependent on the level of production or sales, but also include a fixed portion that remains constant regardless of activity levels. The variable portion, on the other hand, fluctuates in direct proportion to changes in activity (Figure 2.3).

To better understand semi-variable costs, let's consider an example. Imagine a manufacturing company that produces widgets. The company incurs a monthly rent expense of $2,000 for its factory space. This fixed cost remains constant regardless of the number of widgets produced.

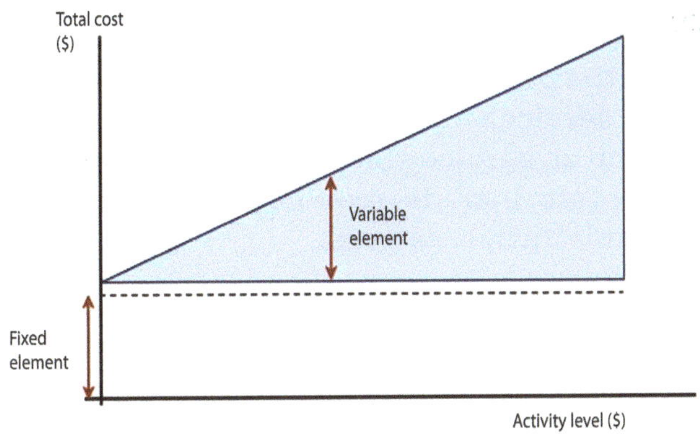

Figure 2.3. *An illustration of semi-variable costs.*

Source: Malek (2013).

In addition to the rent, the company also has a variable cost component. This variable cost is the wages paid to the workers who assemble the widgets. The company pays its workers an hourly rate of $15, and this cost increases as more widgets are produced.

To calculate the total cost incurred by the company, we can use the following formula:

Total Cost = Fixed Cost + (Variable Cost per Unit × Number of Units)

Using the example above, let's say the company produces 100 widgets in a month. The fixed cost remains at $2,000, while the variable cost per unit is $15. Plugging these values into the formula, we can calculate the total cost as follows:

Total Cost = $2,000 + ($15 × 100)

Total Cost = $2,000 + $1,500

Total Cost = $3,500

Therefore, the total cost incurred by the company for producing 100 widgets is $3,500. By understanding semi-variable costs, businesses can make informed decisions regarding their financial planning and budgeting. They can determine the fixed and variable portions of their costs, enabling them to better forecast and control expenses (Kioko & Marlowe, 2023).

2.1.4. Direct Costs

Direct costs are expenses that can be directly attributed to a specific product or service. These costs are directly linked to the production process and can be easily traced back to the final product. Examples of direct costs include raw materials, labor, and equipment.

To illustrate direct costs, let's consider a manufacturing company that produces bicycles. The direct costs associated with manufacturing a bicycle include the cost of raw materials, such as metal, rubber, and plastic, as well as the wages of the workers directly involved in the manufacturing process. These costs can be easily traced back to the production of bicycles and are considered direct costs.

To calculate the total direct costs for manufacturing bicycles, we can use the following formula:

Total Direct Costs = Cost of Raw Materials + Direct Labor Costs

For example, if the cost of raw materials for manufacturing one bicycle is $100 and the direct labor costs for producing one bicycle is $50, the total direct costs for manufacturing one bicycle would be $150.

According to Mandíková, (2021), direct costs are essential for businesses to accurately determine the cost of producing a specific product or service. By identifying and tracking these costs, businesses can make informed decisions regarding pricing, profitability, and overall financial performance.

Quick Fact

According to the Bureau of Labor Statistics, labor costs account for approximately 70% of the total production costs in most industries.

2.1.5. Indirect Costs

Indirect costs are expenses that are not directly associated with the production of goods or services. These costs are not easily traceable to a specific product or service and are often referred to as overhead costs. Indirect costs include expenses such as rent, utilities, insurance, and administrative salaries.

To illustrate this, let's consider a manufacturing company. The company has various departments, including production, administration, and sales. The salaries of the employees in each department would be considered indirect costs. These salaries are necessary to keep the company running as a whole, but they cannot be directly attributed to a specific product or service.

To calculate the indirect costs, we can use the following formula:

Indirect Costs = Total Costs – Direct Costs

Total costs include both direct and indirect costs. Direct costs are expenses that can be directly linked to a specific project or product. By subtracting the direct costs from the total costs, we can determine the indirect costs.

For example, let's say the manufacturing company has total costs of $5,00,000, and direct costs of $3,00,000. Using the formula, we can calculate the indirect costs:

Indirect Costs = $5,00,000 – $3,00,000

Indirect Costs = $2,00,000

Therefore, the indirect costs for this manufacturing company would be $2,00,000.

Indirect costs are important to consider when calculating the total labor. They are necessary for the business to operate efficiently, but they are not directly tied to the production process. By understanding and properly allocating indirect costs, businesses can accurately determine the true cost of their products or services (Mandíková, 2021) (Figure 2.4).

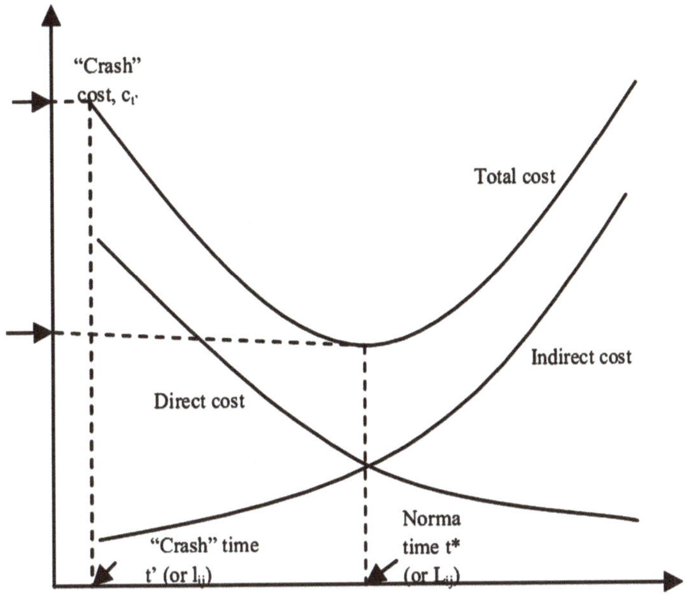

Figure 2.4. *Graphs of the direct, the indirect and total costs for an activity when there is no inflation.*

Source: Tirgari (2013).

2.1.6. Opportunity Costs

Opportunity costs are an essential concept in economics that refers to the benefits or value of what is given up when choosing one option over another (Figure 2.5).

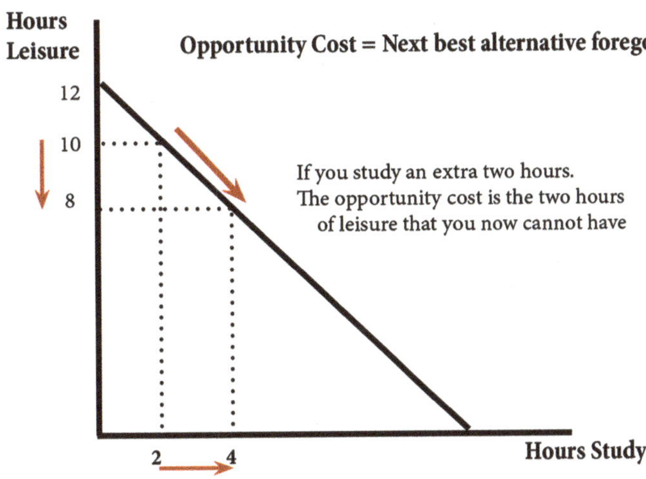

Figure 2.5. *An illustration of opportunity costs.*

Source: Pettinger (2019).

To better understand this concept, let's consider a simple illustration. To illustrate this concept, let's consider a hypothetical scenario. Imagine you have $100, and you are trying to decide between buying a new video game or going out to dinner with friends. The cost of the video game is $60, while the cost of dinner is $40.

If you choose to buy the video game, the opportunity cost is the value of the dinner that you gave up. In this case, the opportunity cost is $40.

On the other hand, if you choose to go out to dinner, the opportunity cost is the value of the video game that you could have purchased. In this case, the opportunity cost is $60.

To calculate opportunity cost, you can use the following formula:

Opportunity Cost = Value of the Next Best Alternative - Value of the Chosen Option

In our example, the formula would be:

Opportunity Cost = $40 (Value of dinner) - $60 (Value of video game) = -$20

This negative value indicates that the opportunity cost of choosing the video game over dinner is $20.

Understanding opportunity costs allows us to make more informed decisions by weighing the benefits and drawbacks of each option. By considering what we are giving up, we can prioritize our choices and allocate our resources more effectively.

2.1.7. Sunk Costs

Sunk costs are expenses that have already been incurred and cannot be recovered. They are irrelevant in decision-making because they cannot be changed or undone (Drury, 2013) (Figure 2.6).

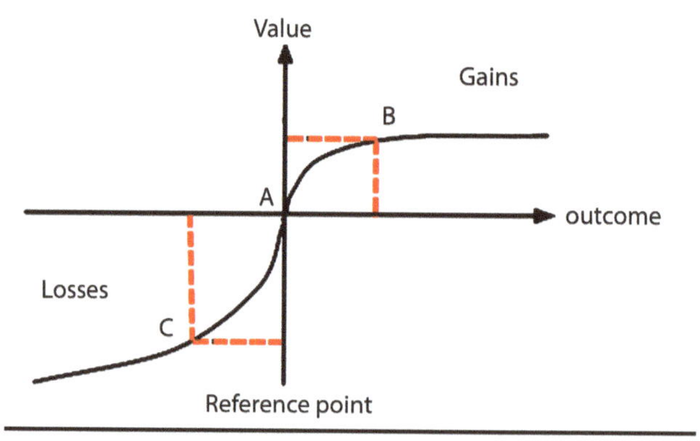

Figure 2.6. *Illustration of sunk costs.*

Source: Lam (2023).

To better understand this concept, let's consider an example. Imagine you have opened a small cafe, and you invested $10,000 in purchasing equipment and renovating the space. After a year of operation, you realize that the cafe is not as profitable as you had hoped. At this point, the $10,000 you initially spent is considered a sunk cost. It cannot be retrieved, regardless of whether you continue operating the cafe or decide to close it down.

To calculate the sunk cost, you can use the following formula:

Sunk Cost = Initial Investment + Additional Expenses

In our cafe example, the initial investment was $10,000. If you also spent an additional $2,000 on maintenance and repairs throughout the year, the sunk cost would be $12,000.

Remember, when making decisions about the future of your cafe, such as whether to continue operating or shut it down, you should not consider the sunk cost of $12,000. Instead, focus on the potential profits or losses you may incur moving forward. By doing so, you can make more informed decisions that are not influenced by past expenditures that cannot be recovered (Drury, 2013).

Did You Understand?

1. What are fixed costs and how are they calculated?
2. What are variable costs and how do they change with production?
3. What are semi-variable costs and how are they calculated?
4. What are direct costs and how are they determined?
5. What are indirect costs and how are they calculated?
6. What are opportunity costs and how are they calculated?
7. What are sunk costs and why are they irrelevant in decision-making?

Answer 1: Fixed costs are expenses that remain constant regardless of the level of production or sales. Examples of fixed costs include rent, insurance premiums, salaries of permanent employees, and property taxes.

To calculate the total fixed costs, you add up all the individual fixed costs. For example, if a company has fixed costs of $2,000 for rent, $5,000 for salaries, and $1,500 for insurance, the total fixed costs would be $8,500 per month.

Answer 2: Variable costs are expenses that fluctuate in direct proportion to the level of production or sales. As production increases, variable costs also increase, and as production decreases, variable costs decrease. Examples of variable costs include the cost of raw materials, labor wages, and electricity. To calculate the total variable costs, you add up all the individual variable costs. For example, if the cost of raw materials for each bicycle is $50, labor wages are $20, and electricity costs amount to $10, the variable costs per bicycle would be $80.

If the company decides to increase its production to 200 bicycles, the total variable costs would be $16,000.

Answer 3: Semi-variable costs, also known as mixed costs, consist of both fixed and variable components. The fixed portion remains constant regardless of activity levels, while the variable portion fluctuates in direct proportion to changes in activity. An example of a semi-variable cost is the rent of a factory space, which remains constant regardless of the number of widgets produced, while the wages of workers who assemble the widgets increase as more widgets are produced.

To calculate the total cost, you add the fixed cost to the variable cost per unit multiplied by the number of units produced. For example, if the fixed cost is $2,000, the variable cost per unit is $15, and the company produces 100 widgets, the total cost would be $3,500.

Answer 4: Direct costs are expenses that can be directly attributed to a specific product or service. They are directly linked to the production process and can be easily traced back to the final product. Examples of direct costs include raw materials, labor, and equipment.

To determine the total direct costs, you add up the cost of raw materials and the direct labor costs.

For example, if the cost of raw materials for manufacturing one bicycle is $100 and the direct labor costs are $50, the total direct costs for manufacturing one bicycle would be $150.

Answer 5: Indirect costs are expenses that are not directly associated with the production of goods or services. They are often referred to as overhead costs and include expenses such as rent, utilities, insurance, and administrative salaries. To calculate the indirect costs, you subtract the direct costs from the total costs. For example, if the total costs are $5,00,000 and the direct costs are $3,00,000, the indirect costs would be $2,00,000.

Answer 6: Opportunity costs refer to the benefits or value of what is given up when choosing one option over another. To calculate the opportunity cost, you subtract the value of the chosen option from the value of the next best alternative. For example, if the value of dinner is $40 and the value of a video game is $60, the opportunity cost of choosing the video game over dinner would be – $20.

Answer 7: Sunk costs are expenses that have already been incurred and cannot be recovered. They are irrelevant in decision-making because they cannot be changed or undone. For example, if you invested $10,000 in a cafe and later realized it is not profitable, the $10,000 is considered a sunk cost. When making decisions about the future of the cafe, you should not consider the sunk cost, but instead focus on potential profits or losses moving forward.

2.2. COST BEHAVIOR AND ITS IMPACT ON DECISION-MAKING

Learning Objectives

- Learn more about types of cost behavior;
- Understand how to manage cost behavior;
- To understand cost behavior analysis techniques;
- Learn more on how cost behavior impact decision-making.

Cost behavior refers to how costs change in response to changes in activity levels. Understanding cost behavior is essential for effective cost management and decision-making. Understanding cost behavior allows managers to make informed decisions regarding cost control and cost reduction. By analyzing cost behavior patterns, managers can identify opportunities to reduce costs and improve profitability. Additionally, understanding cost behavior helps in budgeting and forecasting, as it allows for more accurate estimations of future costs based on projected activity levels (Sinambela & Djaelani, 2022).

2.2.1. Types of Cost Behavior

There are three main types of cost behavior: variable costs, fixed costs, and mixed costs.

1. **Variable Costs:** As discussed above, these are costs that vary in direct proportion to changes in activity levels. Examples of variable costs include:
   - Direct materials;
   - Direct labor;
   - Sales commissions.

As activity levels increase, variable costs increase, and as activity levels decrease, variable costs decrease.

2. **Fixed Costs:** These are costs that remain constant regardless of changes in activity levels. Examples of fixed costs include;
   - Rent;

- Insurance;
- Salaries.

Fixed costs do not change with increases or decreases in activity levels.

3. **Mixed or Semi-Variable Costs:** These are costs that have both variable and fixed components. Examples of mixed costs include;
   - Utilities;
   - Maintenance;
   - Advertising.

The fixed component of mixed costs remains constant, while the variable component changes with activity levels.

Keyword

Break-Even Point – It is the point at which a company's total revenue equals its total costs, resulting in neither profit nor loss.

2.2.2. Managing Cost Behavior

Managing cost behavior is a crucial aspect of financial management. Understanding how costs behave and being able to predict and control them can greatly impact the success of a business. By analyzing cost behavior, managers can make informed decisions regarding pricing strategies, budgeting, and resource allocation.

One important concept in managing cost behavior is the distinction between fixed costs and variable costs. Fixed costs are expenses that do not change with the level of production or sales. Examples of fixed costs include rent, insurance, and salaries. Variable costs, on the other hand, fluctuate with the level of production or sales. Examples of variable costs include raw materials, direct labor, and sales commissions (Sinambela & Djaelani, 2022).

To effectively manage cost behavior, managers need to accurately identify and classify costs. This involves:

- Analyzing historical data;
- Conducting cost-volume-profit analysis;
- Using other techniques to determine the fixed and variable components of costs.

Once costs are classified, managers can use this information to make informed decisions. For example, understanding cost behavior can help managers determine the most profitable pricing strategy. By knowing the fixed and variable costs associated with producing a product or providing a service, managers can calculate the break-even point and set prices accordingly. This ensures that revenues cover all costs and allows the business to generate a profit.

Additionally, managing cost behavior can help with budgeting. By understanding how costs behave, managers can accurately forecast expenses and allocate resources accordingly. This allows for more effective planning and control of costs, which can lead to improved financial performance (Novák et al., 2017).

2.2.3. Cost Behavior Analysis Techniques

Cost behavior analysis techniques are used to understand how costs change in relation to changes in activity levels. It helps businesses determine the fixed and variable components of their costs and predict future costs. By analyzing cost behavior, companies can make informed decisions about pricing, product mix, and resource allocation. Some commonly used techniques include:

- Scatter diagrams;
- Regression analysis;
- High-low method.

These techniques enable businesses to identify cost patterns and make accurate cost predictions. Overall, cost behavior analysis techniques are valuable tools for managing costs and improving financial performance.

2.2.3.1. Scatter Diagrams

Scatter diagrams are a useful tool in cost behavior analysis. They help to visually represent the relationship between two variables, such as cost and volume. By plotting the data points on a graph, patterns, and trends can be identified.

To create a scatter diagram, the cost is plotted on the y-axis and the volume is plotted on the x-axis. Each data point represents a specific cost and volume combination. By analyzing the pattern of the data points, one can determine if there is a correlation between cost and volume.

Scatter diagrams are particularly helpful in determining if costs are fixed or variable. If the data points cluster around a straight line, it suggests a linear relationship and indicates that costs are variable. On the other hand, if the data points are spread out and do not form a clear pattern, it suggests that costs are fixed.

To illustrate how to create one, let's consider a real-life scenario. Suppose we want to examine the relationship between the number of hours studied and the corresponding test scores of a group of students. We have collected data from 30 students, recording the number of hours they studied and their respective test scores.

To plot a scatter diagram, we start by labeling the x-axis as "Number of Hours Studied" and the y-axis as "Test Scores." We then plot each student's data point on the graph, with the number of hours studied on the x-axis and the corresponding test score on the y-axis.

For example, let's say the first student studied for 4 hours and scored 85 on the test. We would mark a point at (4, 85) on the graph. We repeat this process for each student, plotting their data points accordingly.

Once all the data points are plotted, we can observe the pattern or trend in the relationship between the two variables. If the points on the graph are scattered randomly, it suggests that there is no significant relationship between the number of hours studied and test scores. However, if the points form a clear pattern, such as a positive or negative slope, it indicates a correlation between the variables.

By analyzing the scatter diagram, we can draw conclusions about the relationship between the number of hours studied and test scores. This information can be valuable for understanding the impact of studying on academic performance and making informed decisions in educational settings (Sinambela & Djaelani, 2022) (Figure 2.7).

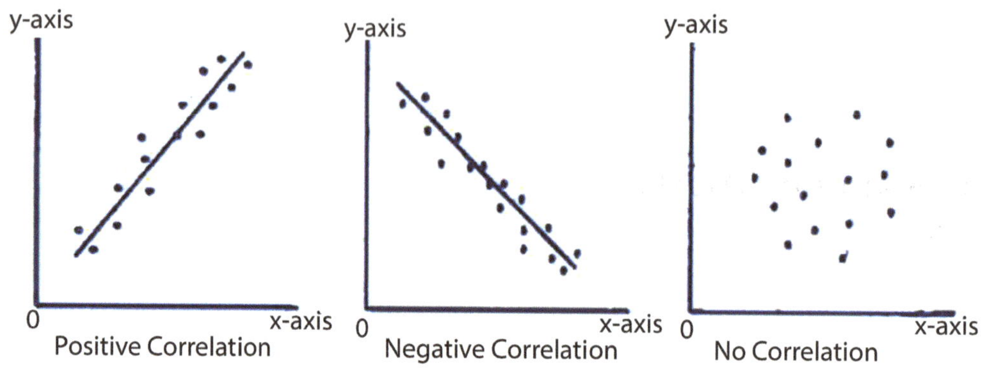

Figure 2.7. *Different correlations in scatter diagram.*

Source: Ezera (2023).

2.2.3.2. Regression Analysis

Regression analysis is a statistical method that examines the relationship between two variables: the dependent variable and the independent variable. In the context of cost behavior analysis, the dependent variable is the cost, while the independent variable is the activity level (Novák et al., 2017).

The purpose of regression analysis in cost behavior analysis is to determine the cost equation or the cost function. The cost equation represents the relationship between the cost and the activity level. It helps managers predict costs at different activity levels and make informed decisions.

To perform regression analysis for cost behavior analysis, data on costs and activity levels are collected and analyzed. The data is then plotted on a scatter plot, with the activity level on the x-axis and the cost on the y-axis. A line of best fit is drawn through the data points, representing the relationship between the cost and the activity level.

The equation of the line of best fit is determined using statistical techniques. This equation represents the cost equation or the cost function. It can be used to estimate costs at different activity levels and provide valuable insights for decision-making.

To illustrate the application of regression analysis in cost behavior analysis, consider the following example:

A manufacturing company wants to determine the relationship between its production volume and its total manufacturing overhead costs. The company collects data on its production volume and corresponding manufacturing overhead costs for the past six months. Using regression analysis, the company can analyze this data to determine the equation that best represents the relationship between production volume and manufacturing overhead costs.

The formula used for regression analysis is:

Y = a + bX

where; 'Y' represents the dependent variable (manufacturing overhead costs); 'X' represents the independent variable (production volume); 'a' represents the intercept (the value of Y when X is equal to zero); and 'b' represents the slope (the change in Y for each unit change in X)

By applying regression analysis to the collected data, the manufacturing company can determine the equation that best represents the relationship between production volume and manufacturing overhead costs. This equation can then be used to predict future manufacturing overhead costs based on different levels of production volume.

2.2.3.3. High-Low Method

The high-low method involves analyzing cost data from two extreme points:

- The highest level of activity; and
- The lowest level of activity.

By comparing the costs at these two points, businesses can determine the fixed and variable components of their costs.

To calculate the variable cost per unit, the high-low method uses the formula:

Variable cost per unit = (Cost at highest level of activity – Cost at lowest level of activity) / (Highest level of activity – Lowest level of activity)

Once the variable cost per unit is determined, businesses can calculate the total fixed costs by subtracting the variable costs from the total costs at either the highest or lowest level of activity.

To illustrate the high-low method in cost behavior analysis, we will perform an analysis of utility costs for a manufacturing company.

In this example, the company collects data on utility costs and the number of units produced for each month over a six-month period. The data is as follows:

Month	Units Produced	Utility Costs
January	1,000	$5,000
February	1,500	$6,500
March	2,000	$7,500
April	2,500	$8,500
May	3,000	$9,500
June	3,500	$10,500

To apply the high-low method, we first determine the highest and lowest levels of activity. In this case, the highest level of activity is 3,500 units produced in June, and the lowest level is 1,000 units produced in January.

Next, we calculate the variable cost per unit by subtracting the lowest total cost from the highest total cost and dividing it by the difference in units produced. Using the data from June and January:

Variable cost per unit = (Total cost in June – Total cost in January) / (Units produced in June – Units produced in January)

= ($10,500 – $5,000) / (3,500 – 1,000)

= $5,500 / 2,500

= $2.20

Now that we have the variable cost per unit, we can calculate the fixed cost by subtracting the variable cost per unit times the lowest level of activity from the total cost in January:

Fixed cost = Total cost in January – (Variable cost per unit × Units produced in January)

= $5,000 – ($2.20 × 1,000)

= $5,000 – $2,200

= $2,800

Therefore, the cost equation for utility costs in this example is:

Total cost = $2.20 × Units produced + $2,800

By using the high-low method, the manufacturing company can separate the fixed and variable components of their utility costs. This information can be used to better understand and manage their costs, make more informed pricing decisions, and improve overall profitability (Sinambela & Djaelani, 2022).

2.2.4. How Does Cost Behavior Impact Decision-Making?

Cost behavior plays a crucial role in decision-making. It refers to the way costs change in response to changes in activity levels. Understanding cost behavior is essential for making informed decisions that can positively impact a company's financial performance (Novák et al., 2017).

One important aspect of cost behavior is whether costs are fixed or variable. Fixed costs remain constant regardless of changes in activity levels, while variable costs fluctuate in proportion to changes in activity. This distinction is important because it affects how costs are allocated and how they impact profitability.

When making decisions, managers need to consider the behavior of costs to determine the financial implications of their choices. For example, if a company is considering increasing production, understanding the behavior of costs can help determine whether the increase in revenue will outweigh the increase in costs.

Additionally, understanding cost behavior can help managers identify areas where costs can be reduced or optimized. By analyzing the relationship between costs and activity levels, managers can identify opportunities for cost savings and make decisions that improve the company's bottom line (Sinambela & Djaelani, 2022).

Did You Understand?

1. What are the three main types of cost behavior?
2. How can managers effectively manage cost behavior?
3. What are some cost behavior analysis techniques?
4. How do scatter diagrams help in cost behavior analysis?
5. What is the high-low method and how does it work?

Answer 1: The three main types of cost behavior are variable costs, fixed costs, and mixed costs.

Answer 2: To effectively manage cost behavior, managers need to accurately identify and classify costs. This involves analyzing historical data, conducting cost-volume-profit analysis, and using other techniques to determine the fixed and variable components of costs. Once costs are classified, managers can use this information to make informed decisions regarding pricing strategies, budgeting, and resource allocation.

Answer 3: Some commonly used cost behavior analysis techniques include scatter diagrams, regression analysis, and the high-low method. These techniques help businesses identify cost patterns, determine the fixed and variable components of costs, and make accurate cost predictions.

Answer 4: Scatter diagrams are a useful tool in cost behavior analysis as they visually represent the relationship between two variables, such as cost and volume. By plotting the data points on a graph, patterns, and trends can be identified. Scatter diagrams can help determine if costs are fixed or variable based on the clustering or spread of the data points.

Answer 5: The high-low method is a cost behavior analysis technique that involves analyzing cost data from two extreme points: the highest level of activity and the lowest level of activity. By comparing the costs at these two points, businesses can determine the fixed and variable components of their costs. The high-low method calculates the variable cost per unit by dividing the difference in costs by the difference in activity levels. This information can then be used to calculate the total fixed costs and create a cost equation.

2.3. COST-VOLUME-PROFIT (CVP) ANALYSIS

Cost-volume-profit (CVP) analysis is a powerful tool that helps businesses understand the relationship between their costs, sales volume, and profits. By examining these three factors, businesses can make informed decisions about pricing, production levels, and overall profitability.

CVP analysis is based on several key assumptions. First, it assumes that all costs can be divided into fixed costs and variable costs. Fixed costs are those that do not change with the level of production or sales volume, such as rent or salaries. Variable costs, on the other hand, vary directly with production or sales volume, such as raw materials or direct labor (Hoque, 2005).

Second, CVP analysis assumes that the sales price per unit, variable cost per unit, and fixed costs remain constant. This assumption allows businesses to simplify their analysis and focus on the relationships between these three variables.

The basic equation used in CVP analysis is:

Profit = (Sales price per unit × Sales volume) – (Variable cost per unit × Sales volume) – Fixed costs

By manipulating this equation, businesses can determine several important metrics. The break-even point, for example, is the level of sales volume at which a business neither makes a profit nor incurs a loss. This can be calculated by setting the profit equal to zero and solving for the sales volume.

Another important metric is the contribution margin, which represents the amount of each sales dollar that is available to cover fixed costs and contribute to profit. The contribution margin can be calculated by dividing the difference between the sales price per unit and the variable cost per unit by the sales price per unit.

CVP analysis can also be used to determine the impact of changes in sales volume on profitability. By calculating the profit at different sales volumes, businesses can identify their profit-maximizing level of production or sales volume (Hoque, 2005).

CASE STUDY

- **Introduction:**

FarmEurope is a leading agricultural company that specializes in the production of crops and livestock. The company operates multiple farms across Europe and is known for its high-quality products. In order to maintain profitability and make informed business decisions, FarmEurope must have a clear understanding of cost concepts and behavior.

- **Cost Concepts:**

Cost concepts are essential for any business, as they help in determining the expenses associated with production. FarmEurope recognizes three main cost concepts: fixed costs, variable costs, and semi-variable costs. Fixed costs are expenses that remain constant regardless of the level of production. These costs include rent, insurance, and salaries. For example, FarmEurope pays a fixed amount for rent each month, regardless of the number of crops or livestock produced.

Variable costs, on the other hand, fluctuate with the level of production. These costs include seeds, fertilizers, and animal feed. As FarmEurope produces more crops or livestock, the variable costs increase accordingly. Semi-variable costs are a combination of fixed and variable costs. These costs have both a fixed component and a variable component. An example of a semi-variable cost for FarmEurope is electricity. The company pays a fixed amount for electricity each month, but the usage of electricity varies with the level of production.

- **Cost Behavior:**

Understanding cost behavior is crucial for FarmEurope to make informed decisions regarding production and pricing. Cost behavior refers to how costs change in response to changes in production levels.

Fixed costs remain constant regardless of the level of production. For FarmEurope, this means that the total fixed costs will not change even if the company increases or decreases its production. Variable costs, on the other hand, change in direct proportion to the level of production. As FarmEurope produces more crops or livestock, the variable costs will increase, and vice versa.

Semi-variable costs exhibit both fixed and variable components. The fixed component remains constant, while the variable component changes with the level of production. For FarmEurope, this means that the total semi-variable costs will increase as production increases, but the fixed component will remain the same.

- **Conclusion:**

FarmEurope understands the importance of cost concepts and behavior in managing its agricultural business. By recognizing and analyzing fixed costs, variable costs, and semi-variable costs, the company can make informed decisions regarding production, pricing, and profitability. This knowledge allows FarmEurope to effectively manage its resources and maintain its position as a leading agricultural company in Europe.

SUMMARY

The cost of a product or service is a crucial factor in purchasing decisions, affecting both businesses and consumers. Factors such as raw materials, production expenses, overhead costs, and shipping or taxes contribute to the cost. Businesses must calculate these costs to set a competitive price. Other factors include market demand, competition, and profit margins. The cost can vary depending on quality or customization, with higher-quality products or services often cost more. Consumers should weigh the price against perceived value, considering factors like durability, reliability, and customer support. There are three types of costs: fixed costs, variable costs, and semi-variable costs. Understanding these costs is essential for effective financial management and making informed decisions about pricing, production levels, and overall financial performance.

Semi-variable costs are expenses that remain constant regardless of production or sales levels, while variable costs fluctuate in proportion to changes in activity. For example, a manufacturing company producing widgets incurs a monthly rent expense of $2,000, while the variable cost per unit is $15. To calculate the total cost, use the formula: Total Cost = Fixed Cost + (Variable Cost per Unit × Number of Units).

Direct costs are expenses directly attributed to a specific product or service, such as raw materials, labor, and equipment. Indirect costs are expenses not directly linked to the production process, such as rent, utilities, insurance, and administrative salaries. By understanding and properly allocating indirect costs, businesses can accurately determine the true cost of their products or services.

Opportunity costs refer to the benefits or value of what is given up when choosing one option over another. Understanding opportunity costs and sunk costs is crucial for making informed decisions in business. Opportunity costs are expenses that cannot be recovered, while sunk costs are incurred and cannot be recovered. Cost behavior, which refers to how costs change in response to changes in activity levels, is essential for effective cost management and decision-making. There are three main types of cost behavior: variable costs, fixed costs, and mixed costs. Managing cost behavior involves accurately identifying and classifying costs, analyzing historical data, conducting cost-volume-profit analysis, and using other techniques. This information helps managers make informed decisions about pricing strategies, budgeting, and resource allocation. Cost behavior analysis techniques, such as scatter diagrams, regression analysis, and the high-low method, help businesses identify cost patterns and make accurate predictions.

Scatter diagrams and regression analysis are essential tools in cost behavior analysis to visually represent the relationship between two variables, such as cost and volume. Scatter diagrams plot data points on a graph, identifying patterns and trends to determine if there is a correlation between the two variables. Regression analysis examines the relationship between the dependent variable (cost) and the independent variable (activity level), determining the cost equation or cost function. This helps managers predict costs at different activity levels and make informed decisions. For example, a manufacturing company can use regression analysis to determine the best equation for predicting future manufacturing overhead costs based on different levels of production volume.

The high-low method is a cost behavior analysis method that involves comparing costs at two extreme points: the highest and lowest levels of activity. It helps businesses determine the fixed and variable components of their costs. For example, a manufacturing company can use the high-low method to analyze utility costs, separating fixed and variable components. Understanding cost behavior is crucial for making informed decisions and improving profitability. It helps identify areas for cost reduction or optimization and helps managers make decisions that improve the company's bottom line. Cost-volume-profit (CVP) analysis is a powerful tool that helps businesses understand the relationship between costs, sales volume, and profits. It assumes that all costs can be divided into fixed and variable costs, and that sales price per unit, variable cost per unit, and fixed costs remain constant.

MULTIPLE CHOICE QUESTIONS

1. **What factors can contribute to the cost of a product or service?**
   a. Market demand and competition
   b. Raw materials and production expenses
   c. Overhead costs and additional charges
   d. All of the above
2. **What are fixed costs?**
   a. Expenses that change with the level of production or sales
   b. Expenses that remain constant regardless of the company's output
   c. Expenses that fluctuate in direct proportion to changes in activity
   d. Expenses that can be directly attributed to a specific product or service
3. **What are variable costs?**
   a. Expenses that change with the level of production or sales
   b. Expenses that remain constant regardless of the company's output
   c. Expenses that fluctuate in direct proportion to changes in activity
   d. Expenses that can be directly attributed to a specific product or service
4. **What are semi-variable costs?**
   a. Expenses that change with the level of production or sales
   b. Expenses that remain constant regardless of the company's output
   c. Expenses that consist of both fixed and variable components
   d. Expenses that can be directly attributed to a specific product or service
5. **What are opportunity costs?**
   a. The benefits or value of what is given up when choosing one option over another
   b. Expenses that have already been incurred and cannot be recovered
   c. The value of the next best alternative minus the value of the chosen option
   d. Expenses that can be directly attributed to a specific product or service

6. **What is cost behavior?**
   a. How costs change in response to changes in activity levels.
   b. How costs are classified and managed.
   c. How costs impact decision-making.
   d. How costs are allocated and budgeted.
7. **Which of the following is an example of a variable cost?**
   a. Rent
   b. Insurance
   c. Direct materials
   d. Salaries
8. **What is the purpose of scatter diagrams in cost behavior analysis?**
   a. To visually represent the relationship between two variables.
   b. To determine the cost equation or cost function.
   c. To calculate the breakeven point.
   d. To analyze historical data.
9. **What is the high-low method used for in cost behavior analysis?**
   a. To calculate the breakeven point.
   b. To determine the cost equation or cost function.
   c. To identify areas for cost reduction.
   d. To analyze cost data from two extreme points.
10. **What is the purpose of CVP analysis?**
   a. To determine the fixed and variable components of costs.
   b. To predict future costs based on activity levels.
   c. To understand the relationship between costs, sales volume, and profits.
   d. To calculate the breakeven point.

Answers to Multiple Choice Questions

1. (d); 2. (b); 3. (a); 4. (c); 5. (c); 6. (a); 7. (c); 8. (a); 9. (d); 10. (c)

REFERENCES

1. Drury, C., (2013). *Costing: An Introduction*. Springer.
2. Ezera, A., (2023). *Scatter Plots Help the World Make Sense*. Infogram. https://infogram.com/blog/scatter-plots/ (accessed on 04 April 2024).
3. Hoque, Z., (2005). An introduction to cost terminology, cost flows, and cost behavior. *Handbook of Cost and Management Accounting*, 9.
4. Kioko, S., & Marlowe, J., (2023). Cost analysis. *Financial Strategy for Public Managers*.

5. Lam, K., (2023). *How Prospect Theory Affects Product Marketing and Sales*. https://www.linkedin.com/pulse/how-prospect-theory-affects-product-marketing-sales-keith-lam/ (accessed on 04 April 2024).

6. Malek, F., (2013). *Cost Classification, Variable, Fixed, Semi-Variable Costs*. Pinterest. https://www.pinterest.co.uk/pin/759771399609586638/ (accessed on 04 April 2024).

7. Mandíková, B., (2021). *A Cost Analysis of a Selected Company*. 13-52

8. Novák, P., Dvorský, J., Popesko, B., & Strouhal, J., (2017). Analysis of overhead cost behavior: Case study on decision-making approach. *Journal of International Studies*.

9. Pettinger, T., (2019). *Opportunity Cost Definition*. Economics Help. https://www.economicshelp.org/blog/2177/economics/opportunity-cost-definition/ (accessed on 04 April 2024).

10. Surbhi. S., (2023). *Difference Between Fixed Cost and Variable Cost (with Example and Comparison Chart)*. Key Differences. https://keydifferences.com/difference-between-fixed-cost-and-variable-cost.html (accessed on 04 April 2024).

11. Sinambela, E. A., & Djaelani, M., (2022). Cost behavior analysis and categorization. *Journal of Social Science Studies (JOS3)*, *2*(1), 13–16.

12. Tirgari, V., (2013). *Information Technology Policies and Procedures Against Unstructured Data: A Phenomenological Study of Information Technology Professionals* ResearchGate. https://www.researchgate.net/publication/261026952_INFORMATION_TECHNOLOGY_POLICIES_AND_PROCEDURES_AGAINST_UNSTRUCTURED_DATA_A_PHENOMENOLOGICAL_STUDY_OF_INFORMATION_TECHNOLOGY_PROFESSIONALS (accessed on 04 April 2024).

CHAPTER

3 Cost-Volume-Profit Analysis

LEARNING OBJECTIVES

After studying this chapter, you will be able to:

- Contribution margin analysis;
- Breakeven point analysis;
- Target profit analysis;
- Assumptions and limitations of CVP analysis.

INTRODUCTORY EXAMPLE

Cost-volume-profit (CVP) analysis is a valuable tool for businesses to understand the relationship between costs, volume, and profit. By analyzing these factors, businesses can make informed decisions to maximize their profitability. To illustrate the concept of CVP analysis, let's consider the example of a company that manufactures and sells a single product.

Nadia Manufacturing Company produces a widget that sells for $10 per unit. The variable cost to produce each widget is $5, which includes direct materials, direct labor, and variable overhead. The company also incurs fixed costs of $20,000 per month, which include rent, utilities, and administrative expenses.

To determine the breakeven point, we need to calculate the number of widgets the company needs to sell in order to cover its fixed and variable costs. The breakeven point can be calculated using the following formula:

Breakeven point (in units) = Fixed costs / (Seling price per unit – Variable cost per unit)

In this case, the breakeven point is:

Breakeven point = $20,000 / ($10 – $5) = $20,000 / $5 = 4,000 units

This means that Nadia Manufacturing Company needs to sell 4,000 widgets in order to cover all its costs and achieve a breakeven point. Any units sold beyond this point will contribute to the company's profit.

To calculate the profit at a given level of sales, we can use the following formula:

Profit = (Seling price per unit – Variable cost per unit) × Number of units sold – Fixed costs

For example, if the company sells 5,000 widgets in a month, the profit would be:

Profit = ($10 – $5) × 5,000 – $20,000 = $5 × 5,000 – $20,000 = $25,000 – $20,000 = $5,000

By using CVP analysis, Nadia Manufacturing Company can determine its breakeven point and make decisions that will maximize its profitability. This example demonstrates the importance of understanding the relationship between costs, volume, and profit in business decision-making.

UNIT INTRODUCTION

Businesses need to use cost-volume-profit (CVP) analysis to comprehend how costs, volume, and profit are related to one another. It supports businesses in making viable decisions regarding pricing, production rates, and marketing tactics. The contribution margin, or the difference between sales revenue and variable costs, is a fundamental concept in CVP analysis. Businesses can find out how much each unit contributes to covering fixed costs and making a profit by computing the contribution margin ratio. Finding the breakeven point, or the sales volume at which total revenue and total costs equal, is another step in the CVP analysis process. With the use of this information, businesses can establish the minimal level of sales required to pay for all expenses and start generating a profit.

Moreover, target profit can be evaluated using CVP analysis. This involves determining the level of sales required to achieve a desired profit target. Businesses can set achievable goals and create efficient plans to achieve them by knowing the relationship between costs, volume, and profits (Trifan & Anton, 2011).

3.1. CONTRIBUTION MARGIN

Learning Objectives

- To understand the formula and calculation of contribution margin;
- To understand illustration of contribution margin;
- To learn more about the uses of contribution margin.

The Contribution Margin is a financial metric that is used to measure the profitability of a product or service. It is calculated by subtracting the variable costs associated with producing the product or service from the revenue generated. The resulting Figure 3.1 represents the amount of money that is available to cover fixed costs and contribute to the company's profit.

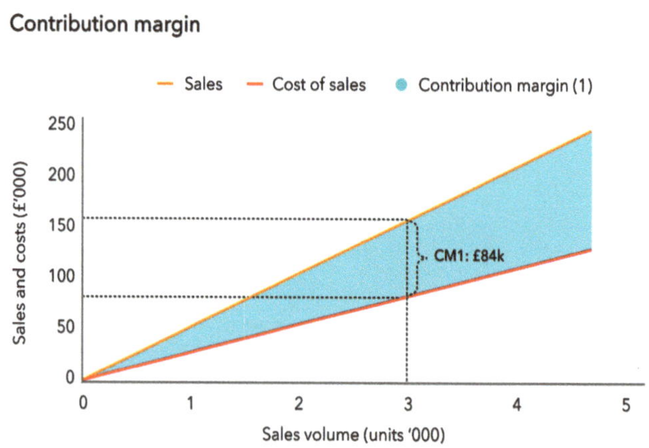

Figure 3.1. *An illustration of contribution margin.*

Source: Fca (2023).

The Contribution Margin is an important tool for businesses as it helps them understand the profitability of their products or services. By analyzing the Contribution Margin, businesses can determine which products or services are generating the most profit and which ones may need to be reevaluated or discontinued (Trifan & Anton, 2011). To calculate the Contribution Margin, one must first determine the revenue generated by a product or service. This can be done by multiplying the price of the product or service by the quantity sold. Next, the variable costs associated with producing the product or service must be identified. Variable costs are costs that change in direct proportion to the quantity produced or sold. Examples of variable costs include raw materials, direct labor, and sales commissions.

Once the revenue and variable costs have been determined, the Contribution Margin can be calculated by subtracting the variable costs from the revenue.

The Contribution Margin can be expressed as a percentage by dividing it by the revenue and multiplying by 100. This allows businesses to compare the profitability of different products or services more easily. A higher Contribution Margin indicates a greater ability to cover fixed costs and generate profit.

Understanding the Contribution Margin is essential for businesses to make informed decisions about pricing, product mix, and cost management. By analyzing the Contribution Margin, businesses can determine the impact of changes in pricing or costs on their profitability. For example, if a business increases the price of a product, the Contribution Margin will increase, resulting in higher profitability. On the other hand, if a business reduces the variable costs associated with producing a product, the Contribution Margin will also increase, leading to higher profitability.

In addition to helping businesses make pricing and cost management decisions, the Contribution Margin can also be used to perform a breakeven analysis. The breakeven point is the level of sales at which a business covers all of its costs and neither makes a profit nor incurs a loss. By comparing the Contribution Margin to the fixed costs, businesses can determine the level of sales needed to reach the breakeven point. This information is valuable for setting sales targets and evaluating the financial viability of a product or service (LE et al., 2020).

3.1.1. Formula and Calculation of Contribution Margin

To calculate the contribution margin, you need to subtract the variable costs from the sales revenue. The formula for contribution margin is as follows:

Contribution Margin = Sales Revenue - Variable Costs

Sales revenue refers to the total amount of money generated from selling products or services. Variable costs are expenses that vary in direct proportion to the level of production or sales. These costs include:

- Materials;
- Direct labor;
- Any other expenses directly related to producing the goods or services.

Once you have the contribution margin, you can use it to analyze the profitability of individual products or services. A higher contribution margin indicates that a product or service is generating more revenue to cover its variable costs and contribute to the overall profitability of the business.

By calculating the contribution margin, businesses can make informed decisions about:

- Pricing;
- Cost control;
- Product mix.

It helps them identify which products or services are most profitable and which ones may need adjustments to improve their contribution margin.

3.1.2. An Illustration of Contribution Margin

To illustrate this concept, let's consider a hypothetical company called XYZ Electronics.

XYZ Electronics manufactures and sells smartphones. The company has determined that the variable costs associated with producing each smartphone amount to $300, including direct materials, direct labor, and other variable expenses. Now, let's assume that XYZ Electronics sells its smartphones for $600 each. To calculate the contribution margin, we subtract the variable costs per unit from the selling price per unit. In this case, the contribution margin per smartphone would be:

$600 - $300 = $300.

The contribution margin of $300 indicates that for every smartphone sold, XYZ Electronics is left with $300 to cover its fixed costs and generate a profit. Fixed costs are expenses that do not vary with the level of production or sales volume, such as rent, salaries, and insurance.

Let's further explore the significance of contribution margin by examining how it can help XYZ Electronics make informed business decisions. Suppose the company is considering launching a new smartphone model with additional features that would increase the variable costs per unit to $350.

By calculating the contribution margin for the new smartphone model, XYZ Electronics can assess its profitability potential. Using the selling price of $600 and the increased variable costs of $350, the contribution margin per unit for the new model would be $600 – $350 = $250.

Comparing the contribution margin of the new model ($250) with the existing model ($300), XYZ Electronics can evaluate the impact of the increased variable costs on its profitability. A lower contribution margin suggests that the new model may be less profitable than the existing one. This information can guide the company in making informed decisions about product pricing, production volume, and resource allocation.

3.1.3. The Uses of Contribution Margin

One of the primary uses of the contribution margin is in determining the profitability of individual products or services. By calculating the contribution margin for each product, businesses can identify which ones are generating the most profit and which ones may be dragging down overall profitability. This information can then be used to make informed decisions about pricing, production volume, and product mix. The contribution margin can also be used to perform breakeven analysis. Breakeven analysis is a tool that helps businesses determine the level of sales they need to cover all their costs and achieve a profit of zero. By dividing the total fixed costs by the contribution margin ratio (contribution margin divided by revenue), businesses can calculate the breakeven point in terms of sales volume or revenue. This information is valuable in setting sales targets and understanding the level of sales needed to achieve profitability (Trifan & Anton, 2011).

Furthermore, the contribution margin can be used to evaluate the impact of changes in sales volume on profitability. By analyzing the contribution margin, businesses can determine the effect of increasing or decreasing sales on their bottom line. For example, if the contribution margin ratio is high, a decrease in sales volume may have a significant negative impact on profitability. Conversely, if the contribution margin ratio is low, an increase in sales volume may have a positive impact on profitability.

The contribution margin can also be used to assess the profitability of different sales channels or customer segments. By analyzing the contribution margin for each channel or segment, businesses can identify which ones are the most profitable and allocate resources accordingly. This information can help businesses optimize their marketing and sales strategies to focus on the most profitable channels or segments.

Another use of the contribution margin is in pricing decisions. By understanding the contribution margin for a product, businesses can set prices that not only cover variable costs but also contribute to covering fixed costs and generating profits. This information is particularly valuable when introducing new products or services, as it helps businesses determine the appropriate pricing strategy to ensure profitability (LE et al., 2020). Additionally, the contribution margin can be used to evaluate the impact of cost changes on profitability. By analyzing the contribution margin, businesses can determine how changes in variable costs, such as raw material prices or labor costs, will affect their profitability. This information is crucial in making decisions about cost management and supplier negotiations.

Did You Understand?

1. What is the Contribution Margin and why is it important for businesses?
2. How is the Contribution Margin calculated?
3. What are the uses of the Contribution Margin?

Answer 1: The Contribution Margin is a financial metric used to measure the profitability of a product or service. It is calculated by subtracting the variable costs associated with production from the revenue generated.

The Contribution Margin is important for businesses because it helps them understand the profitability of their products or services. By analyzing the Contribution Margin, businesses can determine which products or services are generating the most profit and which ones may need to be reevaluated or discontinued.

Answer 2: To calculate the Contribution Margin, first determine the revenue generated by a product or service by multiplying the price by the quantity sold. Next, identify the variable costs associated with production, such as raw materials, direct labor, and sales commissions. Subtract the variable costs from the revenue to calculate the Contribution Margin. The resulting figure represents the amount of money available to cover fixed costs and contribute to the company's profit. The Contribution Margin can also be expressed as a percentage by dividing it by the revenue and multiplying by 100.

Answer 3: The Contribution Margin has several uses for businesses. It can be used to determine the profitability of individual products or services, helping businesses identify which ones are generating the most profit. The Contribution Margin can also be used to perform breakeven analysis, which helps determine the level of sales needed to cover all costs and achieve a profit of zero. Additionally, the Contribution Margin can be used to evaluate the impact of changes in sales volume, assess the profitability of different sales channels or customer segments, make pricing decisions, and evaluate the impact of cost changes on profitability.

3.2. BREAK-EVEN POINT ANALYSIS

Learning Objectives

- To know why perform a break-even analysis;
- To understand the standard break-even time period;
- To know when to use a break-even analysis;
- To learn more about factors that increase a company's break-even point;
- To learn how to reduce the break-even point;
- To learn the limitations of a break-even analysis.

Break-even point analysis is a vital tool for businesses to determine the point at which their total revenue equals their total costs, resulting in neither profit nor loss. This analysis helps businesses make informed decisions regarding pricing, production volume, and cost management. By calculating the break-even point, businesses can understand the minimum sales volume required to cover all fixed and variable costs. This information allows businesses to establish realistic sales goals and evaluate the financial feasibility of their operations (Lulaj & Iseni, 2018) (Figure 3.2).

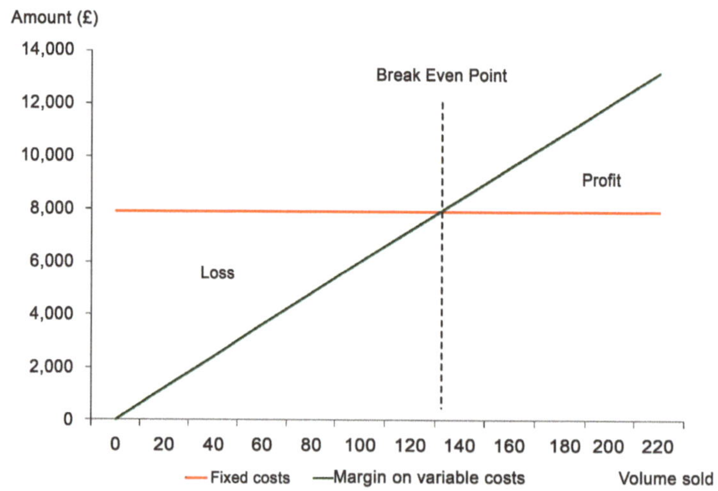

Figure 3.2. *Graphical representation of the breakeven point.*

Source: The Business Plan Shop Ltd. (n.d.).

To calculate the break-even point, businesses need to consider fixed costs and variable costs. Fixed costs are expenses that do not change regardless of the level of sales, such as rent, salaries, and insurance. Variable costs, on the other hand, are expenses that vary with the level of sales, such as raw materials and direct labor.

The formula to calculate the break-even point is as follows:

Break-even point (in units) = Fixed costs / (Seling price per unit – Variable cost per unit)

For example, let's consider a company that sells t-shirts. The fixed costs for this company include rent, utilities, and salaries, which amount to $10,000 per month. The variable costs, which include materials and labor, amount to $5 per t-shirt. The selling price of each t-shirt is $15.

To calculate the break-even point, we need to determine how many t-shirts the company needs to sell in order to cover its fixed and variable costs.

The formula for break-even analysis is:

Break-even point = Fixed costs / (Seling price per unit – Variable cost per unit)

In this case, the break-even point would be:

Break-even point = $10,000 / ($15 – $5)

Break-even point = $10,000 / $10

Break-even point = 1,000 t-shirts

Therefore, in order to cover its costs and start making a profit, the company needs to sell 1,000 t-shirts. Once the company surpasses the break-even point and sells more than 1,000 t-shirts, it will start making a profit. The profit will be equal to the number of units sold minus the break-even point, multiplied by the selling price per unit.

For example, if the company sells 1,500 t-shirts, the profit would be:

Profit = (1,500 – 1,000) × $15

Profit = 500 × $15

Profit = $7,500

This break-even analysis example demonstrates how businesses can use this tool to make informed decisions about pricing, production levels, and sales targets. By understanding their break-even point, businesses can set realistic goals and strategies to ensure profitability (Trifan & Anton, 2011).

3.2.1. Why Perform a Break-Even Analysis?

Performing a break-even analysis is crucial for any business. It helps determine the point at which your business's total revenue equals its total costs, resulting in neither profit nor loss. This analysis allows you to understand the minimum amount of sales needed to cover all expenses and reach the break-even point (LE et al., 2020).

By conducting a break-even analysis, you gain valuable insights into your business's financial health. It helps you assess the viability of your current pricing strategy, production costs, and sales volume. Additionally, it enables you to make informed decisions regarding pricing adjustments, cost reductions, or sales targets.

Furthermore, a break-even analysis is essential for forecasting and budgeting purposes. It provides you with a clear understanding of the sales volume required to achieve your desired profit margins. This information is vital for setting realistic goals and creating an effective financial plan. Moreover, a break-even analysis assists in evaluating the impact of various scenarios on your business's profitability. It allows you to assess the effects of changes in fixed costs, variable costs, or selling prices. By understanding these impacts, you can make proactive decisions to optimize profitability and mitigate potential risks (Abdullahi et al., 2017).

3.2.2. The Standard Break-Even Time Period

The standard break-even time period refers to the amount of time it takes for a business or investment to recoup its initial investment and start making a profit. This is a crucial metric for businesses and investors as it helps determine the viability and profitability of a venture.

Keyword

Financial Feasibility – It is the ability of a project or business venture to generate enough revenue and profit to cover its costs and achieve a satisfactory return on investment.

The break-even time period is calculated by dividing the initial investment by the expected annual profit. For example, if a business invests $1,00,000 and expects to make a profit of $20,000 per year, the break-even time period would be five years ($1,00,000 / $20,000 = 5 years).

Understanding the break-even time period is essential for making informed financial decisions. It allows businesses and investors to assess the risks and potential returns of a venture. A shorter break-even time period indicates a faster return on investment and higher profitability, while a longer break-even time period may indicate a riskier investment with a slower return on investment.

By analyzing the break-even time period, businesses, and investors can evaluate the financial feasibility of a project and make strategic decisions. They can determine if a project is worth pursuing, if adjustments need to be made to increase profitability, or if alternative investments should be considered (Lulaj & Iseni, 2018).

3.2.3. When to Use a Break-Even Analysis?

One instance in which a break-even analysis is useful is when a business is considering launching a new product. By calculating the break-even point, which is the point at which the revenue from selling the product equals the costs of producing and selling it, the business can determine if the product will be profitable. This analysis takes into account factors such as the selling price, variable costs (costs that vary with the level of production), and fixed costs (costs that do not change with the level of production). By comparing the break-even point with the expected sales volume, the business can assess if the product will generate enough revenue to cover costs and make a profit. Another situation in which a break-even analysis is helpful is when a business is considering changing its pricing strategy. By analyzing the break-even point at different price levels, the business can determine the impact on profitability. For example, if the break-even point is too high at the current price, the business may need to consider lowering the price to increase sales volume and reach the break-even point. On the other hand, if the break-even point is already low and the business wants to increase profitability, it may consider raising the price.

Keyword

Sales Mix – It is the proportion of different products or services sold by a company.

A break-even analysis can also be beneficial when a business is evaluating its cost structure. By identifying the fixed and variable costs, the business can assess if there are any opportunities to reduce costs and improve profitability. For example, if the business identifies high fixed costs, it may explore options to decrease these costs, such as renegotiating contracts or finding more cost-effective suppliers (Trifan & Anton, 2011).

3.2.4. Factors That Increase a Company's Break-Even Point

There are several factors that can increase a company's break-even point, making it more challenging to achieve profitability.

One factor is an increase in fixed costs. Fixed costs are expenses that do not change regardless of the level of production or sales. Examples of fixed costs include rent, salaries, and insurance. If a company experiences an increase in fixed costs, such as higher rent or salaries, its break-even point will also increase. This means that the company will need to generate more sales to cover these additional expenses and reach profitability.

Another factor that can increase the break-even point is a decrease in the selling price per unit. The selling price per unit is the amount of money a company receives for each product sold. If the selling price per unit decreases, the company will need to sell more units to cover its costs and break even. This can happen due to various reasons, such as increased competition or changes in market demand.

Additionally, an increase in variable costs can also contribute to a higher break-even point. Variable costs are expenses that change in direct proportion to the level of production or sales. Examples of variable costs include raw materials, direct labor, and packaging. If a company experiences an increase in variable costs, such as higher raw material prices or labor costs, its break-even point will increase. This means that the company will need to sell more products to cover these additional expenses and achieve profitability.

Lastly, changes in the sales mix can also impact the break-even point. If there is a shift in the sales mix towards products with lower profit margins, the break-even point will increase. This is because the company will need to sell more of these lower-margin products to cover its costs and reach profitability (LE et al., 2020).

3.2.5. How to Reduce the Break-Even Point?

Reducing the break-even point can be beneficial for a company, as it allows for faster profitability and increased financial stability. Here are some strategies to help you lower your break-even point:

1. **Cut Costs:** Analyze your expenses and identify areas where you can make cuts. Look for inefficiencies in your operations, negotiate better deals with suppliers, and consider outsourcing non-core activities. By reducing costs, you can decrease the amount of revenue needed to cover your expenses.
2. **Increase Prices:** Evaluate your pricing strategy and determine if you can raise prices without negatively impacting demand. Incremental price increases can help boost your profit margin and lower the break-even point.
3. **Improve Efficiency:** Streamline your processes to increase productivity and reduce waste. Look for ways to automate tasks, eliminate bottlenecks, and improve the overall efficiency of your operations. This will enable you to produce more output with the same amount of resources, effectively lowering your break-even point.
4. **Increase Sales:** Implement marketing strategies to attract new customers and encourage repeat business. Invest in advertising, improve your online presence, and offer promotions or discounts to drive sales. By increasing your sales volume, you can spread your fixed costs over a larger revenue base, thus reducing the break-even point.
5. **Diversify Revenue Streams:** Relying on a single product or service can be risky, as it leaves your business vulnerable to fluctuations in demand. Consider expanding your offerings or targeting new markets to diversify your revenue streams. This can help stabilize your income and lower the break-even point.
6. **Monitor and Adjust:** Continuously monitor your financial performance and adjust your strategies as needed. Regularly review your costs, pricing, efficiency, and sales to identify areas for improvement. By staying proactive and responsive, you can effectively reduce your break-even point over time.

3.2.6. The Limitations of a Break-Even Analysis

A break-even analysis is a valuable tool for businesses to assess the point at which their total revenue equals their total costs, resulting in neither profit nor loss. However, it is important to recognize that this analysis has its limitations.

Firstly, a break-even analysis assumes that all costs and revenues are linear and constant. In reality, costs and revenues are often subject to fluctuations. For example, fixed costs such as rent and salaries may remain constant, but variable costs like raw materials and labor expenses can change due to factors such as inflation or market conditions. Similarly, revenues can be affected by factors like changes in consumer demand or competitor actions. Thus, a break-even analysis may not accurately reflect the actual costs and revenues over time. Secondly, a break-even analysis assumes that the business operates at full capacity. This means that all available resources are being utilized efficiently. However, in reality, businesses often face underutilization or overutilization of resources. Underutilization occurs when the business is not operating at its full potential, leading to increased costs and lower revenues. Overutilization, on the other hand, can result in decreased quality, customer dissatisfaction, and increased costs. These scenarios are not accounted for in a break-even analysis, limiting its applicability.

Furthermore, a break-even analysis does not consider external factors that can impact a business. It does not account for changes in the market, such as shifts in consumer preferences or technological advancements. These external factors can significantly affect a business's profitability and sustainability. Therefore, relying solely on a break-even analysis may lead to inaccurate decision-making.

Lastly, a break-even analysis assumes that all units produced are sold. In reality, businesses may face inventory management issues or experience fluctuations in demand, resulting in unsold units. This can lead to additional costs, such as storage or disposal expenses, which are not considered in a break-even analysis (Trifan & Anton, 2011).

Did You Understand?

1. Why is break-even analysis important for businesses?
2. How do you calculate the break-even point?

Answer 1: Understanding break-even analysis is essential for the success of businesses. Understanding the point at which total revenue equals total costs is crucial for businesses. This balance ensures that there is neither profit nor loss. This analysis offers valuable insights into the minimum sales threshold needed to cover all expenses and begin generating profits. Understanding the break-even point allows businesses to make well-informed decisions regarding pricing, cost management, and sales targets. Break-even analysis plays a crucial role in the financial success of businesses, providing them with valuable insights and direction towards achieving stability and profitability.

Answer 2: Finding the point at which total revenue and total costs equal is the first step in calculating the break-even point. For businesses to evaluate their profitability and make wise decisions, this is an essential metric. The selling price of the good or service, fixed costs, and variable costs must all be taken into account when figuring out the break-even point. You can calculate the number of units or services that must be sold to cover all expenses and reach a break-even point by examining these variables.

Here is the formula to determine the break-even point:

Break-even point (in units) = Fixed costs / (Seling price per unit – Variable cost per unit)

3.3. TARGET PROFIT ANALYSIS

Learning Objectives

- The primary objective in this section is to learn and understand basic information about target profit analysis.

Target profit analysis is a useful tool for businesses to determine the level of sales needed to achieve a desired profit goal. By conducting this analysis, businesses can assess the feasibility of their profit targets and make informed decisions about pricing, costs, and sales volume.

To perform a target profit analysis, businesses need to consider several factors:

- First, they must identify the desired profit level they want to achieve. This could be a specific dollar amount or a percentage of sales.
- Next, they need to determine the fixed and variable costs associated with their products or services.
- Once the profit goal and costs are identified, businesses can calculate the contribution margin, which is the difference between sales revenue and variable costs. By dividing the fixed costs by the contribution margin, businesses can determine the sales volume needed to achieve the target profit.

To illustrate, suppose a company wants to achieve a target profit of $50,000. To calculate the sales required to reach this goal, we need to consider the company's fixed costs, variable costs, and contribution margin.

Fixed costs are expenses that do not change with the level of production or sales. These include rent, salaries, and insurance. Let's assume the company's fixed costs amount to $30,000.

Variable costs, on the other hand, vary with the level of production or sales. They include materials, labor, and direct overhead costs. For our example, let's assume the company's variable costs are $20 per unit.

Contribution margin is the difference between the selling price per unit and the variable cost per unit. It represents the amount of profit available to cover fixed costs and contribute to the target profit. In our example, let's assume the selling price per unit is $50.

To calculate the contribution margin, we subtract the variable cost per unit ($20) from the selling price per unit ($50). This gives us a contribution margin of $30 per unit.

Next, we divide the target profit ($50,000) by the contribution margin per unit ($30) to determine the number of units that need to be sold. In this case, the company needs to sell approximately 1,667 units to reach the target profit.

By using this target profit calculation, businesses can effectively set their sales goals and make informed decisions about pricing, costs, and production levels. It provides a clear target to strive for and helps in assessing the financial health and success of a company (LE et al., 2020).

Keyword

Financial Health – It is the state of business's or one's financial situation and the ability to meet financial obligations and goals.

3.4. ASSUMPTIONS AND LIMITATIONS OF CVP ANALYSIS

Although Cost-Volume-Profit (CVP) analysis is a valuable tool for businesses to assess the relationship between costs, volume, and profit, it is important to recognize the assumptions and limitations associated with it.

Firstly, CVP analysis assumes that costs can be classified as either fixed or variable. While this assumption simplifies the analysis, it may not accurately represent the true nature of costs in reality. Some costs may have both fixed and variable components, making it challenging to accurately assign them to a specific category.

Secondly, CVP analysis assumes that the sales mix remains constant. In other words, it assumes that the proportion of different products or services sold remains the same. However, in practice, businesses often experience changes in their sales mix, which can impact the accuracy of CVP analysis.

Additionally, CVP analysis assumes that all units produced are sold. This assumption may not hold true in situations where there is excess production or unsold inventory. In such cases, the analysis may not accurately reflect the actual profit or loss.

Furthermore, CVP analysis assumes that costs and revenues are linear and can be accurately predicted. However, in reality, costs and revenues may not always follow a linear pattern. Factors such as economies of scale, changes in market conditions, and fluctuations in production levels can affect the accuracy of CVP analysis.

Lastly, CVP analysis assumes that the time frame under consideration is short-term. It does not account for long-term changes in costs, volumes, or prices. Therefore, it is important to use CVP analysis in conjunction with other tools and consider its limitations when making strategic business decisions (Abdullahi et al., 2017).

Did You Understand?

1. What factors need to be considered when performing a target profit analysis?
2. What are some assumptions and limitations of Cost-Volume-Profit (CVP) analysis?

Answer 1: Businesses need to consider the desired profit level, fixed and variable costs, and the contribution margin.

Answer 2: CVP analysis assumes that costs can be classified as fixed or variable, that the sales mix remains constant, that all units produced are sold, that costs and revenues are linear, and that the time frame is short-term.

CASE STUDY

- **Introduction:** This case study focuses on the application of Cost-Volume-Profit (CVP) analysis in the context of Swizcom, a software company. CVP analysis is a managerial accounting technique that helps businesses understand the relationship between costs, volume, and profits. By analyzing these factors, Swizcom can make informed decisions regarding pricing, sales volume, and overall profitability.
- **Background:** Swizcom develops and sells software products to businesses. The company's main product is a project management software, which is sold through a subscription model. Swizcom's management team wants to evaluate the financial implications of potential changes in pricing and sales volume. To accomplish this, they decide to conduct a CVP analysis.
- **CVP Analysis:** The first step in the CVP analysis is to identify the company's fixed and variable costs. Fixed costs are expenses that do not change with the level of production or sales. Examples of fixed costs for Swizcom include rent, salaries, and insurance. Variable costs, on the other hand, fluctuate in direct proportion to the level of production or sales. Examples of variable costs for Swizcom include raw materials, direct labor, and sales commissions.

Once the fixed and variable costs are determined, the next step is to calculate the contribution margin. The contribution margin is the difference between sales revenue and variable costs. It represents the amount of revenue that is available to cover fixed costs and generate profits. By calculating the contribution margin, Swizcom can determine the breakeven point, which is the level of sales at which the company neither makes a profit nor incurs a loss.

- **Results:** After conducting the CVP analysis, Swizcom's management team discovers that the company's current pricing strategy is not generating enough profits. They decide to increase the price of the software product by 10% and analyze the impact on profitability. The CVP analysis shows that the breakeven point decreases, indicating that the company will achieve profitability at a lower sales volume.
- **Conclusion:** CVP analysis is a valuable tool for businesses like Swizcom to evaluate the financial implications of pricing and sales volume changes. By understanding the relationship between costs, volume, and profits, Swizcom can make informed decisions that maximize profitability. In this case study, the CVP analysis helped Swizcom identify the need for a price increase to improve profitability.

SUMMARY

Chapter 3 explores Cost-Volume-Profit (CVP) analysis, which is a crucial tool for businesses to understand the relationship between costs, volume, and profit, making informed decisions about pricing, production levels, and sales strategies. It involves calculating the contribution margin, which is the difference between sales revenue and variable costs. By calculating the contribution margin ratio, businesses can determine how much each unit contributes to covering fixed costs and generating profit.

The CVP analysis also involves calculating the breakeven point, which is the level of sales at which total revenue equals total costs. This information allows businesses to determine the minimum level of sales needed to cover all costs and start generating profit. Additionally, CVP analysis can be used to assess target profit, determining the level of sales required to achieve a desired profit target.

The Contribution Margin is a financial metric that measures the profitability of a product or service by subtracting the variable costs associated with producing the product or service from the revenue generated. It is essential for businesses to make informed decisions about pricing, product mix, and cost management. By analyzing the Contribution Margin, businesses can determine the impact of changes in pricing or costs on their profitability.

Break-even point analysis is a vital tool for businesses to determine the point at which their total revenue equals their total costs, resulting in neither profit nor loss. It helps businesses make informed decisions regarding pricing adjustments, cost reductions, or sales targets. Factors that can increase a company's break-even point include an increase in fixed costs, a decrease in the selling price per unit, an increase in variable costs, and changes in the sales mix.

To reduce the break-even point, businesses can cut costs, increase prices, improve efficiency, increase sales, diversify revenue streams, and monitor and adjust their strategies. By analyzing expenses, identifying inefficiencies, outsourcing non-core activities, streamlining processes, automating tasks, and reducing waste, businesses can decrease the amount of revenue needed to cover expenses.

Another tool discussed here is the target profit analysis. This is a crucial tool for businesses to determine the level of sales needed to achieve a desired profit goal.

However, CVP analysis has several assumptions and limitations, such as the assumption that costs can be classified as either fixed or variable, the assumption that the sales mix remains constant, that all units produced are sold, and that the time frame is short-term. Therefore, it is essential to use CVP analysis in conjunction with other tools and consider its limitations when making strategic business decisions.

MULTIPLE CHOICE QUESTIONS

1. **What is the purpose of cost-volume-profit (CVP) analysis?**
   a. To understand the relationship between costs, volume, and profit
   b. To calculate the breakeven point
   c. To determine the profitability of a product or service
   d. `All of the above
2. **What is the formula to calculate the breakeven point?**
   a. Breakeven point = Fixed costs / Seling price per unit
   b. Breakeven point = Fixed costs / Variable cost per unit
   c. Breakeven point = Fixed costs / (Seling price per unit – Variable cost per unit)
   d. Breakeven point = Seling price per unit / Variable cost per unit
3. **What does the contribution margin represent?**
   a. The difference between sales revenue and fixed costs
   b. The difference between sales revenue and variable costs
   c. The difference between variable costs and fixed costs
   d. The difference between variable costs and total costs
4. **How is the contribution margin expressed as a percentage?**
   a. By dividing it by the revenue and multiplying by 100
   b. By dividing it by the variable costs and multiplying by 100
   c. By dividing it by the fixed costs and multiplying by 100
   d. By dividing it by the total costs and multiplying by 100
5. **What can businesses determine by analyzing the contribution margin?**
   a. The profitability of different products or services
   b. The impact of changes in pricing or costs on profitability
   c. The breakeven point
   d. All of the above
6. **What is the formula to calculate the contribution margin?**
   a. Contribution Margin = Sales Revenue – Fixed Costs
   b. Contribution Margin = Sales Revenue – Variable Costs
   c. Contribution Margin = Variable Costs – Fixed Costs
   d. Contribution Margin = Variable Costs / Sales Revenue
7. **Which of the following is NOT a factor that can increase a company's break-even point?**
   a. Increase in fixed costs
   b. Decrease in selling price per unit

c. Increase in variable costs
d. Increase in sales volume

8. How can a decrease in selling price per unit affect a company's break-even point?

a. It decreases the break-even point
b. It has no impact on the break-even point
c. It increases the break-even point
d. It depends on the level of production or sales

9. What is one strategy to reduce the break-even point?

a. Increase prices
b. Decrease fixed costs
c. Decrease sales volume
d. Increase variable costs

10. What is target profit analysis used for?

a. To assess the relationship between costs, volume, and profit
b. To determine the level of sales needed to achieve a desired profit goal
c. To calculate the break-even point
d. To analyze the efficiency of a company's operations

11. What is one assumption of CVP analysis?

a. Costs can be classified as either fixed or variable
b. The sales mix remains constant
c. All units produced are sold
d. Costs and revenues are linear and can be accurately predicted

Answers to Multiple Choice Questions

1. (d); 2. (c); 3. (b); 4. (a); 5. (d); 6. (b); 7. (d); 8. (c); 9. (b); 10. (b); 11. (a)

REFERENCES

1. Abdullahi, S. R., Bello, S., Mukhtar, I. S., & Musa, M. H., (2017). Cost-volume-profit analysis as a management tool for decision making in small business enterprise within Bayero University, Kano. *IOSR Journal of Business and Management (IOSR-JBM)*, *19*(2), 40–45.
2. Fca, L. S., (2023). *What is Contribution Margin?* Flinder – Smart Finance Functions®. https://www.flinder.co/insights/what-is-contribution-margin (accessed on 04 April 2024).
3. Le, O. T. T., Tran, P. T. T., Tran, T. V., & Nguyen, C. V., (2020). Application of cost-volume-profit analysis in decision-making by public universities in Vietnam. *The Journal of Asian Finance, Economics and Business*, 7(6), 305–316.

4. Lulaj, E., & Iseni, E., (2018). Role of analysis CVP (cost-volume-profit) as important indicator for planning and making decisions in the business environment. *European Journal of Economics and Business Studies*, *4*(2).
5. The Business Plan Shop Ltd., (n.d.). https://www.thebusinessplanshop.com/en/help/glossary/breakeven-point (accessed on 04 April 2024).
6. Trifan, A., & Anton, C., (2011). Using cost-volume-profit analysis by management. *Bulletin of the Transilvania University of Brasov. Economic Sciences. Series V*, *4*(2), 207.

CHAPTER

4 Job Order Costing

LEARNING OBJECTIVES

After studying this chapter, you will be able to:

- Job cost sheets;
- Job order costing systems;
- Overhead allocation.

INTRODUCTORY EXAMPLE

Job Order Costing is a cost accounting system used by companies to track and allocate costs to specific jobs or projects. This system is particularly useful for companies that produce unique, customized products or services.

One example of a company that utilizes Job Order Costing is Jamba Company, a manufacturer of high-end bicycles. Each bicycle produced by Jamba Company is customized according to the customer's specifications, resulting in a unique product for each order.

To effectively track and allocate costs, Jamba Company assigns a unique job number to each bicycle order. This job number allows the company to identify and record all costs associated with that particular order. These costs include direct materials, direct labor, and manufacturing overhead.

Direct materials are the raw materials used to construct the bicycle, such as the frame, wheels, and gears. Jamba Company keeps detailed records of the quantity and cost of each material used for each job.

Direct labor refers to the wages paid to the employees directly involved in the production of the bicycle. Jamba Company records the number of hours worked by each employee on each job, along with their hourly wage rates.

Manufacturing overhead includes all other indirect costs incurred during the production process. This can include expenses such as utilities, depreciation of manufacturing equipment, and factory supervision. Jamba Company allocates these costs to each job based on a predetermined overhead rate.

Once all costs have been recorded, Jamba Company can calculate the total cost of each job by summing up the direct materials, direct labor, and manufacturing overhead. This information is crucial for determining the profitability of each job and making informed pricing decisions.

In conclusion, Job Order Costing is an essential tool for companies like Jamba Company that produce customized products or services. By accurately tracking and allocating costs to specific jobs, companies can make informed decisions about pricing, profitability, and resource allocation.

UNIT INTRODUCTION

Job order costing is a method used by companies to track and allocate costs to specific jobs or projects. This accounting system is commonly used in industries such as construction, manufacturing, and custom product development (Bottomley & Bosman, 2018).

The process begins with the creation of a job order, which includes details about the specific job or project, such as materials needed, labor hours required, and any other relevant expenses. As the job progresses, costs are recorded and accumulated for each job.

One of the key benefits of job order costing is that it allows companies to determine the profitability of individual jobs. By tracking costs at a job level, companies can identify which jobs are generating the most revenue and which ones are not performing as well. This information is crucial for making informed decisions about resource allocation and pricing strategies.

Job order costing also provides accurate and detailed information for financial reporting purposes. By tracking costs at a job level, companies can generate reports that show the total costs incurred for each job, allowing for better cost control and analysis.

Additionally, job order costing enables companies to accurately estimate costs for future jobs. By analyzing historical data from similar jobs, companies can make more accurate predictions about the costs associated with new projects. This helps in setting competitive prices and ensuring profitability.

In job order costing, there are several basic concepts and terminologies that are associated. These include direct materials, direct labor, and manufacturing overhead.

1. Direct materials refer to the materials that are specifically used in the production process for a particular job. These materials can be easily traced and assigned to a specific job. Examples of direct materials include raw materials and components.
2. Direct labor, on the other hand, refers to the labor costs that are directly associated with the production of a specific job. This includes the wages or salaries of the workers who are directly involved in the production process. These costs can also be easily traced and assigned to a specific job.
3. Manufacturing overhead, also known as indirect costs, includes all other costs that are not directly traceable to a specific job. These costs are incurred in the production process but cannot be easily assigned to a specific job. Examples of manufacturing overhead costs include factory rent, utilities, and depreciation of factory equipment.

Understanding these basic concepts and terminologies is essential in job order costing as they help in accurately determining the costs associated with each job. By properly allocating direct materials, direct labor, and manufacturing overhead, businesses can effectively track and control their costs, leading to more accurate pricing and better decision-making (Bottomley & Bosman, 2018).

4.1. JOB COST SHEETS

Learning Objectives

- To learn how to prepare a job cost sheet;
- To learn how to calculate the total cost of a job.

Job cost sheets are essential documents used in project management to track and record the costs associated with completing a specific job or project. These sheets provide a detailed breakdown of all expenses incurred throughout the duration of the job, including direct and indirect costs. By maintaining accurate job cost sheets, businesses can:

- Gain a better understanding of their project costs;
- Identify areas of improvement;
- Make more informed decisions regarding budgeting and resource allocation;
- Job cost sheets can be used for future reference and analysis, allowing businesses to compare actual costs to estimated costs and evaluate the overall profitability of a project.

4.1.1. Preparing a Job Cost Sheet

To prepare a job cost sheet, start by gathering all relevant information about the job. This includes the job number, customer name, and description of the work to be done. Additionally, gather any estimates or quotes for labor, materials, and other expenses.

Next, create a table with columns for each cost category. These categories may include labor, materials, subcontractors, equipment, and overhead costs. Within each category, list the specific costs incurred, along with their corresponding amounts.

When recording labor costs, be sure to include the number of hours worked, the rate per hour, and the total labor cost for each employee involved in the job. For materials, include the quantity used, the unit cost, and the total cost of materials used.

Subcontractor costs should include the name of the subcontractor, the services provided, and the total cost of their services. Equipment costs should include any rental fees or depreciation expenses. Overhead costs, such as utilities or administrative expenses, should also be included.

Once all costs have been recorded, calculate the total cost for each category and the overall total cost of the job. This will provide a comprehensive overview of all expenses incurred throughout the project.

To illustrate the process of creating a job cost sheet, let's consider the following example:

Imagine a construction company that has been hired to build a new office building. The project is estimated to take six months to complete, and the company wants to closely monitor all costs associated with the job.

To begin, the company would create a job cost sheet specifically for this project. The sheet would include the following information:

1. Job Name: "New Office Building Construction"
2. Job Number: 12345
3. Job Description: Detailed description of the project, including specifications and requirements.

Next, the company would start recording all costs associated with the job. This includes direct costs, such as materials and labor, as well as indirect costs, such as overhead expenses.

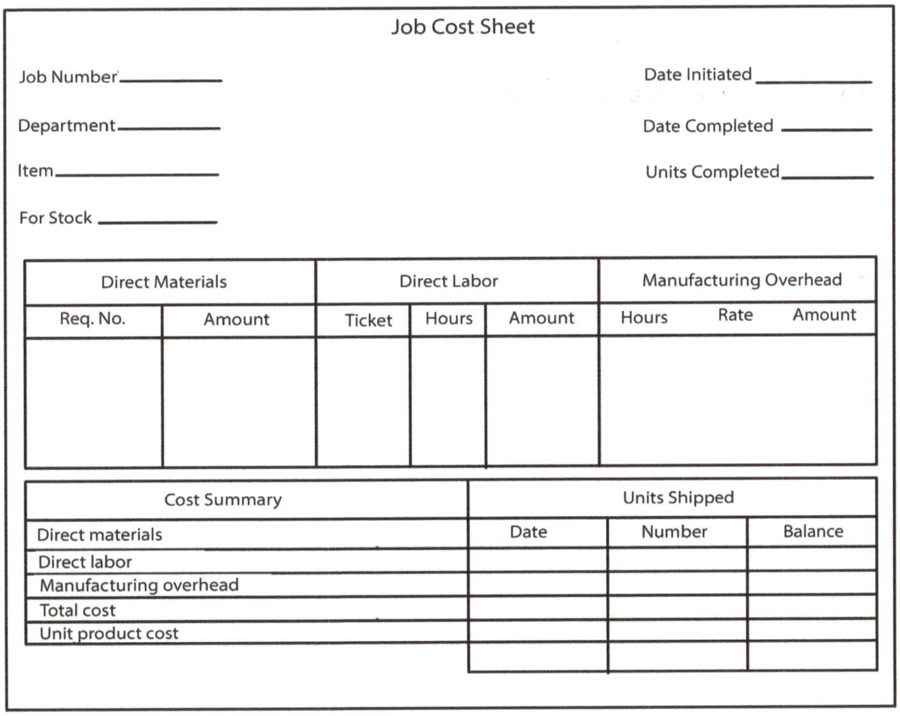

Job Cost Sheet

Job Number ________ Date Initiated ________

Department ________ Date Completed ________

Item ________ Units Completed ________

For Stock ________

Direct Materials		Direct Labor			Manufacturing Overhead		
Req. No.	Amount	Ticket	Hours	Amount	Hours	Rate	Amount

Cost Summary	Units Shipped		
	Date	Number	Balance
Direct materials			
Direct labor			
Manufacturing overhead			
Total cost			
Unit product cost			

Figure 4.1. An example of a job cost sheet.

Source: Tamplin (2023).

For each cost incurred, the company would record the following information on the job cost sheet:

1. Date: The date when the cost was incurred.

2. Description: A brief description of the cost.
3. Quantity: The quantity of materials used, or the number of labor hours worked.
4. Unit Cost: The cost per unit of material or labor.
5. Total Cost: The total cost of the item or service.

By consistently updating the job cost sheet with all incurred costs, the company can keep track of the total expenses associated with the project. This information is crucial for accurate financial reporting and helps businesses make informed decisions regarding future projects (Bottomley & Bosman, 2018) (Figure 4.1).

4.1.2. Calculating the Total Cost of a Job

The importance of accurately calculating the total cost cannot be overstated, as it directly impacts the profitability and success of any project or job. By thoroughly analyzing the various elements that contribute to the total cost, we can gain insight into how to effectively manage and control expenses.

To begin with, it is crucial to define what constitutes the total cost of a job. The total cost encompasses all expenses incurred throughout the entire duration of the project, including both direct and indirect costs.

Here is an example that illustrates how to calculate the cost of a job:

1. Determine the Direct Costs: Direct costs are expenses that can be directly attributed to the job. These may include materials, labor, equipment, and subcontractor fees. To calculate the direct costs, add up the costs of all the items and services required for the job.
2. Consider the Indirect Costs: Indirect costs are expenses that are not directly tied to the job but are necessary for its completion. These may include overhead costs like rent, utilities, insurance, and administrative expenses. To calculate the indirect costs, estimate the percentage of these expenses that can be allocated to the job and add it to the direct costs.
3. Account for Contingency: Contingency costs are unforeseen expenses that may arise during the project. It is important to include a contingency amount to cover any unexpected costs. A common practice is to allocate a percentage of the total direct and indirect costs as the contingency amount.
4. Calculate the Total Cost: To determine the total cost of the job, add the direct costs, indirect costs, and contingency amount together.

Example:

1. Direct Costs:
   - Materials: $500
   - Labor: $1,000
   - Equipment: $200
   - Subcontractor fees: $300

Total Direct Costs: $2,000

2. Indirect Costs:
   - Overhead costs (estimated at 20% of direct costs): $400

Total Indirect Costs: $400

3. Contingency:
   - 10% of total direct and indirect costs: $240

Total Cost of the Job: $2,000 + $400 + $240 = $2,640

By following these steps, you can accurately calculate the cost of a job and ensure that your project remains financially feasible.

Did You Understand?

1. What is the purpose of job cost sheets in project management?
2. How do you calculate the total cost of a job?

Answer 1: The answer is that job cost sheets are essential documents used to track and record the costs associated with completing a specific job or project. They provide a detailed breakdown of all expenses incurred, helping businesses gain a better understanding of project costs, identify areas of improvement, and make informed decisions regarding budgeting and resource allocation. Job cost sheets can also be used for future reference and analysis to evaluate the overall profitability of a project.

Answer 2: The answer is that the total cost includes both direct and indirect costs. Direct costs are expenses directly attributed to the job, such as materials, labor, equipment, and subcontractor fees. Indirect costs are expenses necessary for the job's completion but not directly tied to it, such as overhead costs. To calculate the total cost, add the direct costs, estimated percentage of indirect costs, and a contingency amount for unforeseen expenses. By following these steps, businesses can accurately determine the total cost of a job and ensure financial feasibility.

4.2. JOB ORDER COSTING SYSTEMS

Learning Objectives

- To understand different job order costing systems;
- To learn the differences between job order costing and process costing.

Job order costing systems are used by companies to track the costs associated with producing individual units or batches of products. This system is particularly useful for businesses that produce unique or customized products, as it allows for the allocation of costs to specific jobs or projects (Hoque, 2005).

4.2.1. Different Job Order Costing Systems

There are different job order costing systems, including the job cost sheet, materials requisition form, and time ticket. These systems are essential for accurately tracking costs in a manufacturing environment (Bradford, 2010).

Firstly, the job cost sheet is a vital tool in job order costing. It provides a detailed breakdown of all costs associated with a specific job. The sheet includes information such as direct materials used, direct labor costs, and manufacturing overhead expenses. By recording these costs, the company can determine the total cost of each job and evaluate its profitability.

Materials Requisition
A.B. Co. Ltd.

Department .... Serial No. ....
Job No. .... Date ....

Qty.	Description	Code No.	Bin Card No.	Store Ledger Folio	Rate	Amount

Authorized by .... Received by ....
Storekeeper's Signature .... Checked by ....
Materials Abstract Prepared by ....

Figure 4.2. A specimen of the materials requisition form.

Source: Tamplin (2023).

Secondly, the materials requisition form plays a crucial role in job order costing. This form is used to request materials needed for a particular job. It includes details such as the quantity of materials required, the job number, and the date of the request. By documenting these details, the company can accurately allocate costs to each job and maintain an inventory of materials (Figure 4.2).

Lastly, the time ticket is another essential component of job order costing. This ticket is used to record the amount of time spent by employees on a specific job. It includes information such as the employee's name, the job number, and the hours worked. By tracking this information, the company can calculate the labor cost associated with each job and ensure accurate cost allocation (Figure 4.3).

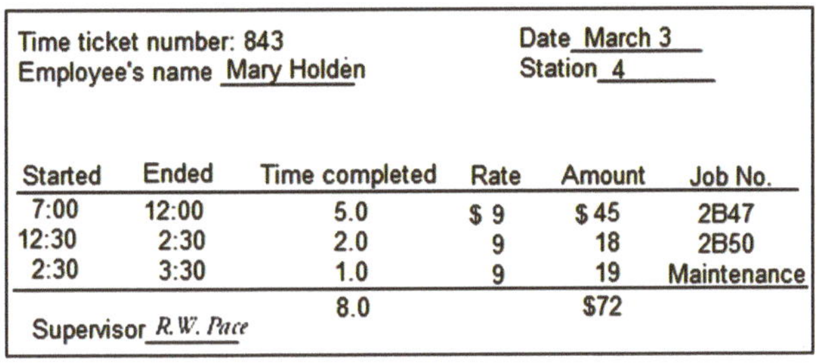

Time ticket number: 843
Employee's name Mary Holden
Date March 3
Station 4

Started	Ended	Time completed	Rate	Amount	Job No.
7:00	12:00	5.0	$ 9	$ 45	2B47
12:30	2:30	2.0	9	18	2B50
2:30	3:30	1.0	9	19	Maintenance
		8.0		$72	

Supervisor R.W. Pace

Figure 4.3. An example of employee time ticket.

Source: Javed (2023).

4.2.2. Job Order Costing vs. Process Costing

Job order costing and process costing are two different methods used by companies to allocate costs to their products or services. Each method has its own advantages and disadvantages, and understanding the differences between them is crucial for effective cost management.

Job order costing is used when a company produces unique products or services that are tailored to the specific needs of individual customers. This method involves tracking the costs associated with each individual job or project. For example, a construction company that builds custom homes would use job order costing to track the costs of each home it builds. The costs would include materials, labor, and overhead expenses specific to that particular project (Bradford, 2010).

Process costing, on the other hand, is used when a company produces homogeneous products or services that are indistinguishable from each other. This method involves allocating costs to each unit produced based on the average cost of producing all units. For example, a company that manufactures soda bottles would use process costing to allocate the costs of producing each bottle. The costs would include materials, labor, and overhead expenses averaged across all bottles produced.

While job order costing provides more detailed cost information for each individual job, process costing provides a broader picture of the overall costs of producing a large number of identical products. This can be useful for companies that produce goods or services on a large scale.

	Advantages	Disadvantages
Job order costing	• Provides a detailed breakdown of costs for each job, allowing for accurate pricing and profitability analysis. • Provides a clear understanding of the resources used for each job, making it easier to identify areas for cost reduction.	• Can be time-consuming and complex. • It requires extensive record-keeping and tracking of costs for each job. This can be challenging for businesses with a high volume of jobs or projects. • May not be suitable for businesses with standard, repetitive production processes.
Process costing	• Provides a simple and efficient way to determine the cost per unit. • It is particularly useful for businesses with continuous production processes, as it allows for easy tracking of costs throughout the production cycle.	• May not provide the same level of accuracy as job order costing. • It does not provide a detailed breakdown of costs for each individual unit, making it difficult to identify specific cost drivers. • May not be suitable for businesses with high variability in their production processes.

To select the most appropriate costing method, companies should consider the nature of their products and the production process. If the products are unique and require individual attention, job order costing is the better choice. However, if the products are standardized and go through similar processes, process costing is more suitable (Bradford, 2010).

Did You Understand?

1. What are the different job order costing systems and how do they help track costs?
2. What is the difference between job order costing and process costing?

Answers 1: The job cost sheet, materials requisition form, and time ticket are the essential tools for accurately tracking costs in a manufacturing environment. The job cost sheet provides a detailed breakdown of costs for each job, the materials requisition form helps allocate costs to each job and maintain an inventory of materials, and the time ticket tracks labor costs associated with each job.

Answer 2: Job order costing is used for unique products or services tailored to individual customers, while process costing is used for homogeneous products or services. Job order costing provides detailed cost information for each job, while process costing provides a broader picture of overall costs for a large number of identical products.

4.3. OVERHEAD ALLOCATION

Learning Objectives

To learn more about methods used in overhead allocation:

- Predetermined overhead rates;
- Activity-based costing (ABC).

Overhead allocation is a method used by companies to distribute their indirect costs to their products or services. The purpose of overhead allocation is to accurately assign these indirect costs to the products or services that caused them. This allows companies to determine the true cost of producing each item and make more informed decisions regarding pricing, profitability, and resource allocation (Greenberg & Schneider, 2010). The two key methods used in overhead allocation are discussed in subsections.

4.3.1. Predetermined Overhead Rates

The predetermined overhead rate is calculated by dividing the estimated overhead costs by the estimated activity level. This rate is then used to allocate overhead costs to products or services. By using a predetermined rate, companies can more accurately assign indirect costs to their products or services, which helps in determining the true cost of production (Greenberg & Schneider, 2010).

One commonly used method of allocating overhead costs is the traditional method. In this method, the predetermined overhead rate is calculated by dividing the estimated total overhead costs by the estimated total direct labor hours or machine hours. This rate is then applied to each product or service based on the actual direct labor hours or machine hours used.

Let's consider an example to better understand this concept. Deptech Manufacturing Company produces widgets. The estimated total manufacturing overhead costs for the year are $5,00,000. The company estimates that it will use 50,000 direct labor hours during the year as the allocation base. To calculate the predetermined overhead rate, we divide the estimated total manufacturing overhead costs by the estimated total amount of the allocation base:

In this case, the predetermined overhead rate would be:

Simplifying the calculation, we find that the predetermined overhead rate is $10 per direct labor hour.

Once the predetermined overhead rate is determined, it is used to allocate the manufacturing overhead costs to individual products or services. This is done by multiplying the predetermined overhead rate by the actual amount of the allocation base used by each product or service.

For example, if a widget requires 5 direct labor hours to produce, the manufacturing overhead cost allocated to that widget would be:

Manufacturing Overhead Cost =Predetermined Overhead Rate × Actual Amount of Allocation Base Used

Manufacturing Overhead Cost = $10 per direct labor hour × 5 direct labor hours

Therefore, the manufacturing overhead cost allocated to the widget would be $50.

The predetermined overhead rate is useful for budgeting and cost control purposes. By estimating the total manufacturing overhead costs and the allocation base, companies can plan and manage their costs more effectively. It also helps in determining the cost of each product or service, which is essential for pricing decisions and profitability analysis.

However, it is important to note that the predetermined overhead rate is an estimate and may not reflect the actual manufacturing overhead costs incurred. Variations in the actual amount of the allocation base used or unexpected changes in manufacturing overhead costs can result in differences between the allocated costs and the actual costs. To address this, companies often perform a year-end adjustment to reconcile the allocated costs with the actual costs (Greenberg & Schneider, 2010).

4.3.2. Activity-Based Costing (ABC)

Activity-based costing (ABC) is a costing method that aims to allocate costs to specific activities within an organization. It provides a more accurate way of determining the true cost of products or services, as it considers the resources consumed by each activity. By doing so, ABC allows for a more precise understanding of the cost drivers and enables better decision-making.

The ABC process involves several steps:

- First, activities are identified and classified into cost pools. Cost pools are groups of activities that share similar cost drivers. For example, in a manufacturing company, activities like machine setup, material handling, and quality control may be grouped together.
- Once the cost pools are established, cost drivers are identified for each activity. Cost drivers are the factors that cause costs to be incurred, such as the number of setups, the number of materials handled, or the number of inspections performed.
- Next, the costs associated with each activity are calculated. This includes both direct costs, which can be easily traced to an activity, and indirect costs, which need to be allocated based on a cost driver.
- Once the costs are assigned to activities, the next step is to allocate them to products or services. This is done by identifying the cost drivers for each product or service

and calculating the cost incurred by each driver. For example, if the cost driver for a product is the number of setups required, the cost of setups will be allocated based on the number of setups performed for that product. By allocating costs based on the actual consumption of resources, ABC provides a more accurate picture of the true cost of each product or service.

To understand ABC better, let's consider an example of a manufacturing company that produces two products: Product A and Product B. Traditionally, the company would allocate overhead costs based on the direct labor hours each product requires. However, this method fails to consider the fact that different activities consume resources at different rates. For instance, Product A may require more machine setup time, while Product B may require more inspection time. By using ABC, the company can allocate costs more accurately by considering the specific activities involved in producing each product.

To implement ABC, the company first identifies the activities involved in the production process. These activities can be divided into two categories: unit-level activities and batch-level activities. Unit-level activities are those that are performed for each unit produced, such as machine setup time. Batch-level activities, on the other hand, are performed for each batch of products, such as inspection time. By identifying these activities, the company can then assign costs to them based on their resource consumption.

Once the activities have been identified, the company needs to determine the cost drivers for each activity. Cost drivers are the factors that cause the activity to occur and, therefore, determine the cost of the activity. For example, the cost driver for machine setup time could be the number of setups required, while the cost driver for inspection time could be the number of batches inspected. By determining the cost drivers, the company can allocate costs more accurately based on the actual consumption of resources.

To illustrate how ABC works, let's consider the following example. The company produces two products: Product A and Product B. The following table shows the activities involved in the production process and their respective cost drivers:

Activity	Cost Driver
Machine setup time	Number of setups
Inspection time	Number of batches

Based on historical data, the company determines that Product A requires 10 machine setups and 5 batches of inspection, while Product B requires 5 machine setups and 10 batches of inspection. The total overhead cost for the period is $10,000.

Using traditional costing, the company would allocate the overhead cost based on the direct labor hours.

Let's assume that Product A requires 100 direct labor hours, while Product B requires 50 direct labor hours. If the overhead rate is $10 per direct labor hour, the company would allocate $1,000 of overhead cost to Product A and $500 to Product B.

However, by using ABC, the company can allocate costs more accurately based on the actual consumption of resources.

Let's assume that the cost driver rates for machine setup time and inspection time are $500 per setup and $200 per batch, respectively. The company would allocate:

$5,000 of overhead cost to Product A (10 setups × $500/setup)

$3,000 to Product B (5 setups × $500/setup + 10 batches × $200/batch)

Resulting in a total of $8,000.

As we can see from this example, ABC provides a more accurate way of allocating costs by considering the specific activities involved in the production process. By identifying the activities and their respective cost drivers, companies can allocate costs based on the actual consumption of resources, resulting in more accurate cost calculations.

The benefits of ABC are numerous.

- Firstly, it provides a more accurate understanding of the cost structure within an organization. This allows managers to make informed decisions regarding pricing, product mix, and process improvements. By identifying the activities that consume the most resources, managers can focus on reducing costs in those areas, leading to increased efficiency and profitability.
- Secondly, ABC helps in identifying and eliminating non-value-added activities. Non-value-added activities are those that do not contribute to the final product or service but still incur costs. By identifying these activities, managers can eliminate or streamline them, resulting in cost savings and improved productivity.
- Lastly, ABC promotes transparency and accountability within an organization. By assigning costs to specific activities, employees become aware of the impact their actions have on costs. This encourages them to find ways to reduce costs and improve efficiency.

Did You Understand?

1. What is the purpose of overhead allocation and how does it help companies in decision-making?
2. What is activity-based costing (ABC) and how does it provide a more accurate way of determining the true cost of products or services?

Answer 1: The purpose of overhead allocation is to accurately assign indirect costs to the products or services that caused them. This allows companies to determine the true cost of producing each item and make more informed decisions regarding pricing, profitability, and resource allocation.

Answer 2: Activity-based costing (ABC) is a costing method that aims to allocate costs to specific activities within an organization. It considers the resources consumed by each activity, providing a more precise understanding of the cost drivers. By allocating costs based on the actual consumption of resources, ABC provides a more accurate picture of the true cost of each product or service.

CASE STUDY

- **Introduction:** Job order costing is a widely used accounting method that helps businesses track the costs associated with producing individual products or providing specific services. This case study focuses on Jehob Company, a manufacturing firm that utilizes job order costing to monitor its production costs and make informed business decisions.
- **Background:** Jehob Company operates in the textile industry and specializes in producing custom-made garments. Each garment is unique and tailored to meet the specific requirements of individual customers. To accurately determine the cost of each garment, Jehob Company employs job order costing.

Job order costing process:

1. Cost Accumulation:
   - Jehob Company identifies each garment order as a separate job and assigns a unique job number to it.
   - All direct materials used in the production of a garment are recorded and allocated to the respective job.
   - Direct labor costs, including wages and benefits, are tracked, and assigned to the appropriate job.
   - Overhead costs, such as rent, utilities, and equipment depreciation, are allocated to each job based on a predetermined overhead rate.
2. Cost Allocation:
   - Once all costs are accumulated, Jehob Company calculates the total cost for each job by adding the direct materials, direct labor, and allocated overhead costs.
   - The total cost is then divided by the number of garments produced for that job, resulting in the cost per unit.
3. Cost Recording:
   - Jehob Company records the cost per unit for each job in its accounting system.
   - This information is crucial for determining the selling price of each garment and evaluating the profitability of individual jobs.

Benefits of Job Order Costing:

Job order costing provides several advantages for Jehob Company:

- **Accurate Cost Determination:** By tracking costs at the individual job level, Jehob Company can accurately determine the cost of each garment, ensuring proper pricing and profitability analysis.

- **Cost Control:** Job order costing enables Jehob Company to identify cost variances and take corrective actions to control expenses.
- **Decision Making:** With detailed cost information, Jehob Company can make informed decisions regarding pricing, resource allocation, and overall business strategy.

Conclusion:

Jehob Company's utilization of job order costing has proven to be an effective method for accurately determining the cost of custom-made garments. By implementing this costing system, Jehob Company can make informed business decisions, control costs, and enhance its overall profitability.

SUMMARY

Job order costing is a method used by companies to track and allocate costs to specific jobs or projects. It is commonly used in industries like construction, manufacturing, and custom product development. The process begins with creating a job order, which includes details about the specific job or project. As the job progresses, costs are recorded and accumulated for each job. Job order costing allows companies to determine the profitability of individual jobs, identify areas of improvement, make informed decisions regarding budgeting and resource allocation, and accurately estimate costs for future jobs. Basic concepts and terminologies in job order costing include direct materials, direct labor, and manufacturing overhead. Job cost sheets are essential documents used in project management to track and record the costs associated with completing a specific job or project. By maintaining accurate job cost sheets, businesses can gain a better understanding of their project costs, identify areas of improvement, and make more informed decisions regarding budgeting and resource allocation.

Accurately calculating the total cost of a job is crucial for project profitability and success. It involves determining direct costs, indirect costs, and contingency amounts. Job order costing systems are essential for tracking costs associated with producing individual units or batches of products. Different systems include the job cost sheet, materials requisition form, and time ticket. Job order costing is used when a company produces unique products or services tailored to individual needs, while process costing is used when a company produces homogeneous products or services. Job order costing provides a detailed breakdown of costs for each job, allowing for accurate pricing and profitability analysis. However, it can be time-consuming, complex, and may not be suitable for businesses with standard, repetitive production processes. Process costing is simple and efficient but may not provide the same level of accuracy as job order costing. To select the most appropriate costing method, companies should consider the nature of their products and production processes.

Overhead allocation is a method used by companies to distribute their indirect costs to their products or services, allowing them to determine the true cost of production and make informed decisions about pricing, profitability, and resource allocation. Two methods are used: predetermined overhead rates and activity-based costing (ABC). Predetermined overhead rates are calculated by dividing the estimated overhead costs by the estimated activity level, while activity-based costing (ABC) allocates costs to specific activities within an organization. Both methods help in budgeting, cost control, and determining the cost of each product or service, but the predetermined overhead rate may not reflect actual costs. Adjustments are often performed to reconcile the allocated costs with actual costs.

ABC (Asset-Based Cost Allocation) is a costing method that helps companies allocate overhead costs more accurately by considering the specific activities involved in producing each product. ABC involves identifying unit-level and batch-level activities, determining cost drivers for each activity, and allocating costs based on actual resource consumption. This approach provides a more accurate understanding of cost structure, enabling managers to make informed decisions about pricing, product mix, and process improvements. It also helps identify and eliminate non-value-added activities, leading to cost savings and improved productivity. ABC promotes transparency and accountability, encouraging employees to reduce costs and improve efficiency.

MULTIPLE CHOICE QUESTIONS

1. Which of the following is NOT a benefit of maintaining accurate job cost sheets?

a. Gain a better understanding of project costs

b. Identify areas of improvement

c. Make more informed decisions regarding budgeting and resource allocation

d. None of the above

2. What information should be included in a job cost sheet?

a. Job number, customer name, and description of work

b. Estimates or quotes for labor, materials, and other expenses

c. Columns for each cost category

d. All of the above

3. What is the purpose of calculating the total cost of a job?

a. To determine the profitability of the project

b. To make informed decisions regarding pricing and resource allocation

c. To evaluate the success of the project

d. All of the above

4. What are the two methods used by companies to allocate costs to their products or services?

a. Job order costing and process costing

b. Job costing and process costing

c. Job order costing and product costing

d. Job costing and product costing

5. When is job order costing used?

a. When a company produces unique products or services

b. When a company produces homogeneous products or services

c. When a company wants a broad picture of overall costs

d. When a company wants to allocate costs based on average cost

6. What is the purpose of process costing?

a. To track costs associated with each individual job or project

b. To allocate costs to each unit produced based on average cost

c. To provide a detailed breakdown of costs for each individual unit

d. To determine the true cost of producing each item

7. What is an advantage of job order costing?

a. Provides a detailed breakdown of costs for each job

b. Provides a simple and efficient way to determine cost per unit

c. Allows for easy tracking of costs throughout the production cycle

d. Provides a clear understanding of the resources used for each job

8. What is a disadvantage of job order costing?

a. Can be time-consuming and complex

b. May not provide the same level of accuracy as process costing

c. Does not provide a detailed breakdown of costs for each individual unit

cd. May not be suitable for businesses with high variability in their production processes

9. What is an advantage of process costing?

a. Provides a clear understanding of the resources used for each job

b. Provides a detailed breakdown of costs for each individual unit

c. Provides a simple and efficient way to determine cost per unit

d. Allows for easy tracking of costs throughout the production cycle

10. What is a disadvantage of process costing?

a. May not provide the same level of accuracy as job order costing

b. Can be time-consuming and complex

c. Does not provide a detailed breakdown of costs for each individual unit

d. May not be suitable for businesses with standard, repetitive production processes

11. What should companies consider when selecting a costing method?

a. The nature of their products and the production process

b. The size of their customer base

c. The level of competition in the market

d. The availability of raw materials

12. What is overhead allocation?

a. A method used by companies to distribute their indirect costs to their products or services

b. A method used by companies to distribute their direct costs to their products or services

c. A method used by companies to determine the true cost of production

d. A method used by companies to determine pricing and profitability

13. How is the predetermined overhead rate calculated in the traditional method?

a. By dividing estimated total overhead costs by estimated total direct labor hours or machine hours

b. By dividing actual total overhead costs by actual total direct labor hours or machine hours

c. By dividing estimated total direct labor hours or machine hours by estimated total overhead costs

d. By dividing actual total direct labor hours or machine hours by actual total overhead costs

14. What are the steps involved in the ABC process?

a. Identifying activities, identifying cost drivers, calculating costs, allocating costs

b. Allocating costs, calculating costs, identifying activities, identifying cost drivers

c. Calculating costs, identifying cost drivers, identifying activities, allocating costs

d. Identifying cost drivers, identifying activities, calculating costs, allocating costs

15. What is an advantage of using ABC?

a. Provides a more accurate understanding of the cost structure within an organization

b. Provides a detailed breakdown of costs for each individual unit

c. Provides a simple and efficient way to determine cost per unit

d. Provides a clear understanding of the resources used for each job

Answers to Multiple Choice Questions

1. (d); 2. (d); 3. (d); 4. (a); 5. (a); 6. (b); 7. (a); 8. (a); 9. (c); 10. (a); 11. (a); 12. (a); 13. (a); 14. (a); 15. (a)

REFERENCES

1. Bottomley, B., & Bosman, R., (2018). Job Costing: An Analysis of the Construction Industry. VOLUME 1 NO. 2
2. Bradford, B. M., (2010). Job order costing at sogel aviation. National Accounting Journal, 12(1).
3. Greenberg, R. K., & Schneider, A., (2010). Job order costing: A simulation and vehicle for conceptual discussion. Academy of Educational Leadership Journal, 14(3), 39–57.
4. Hoque, Z., (2005). Job order costing. Handbook of Cost and Management Accounting (pp. 61–67) London.
5. Javed, R., (2023). Measuring and Recording Direct Labor Cost. Accounting for Management. https://www.accountingformanagement.org/measuring-and-recording-direct-labor-cost/ (accessed on 04 April 2024).

6. Tamplin, T., (2023). Job Cost Sheet; Advantages, Format, Calculation, and Example. Finance Strategists. https://www.financestrategists.com/accounting/cost-accounting/job-costing/job-cost-sheet/ (accessed on 04 April 2024).

7. Tamplin, T., (2023). Material Requisition; Definition, Explanation and Format. Finance Strategists. https://www.financestrategists.com/accounting/cost-accounting/material-costing/material-requisition/ (accessed on 04 April 2024).

CHAPTER

5 Process Costing

LEARNING OBJECTIVES

After studying this chapter, you will be able to:

- The various steps in process costing;
- Types of process costing;
- The pros and cons of process costing;
- Cost flow in process costing.

INTRODUCTORY EXAMPLE

Process costing is a widely used accounting method employed by companies to determine the cost of producing goods in a continuous production process. This method is particularly useful for industries such as pharmaceuticals, where products are manufactured in large quantities over extended periods.

To better understand the concept of process costing, let's consider an example from Merck, a leading pharmaceutical company. Merck produces a variety of drugs and medications, and the production process involves multiple stages.

Firstly, the company obtains the necessary raw materials, such as chemicals and active ingredients, from suppliers. These materials are then transferred to the production department, where they undergo various processes, including mixing, heating, and cooling. Each process adds value to the materials and brings them closer to becoming a finished product.

Throughout the production process, costs are accumulated at each stage. These costs include direct materials, direct labor, and manufacturing overhead.

Once the production process is complete, the finished products are transferred to the packaging department, where they are prepared for distribution. The costs incurred during the packaging process are also accumulated and added to the overall production cost.

At the end of each accounting period, Merck calculates the total cost of production by summing up the costs incurred at each stage. This total cost is then divided by the number of units produced to determine the cost per unit.

Process costing provides valuable insights for companies like Merck, enabling them to track the cost of production accurately. This information is essential for decision-making, pricing strategies, and financial reporting.

UNIT INTRODUCTION

Process costing is a method used by companies to calculate the cost of producing goods or services in a continuous production process. It is commonly used in industries such as:

- Manufacturing;
- Chemical processing;
- Food processing, where goods are produced in large quantities and go through multiple stages of production.

In process costing, the total cost of production is divided by the total number of units produced to determine the cost per unit. This allows companies to have a better understanding of the cost of each unit and make informed decisions regarding pricing and profitability (Basu, 2020).

The process costing method involves tracking the costs incurred at each stage of production, including:

- Direct materials;
- Direct labor;
- Overhead costs.

These costs are accumulated and allocated to each unit produced, providing a comprehensive picture of the total cost involved in the production process.

Some key features of process costing include:

- The use of cost centers, which are specific areas or departments within a company where costs are incurred. By assigning costs to these cost centers, companies can analyze the efficiency and effectiveness of each department and identify areas for improvement.
- Process costing also allows for the calculation of the cost of unfinished goods, known as work-in-progress (WIP). This helps companies monitor the value of inventory at each stage of production and accurately report their financial position.

The importance of process costing cannot be overstated. It is a vital tool for businesses to accurately determine the cost of production for each unit of output. By tracking and allocating costs to specific processes, companies are able to make informed decisions regarding pricing, resource allocation, and overall profitability.

One of the key benefits of process costing is its ability to provide a detailed breakdown of costs at each stage of production. This allows businesses to identify areas where costs can be reduced, leading to increased efficiency and lower overall expenses. Additionally, process costing enables companies to accurately calculate the cost per unit, which is essential for pricing decisions.

Process costing also plays a crucial role in resource allocation. By understanding the costs associated with each process, businesses can allocate resources more effectively, ensuring that each process receives the necessary resources to operate efficiently. This leads to improved productivity and reduced waste.

Keyword

Inventory Control – It is an essential aspect of managing a business that involves keeping track of the goods and materials a company has in stock, as well as monitoring their movement in and out of the business.

Furthermore, process costing provides valuable insights into the profitability of different products or services. By comparing the costs and revenues associated with each process, businesses can identify which products or services are generating the highest profits and focus their efforts accordingly.

There are several reasons why businesses should consider implementing this method in their operations.

1. It allows for better monitoring of profit margins. By tracking the costs incurred at each stage of the production process, businesses can accurately determine the profitability of their products. This information is crucial for making informed decisions and improving overall financial performance.
2. Process costing helps with inventory control. By assigning costs to each process, businesses can easily identify any discrepancies or inefficiencies in their inventory management. This allows for more effective planning and allocation of resources, ultimately leading to cost savings and improved efficiency.
3. Process costing promotes uniformity in reporting. With a standardized method of cost allocation, businesses can ensure consistency and comparability in their financial statements. This makes it easier for internal and external stakeholders to analyze and evaluate the company's performance.

Key Takeaways from Process Costing:

1. Process costing is a method used to determine the cost of producing a product or service in a continuous production process.
2. It is commonly used in industries such as manufacturing, chemicals, and food processing, where products go through multiple stages of production.
3. Process costing involves allocating costs to different stages of production, such as materials, labor, and overhead, to determine the total cost of each unit produced.
4. Process costing provides valuable information for decision-making, such as pricing decisions, cost control, and performance evaluation.
5. Process costing is different from job costing, which is used for unique or customized products or services.
6. It is important to accurately track and allocate costs in process costing to ensure accurate cost calculations and decision-making.
7. Process costing can be complex, especially in industries with multiple production processes or high overhead costs.
8. However, with proper implementation and regular monitoring, process costing can provide valuable insights into the cost of production and help businesses make informed decisions.

5.1. STEPS IN PROCESS COSTING

Learning Objectives:

The main objective of this section to learn various steps in process costing, including:

- Analyzing inventory;
- Calculating equivalent units;
- Calculating applicable costs;
- Calculating the cost per unit;
- Allocating costs to complete and incomplete products.

5.1.1. Analyzing Inventory

The first step in process costing is to analyze the inventory. This involves examining the different types of costs that are incurred during the production process. These costs can be classified into three categories:

1. Direct Materials: These are the materials that are directly used in the production process. Examples include raw materials, components, and packaging materials.
2. Direct Labor: This refers to the wages and salaries of the workers who are directly involved in the production process. It includes the time spent on assembling, testing, and packaging the product.
3. Overhead Costs: These are the indirect costs that are not directly related to the production process. Examples include rent, utilities, and depreciation of equipment.

To illustrate this process, let's consider an example of a chocolate manufacturing company. The company produces chocolate bars in a continuous production process. The first step is to analyze the inventory of the chocolate bars.

- The direct materials for the chocolate bars include cocoa beans, sugar, milk, and packaging materials.
- The direct labor includes the wages of the workers who are involved in the production process, such as the chocolatiers and the packaging workers.

- The overhead costs include the rent of the production facility, the utilities, and the depreciation of the production equipment.

By analyzing the inventory, the company can determine the total cost of producing the chocolate bars. This information is important for decision-making purposes, such as setting the selling price of the product and determining the profitability of the company (Basu, 2020).

Quick Fact

Approximately 34% of businesses have encountered situations where they unintentionally sold a product that was unavailable in their inventory, resulting in delayed order shipments.

5.1.2. Calculating Equivalent Units

The second most important step in process costing is calculating the equivalent units. Equivalent units refer to the number of units that have been partially completed and are expressed in terms of fully completed units. This is necessary because in a continuous manufacturing process, not all units are completed at the same time. Some units may be partially completed while others are still in progress (Parkinson, 2015).

To calculate the equivalent units, the following steps can be followed:

1. Determine the number of units that are fully completed. These units do not require any additional work and can be considered fully finished.
2. Determine the number of units that are partially completed. These units require further work before they can be considered fully finished.
3. Convert the partially completed units into equivalent units. This is done by multiplying the number of partially completed units by the percentage of completion. For example, if there are 100 partially completed units and they are 50% complete, the equivalent units would be 50 units.
4. Add the fully completed units and the equivalent units together to get the total number of units produced.

To illustrate this process, let's consider an example:

Company X is a furniture manufacturer that produces chairs. In a particular month, Company X started with 500 chairs in production. During the month, 1,000 chairs were started, and 800 chairs were completed. At the end of the month, there were 700 chairs still in progress.

Using the steps outlined above, we can calculate the equivalent units:

1. Fully completed units: 800 chairs.

2. Partially completed units: 700 chairs.
3. Equivalent units: 700 chairs × 100% = 700 chairs.

Adding the fully completed units and the equivalent units together, we find that a total of 1,500 units were produced during the month.

By calculating the equivalent units, companies can accurately determine the cost per unit and make informed decisions regarding pricing and production. This information is crucial for effective cost management and overall profitability.

5.1.3. Calculating Applicable Costs

Process costing is a method used to determine the cost of producing a product or service in a continuous manufacturing process. This process involves several steps that need to be followed in order to accurately calculate the applicable costs.

- Step 1: Determine the number of units produced during the period. This can be done by counting the finished units or by estimating the number of units based on the production schedule.
- Step 2: Calculate the total cost of production. This includes both direct and indirect costs. Direct costs are those that can be directly traced to the production process, such as raw materials and direct labor. Indirect costs are those that cannot be directly traced to the production process, such as factory overhead and administrative expenses.
- Step 3: Determine the cost per unit. To do this, divide the total cost of production by the number of units produced. This will give you the cost per unit.
- Step 4: Allocate the costs to the different production departments or processes. This step involves assigning the costs to the various departments or processes based on their usage of resources. This can be done using different allocation methods, such as the weighted average method or the first-in, first-out method.
- Step 5: Calculate the cost of goods completed and transferred out. This is the cost of the units that have been completed during the period and transferred to the next department or process. To calculate this, multiply the number of completed units by the cost per unit.
- Step 6: Calculate the cost of goods in process. This is the cost of the units that are still in the production process at the end of the period. To calculate this, multiply the number of units in process by the cost per unit.

To illustrate these steps, let's consider an example. ABC Manufacturing Company produces widgets. During the month of January, they produced 1,000 widgets. The total cost of production for the month was $10,000, which includes $6,000 in direct costs and $4,000 in indirect costs. The cost per unit is calculated by dividing the total cost of production by the number of units produced, which is $10 per unit.

ABC Manufacturing has two production departments: Department A and Department B. Department A produced 600 units, while Department B produced 400 units. To allocate the costs, ABC Manufacturing uses the weighted average method. The cost of goods completed and transferred out from Department A is $6,000 (600 units × $10 per unit), while the cost of goods completed and transferred out from Department B is $4,000 (400 units × $10 per unit).

At the end of January, there were 200 units still in process in Department A and 100 units still in process in Department B. The cost of goods in process for Department A is $2,000 (200 units × $10 per unit), and the cost of goods in process for Department B is $1,000 (100 units × $10 per unit).

By following these steps and using the example provided, ABC Manufacturing Company can accurately calculate the applicable costs for their production process.

5.1.4. Calculating the Cost Per Unit

Calculating the cost per unit is particularly useful in industries where products are produced in large quantities, such as the food processing or chemical industries. To calculate the cost per unit in process costing, there are several steps that need to be followed.

First, the total cost of production for a given period is determined. This includes both direct costs, such as raw materials and direct labor, as well as indirect costs, such as factory overhead.

Next, the total number of units produced during the period is determined. This can be done by counting the number of units completed or by using an estimate based on the amount of work done. Once the total cost and total number of units are known, the cost per unit can be calculated by dividing the total cost by the total number of units.

For example, if the total cost of production is $10,000 and 1,000 units were produced, the cost per unit would be $10.

Understanding the cost per unit is important for a variety of reasons. It allows companies to determine the profitability of their products and make informed decisions about pricing and production. Additionally, it provides valuable information for financial reporting and budgeting purposes (Parkinson, 2015).

5.1.5. Allocating Costs to Complete and Incomplete Products

Process costing involves allocating costs to both complete and incomplete products through a series of steps.

The first step in process costing is to identify the different production departments or stages involved in the manufacturing process. Each department is assigned a unique cost center, which allows for accurate cost allocation. Once the cost centers are established, the next step is to determine the total costs incurred in each department. These costs include direct materials, direct labor, and manufacturing overhead. Direct materials refer to the raw materials directly used in the production process, while direct labor includes the wages of employees directly involved in manufacturing the product. Manufacturing overhead covers all other indirect costs, such as utilities, rent, and depreciation.

After the total costs are determined, they are allocated to the units produced in each department. This is done by dividing the total costs by the number of units produced.

For example, if a department incurs $10,000 in costs and produces 1,000 units, the cost per unit would be $10 ($10,000 divided by 1,000 units).

In process costing, it's important to note that costs are allocated to both complete and incomplete products. This means that costs are assigned to products that are still in progress and have not yet reached the final stage of production. This is different from job costing, where costs are only allocated to completed products. To illustrate this process, let's consider a company that manufactures cookies. The production process involves two departments: mixing and baking. In the mixing department, the company incurs $5,000 in costs and produces 2,000 units. This results in a cost per unit of $2.50 ($5,000 divided by 2,000 units).

In the baking department, the company incurs $7,500 in costs and produces 3,000 units. This gives a cost per unit of $2.50 ($7,500 divided by 3,000 units).

By allocating costs to both complete and incomplete products, process costing provides a comprehensive view of the costs incurred at each stage of production. This information is valuable for decision-making, cost control, and pricing purposes (Basu, 2020).

Did You Understand?

1. What are the three categories of costs in the production process?
2. How can equivalent units be calculated in process costing?
3. What are the steps involved in calculating applicable costs in process costing?
4. Why is calculating the cost per unit important in process costing?

Answer 1: The three categories of costs in the production process are direct materials, direct labor, and overhead costs.

Answer 2: Equivalent units can be calculated by determining the number of fully completed units, the number of partially completed units, and converting the partially completed units into equivalent units based on their percentage of completion.

Answer 3: The steps involved in calculating applicable costs in process costing are determining the number of units produced, calculating the total cost of production, determining the cost per unit, allocating costs to different production departments or processes, calculating the cost of goods completed and transferred out, and calculating the cost of goods in process.

Answer 4: Calculating the cost per unit is important in process costing because it allows companies to determine the profitability of their products, make informed decisions about pricing and production, and provides valuable information for financial reporting and budgeting purposes.

5.2. TYPES OF PROCESS COSTING

Learning Objectives

To learn and understand various types of process costing, including:

- Weighted average costs;
- Standard costs;
- First-in, first-out (FIFO).

5.2.1. Weighted Average Costs

One of the common methods used in process costing is weighted average costs. In method, the costs incurred in each process are averaged out over the units produced. This means that the cost per unit is determined by dividing the total costs incurred in a process by the total number of units produced in that process. The weighted average cost per unit is then used to determine the cost of the finished goods (Drury, 2013).

To illustrate how weighted average costs work, let's consider an example.

Suppose a company has two processes involved in the production of a product: Process A and Process B. In Process A, 1,000 units are produced with total costs incurred of $10,000. In Process B, 2,000 units are produced with total costs incurred of $15,000.

To determine the weighted average cost per unit, we add up the total costs incurred in both processes ($10,000 + $15,000 = $25,000) and divide it by the total number of units produced (1,000 + 2,000 = 3,000). The weighted average cost per unit is therefore $25,000/3,000 = $8.33.

Using this weighted average cost per unit, we can calculate the cost of the finished goods. For example, if 500 units are completed in Process B, the cost of these units would be 500 units × $8.33 = $4,165.

5.2.2. Standard Costs

Standard costs are an important component of process costing. They are predetermined costs that companies establish for each product or service. Standard costs are based on factors such as historical data, industry standards, and management's expectations.

To understand the concept of standard costs in process costing, let's consider an example.

Imagine a company that manufactures widgets. The company has determined that the standard cost per widget is $10. This includes:

- $3 for direct materials.
- $4 for direct labor.
- $3 for overhead.

During a specific period, the company produces 1,000 widgets. The actual costs incurred during this period are $3,200 for direct materials, $4,500 for direct labor, and $3,800 for overhead. To calculate the cost per widget using standard costs, we would divide the total actual costs by the number of widgets produced. In this case;

The cost per widget would be ($3,200 + $4,500 + $3,800) / 1,000 = $11.50.

By comparing the standard cost per widget ($10) to the actual cost per widget ($11.50), the company can identify any variances and take appropriate actions. Variances may occur due to factors such as:

- Changes in material prices.
- Labor inefficiencies.
- Overhead expenses.

5.2.3. First-In, First-Out (FIFO)

First-in, First-out (FIFO) is a particularly useful method when the production process involves multiple stages or departments. This method assumes that the costs of the earliest units produced are the first to be assigned to the cost of goods sold or completed units. In other words, the costs of the units that enter the process first are transferred to the next stage or department first (Figure 5.1).

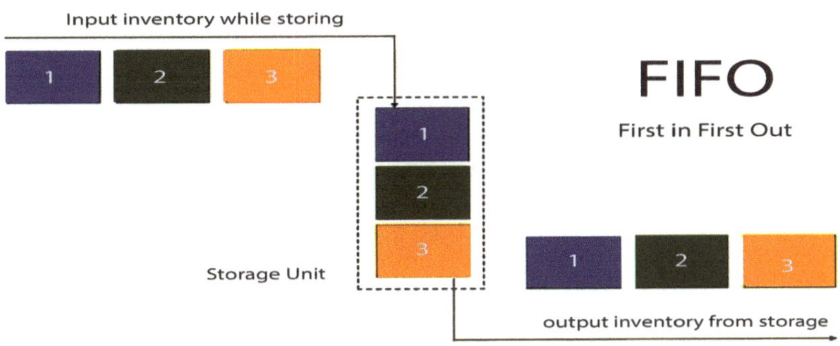

Figure 5.1. An illustration of FIFO.

Source: Team (2020).

To better understand how the FIFO method works, let's consider an example.

Imagine a company that produces widgets. The production process involves three stages: Stage A, Stage B, and Stage C. In Stage A, raw materials are converted into partially completed widgets. The cost of these partially completed widgets is $10,000.

These partially completed widgets then move to Stage B, where additional materials and labor are added. The cost of these additional materials and labor is $5,000. Finally, the partially completed widgets move to Stage C, where the final touches are added. The cost of these final touches is $2,000.

Using the FIFO method, we would assign the costs in the following order:

1. The cost of the partially completed widgets in Stage A ($10,000) would be transferred to Stage B first.
2. Then, the cost of the additional materials and labor in Stage B ($5,000) would be added to the cost of the partially completed widgets from Stage A.
3. Finally, the cost of the final touches in Stage C ($2,000) would be added to the total cost.

By using the FIFO method, we can accurately allocate costs to each stage of the production process, providing valuable information for decision-making and cost control.

Did You Understand?

1. How is the cost per unit determined in the weighted average costs method?
2. How do you calculate the weighted average cost per unit?
3. What are standard costs based on?
4. When is the FIFO method useful?

Answer 1: The cost per unit is determined by dividing the total costs incurred in a process by the total number of units produced in that process.

Answer 2: To calculate the weighted average cost per unit, add up the total costs incurred in both processes and divide it by the total number of units produced.

For example, if you have 100 units that cost $10 each and 200 units that cost $15 each, the calculation would be as follows:

(100 units x $10) + (200 units x $15) = $1000 + $3000 = $4000

Total cost = $4000

Total number of units = 100 + 200 = 300 units

Weighted average cost per unit = $4000 / 300 units = $13.33

Answer 3: Standard costs are based on factors such as historical data, industry standards, and management's expectations.

Answer 4: The FIFO method is useful when the production process involves multiple stages or departments.

5.3. PROS AND CONS OF PROCESS COSTING

Learning Objectives

- The main objective in this section is to understand various pros and cons of process costing.

While process costing has its advantages, it also comes with certain drawbacks. In this section, we will explore the pros and cons of process costing.

5.3.1. Pros of Process Costing

- Cost Allocation: Process costing allows businesses to allocate costs to each unit produced, providing a clear understanding of the cost per unit.
- Cost Control: By tracking costs at each stage of the production process, process costing enables businesses to identify areas of inefficiency and take corrective measures.
- Pricing Decisions: Process costing helps businesses determine the selling price of their products by considering the cost per unit and desired profit margin.
- Inventory Valuation: Process costing provides an accurate valuation of work-in-progress inventory, which is essential for financial reporting and decision-making.
- Performance Evaluation: Process costing allows businesses to evaluate the performance of each department or process within the organization, facilitating improvements and accountability.
- Standardization: Process costing promotes standardization of processes, leading to increased efficiency and productivity.
- Cost Comparison: Process costing enables businesses to compare costs across different production processes, helping them make informed decisions regarding resource allocation.
- Budgeting: Process costing provides valuable data for budgeting purposes, allowing businesses to allocate resources effectively and plan for future growth.
- Cost Reduction: By identifying areas of waste and inefficiency, process costing helps businesses reduce costs and improve profitability.
- Cost Transparency: Process costing provides transparency in cost allocation,

allowing businesses to communicate and justify their pricing strategies to customers and stakeholders.

5.3.2. Cons of Process Costing

- Complexity: Process costing can be complex, especially in industries with multiple processes and cost centers, requiring careful tracking and allocation of costs.
- Time-Consuming: The detailed tracking and allocation of costs in process costing can be time-consuming, requiring dedicated resources and expertise.
- Lack of Accuracy: Process costing relies on assumptions and averages, which may not accurately represent the actual costs incurred in producing each unit.
- Limited Flexibility: Process costing may not be suitable for businesses that produce customized or unique products, as it focuses on the average cost per unit.
- Difficulty in Cost Control: Process costing may make it challenging to identify and control costs at each individual unit level, as it emphasizes the overall cost of the process.
- Overhead Allocation: Process costing often relies on predetermined overhead rates, which may not accurately reflect the actual overhead costs incurred.
- Incomplete Cost Information: Process costing may not provide detailed cost information for each individual unit, making it difficult to analyze profitability on a per-unit basis.
- Inefficiency Identification: Process costing may not effectively identify specific areas of inefficiency within a process, as it focuses on the overall cost of the process.
- Inaccurate Pricing: Process costing alone may not provide accurate pricing information, as it does not consider market demand and competition.
- Limited Decision-Making Support: Process costing may not provide sufficient information for complex decision-making, such as product mix or outsourcing decisions.

Keyword

Overhead Rates – These refer to the percentage of indirect costs incurred by a business in relation to its total direct costs.

5.4. COST FLOW IN PROCESS COSTING

Learning Objectives

- Understanding the cost flow in process costing which is essential for effective cost management and decision-making.

In process costing, costs are accumulated and assigned to each production department or process. These costs include direct materials, direct labor, and manufacturing overhead. The costs are then allocated to the units produced based on the number of units or the amount of work done in each process (Parkinson, 2015).

To illustrate the cost flow in process costing, consider Figure 5.2.

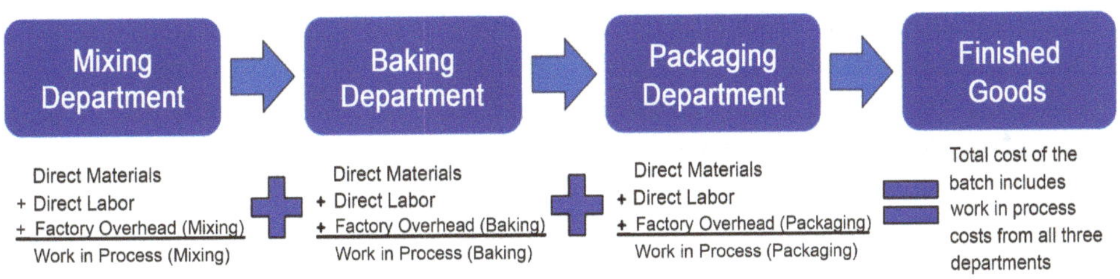

Figure 5.2. The cost flows in a process cost system that processes the products in a specified sequential order.

Source: Flow of Costs (Process Costing); Accounting for Managers (n.d.).

In the image, you can see the different stages or processes involved in the production of a product. Each process has its own cost accumulation and allocation. The costs incurred in each process are added to the units produced in that process. This continues until the final product is completed.

The image also shows the flow of costs between processes. As the units move from one process to another, the costs associated with those units also move. This allows for accurate costing of each process and helps identify any inefficiencies or areas for improvement.

Understanding the cost flow in process costing is crucial for managers and decision-makers. It provides valuable insights into the cost structure of a product and helps in determining the most cost-effective production methods. By analyzing the cost flow, managers can identify bottlenecks, reduce costs, and improve overall efficiency (Horngren et al., 2002).

Did You Understand?

1. What are some advantages of process costing?
2. What are some disadvantages of process costing?
3. Why is understanding the cost flow in process costing important?

Answer 1: Some advantages of process costing include cost allocation, cost control, pricing decisions, inventory valuation, performance evaluation, standardization, cost comparison, budgeting, cost reduction, and cost transparency.

Answer 2: Some disadvantages of process costing include complexity, time-consuming nature, lack of accuracy, limited flexibility, difficulty in cost control, reliance on predetermined overhead rates, incomplete cost information, inefficiency identification, inaccurate pricing, and limited decision-making support.

Answer 3: Understanding the cost flow in process costing is important because it allows for effective cost management and decision-making. It provides insights into the cost structure of a product, helps determine cost-effective production methods, identifies bottlenecks, reduces costs, and improves overall efficiency.

CASE STUDY

Introduction: The purpose of this case study is to analyze the process costing system used by ExxonMobil, one of the world's largest publicly traded international oil and gas companies. Process costing is a method used by companies that produce homogeneous products in large quantities through a continuous production process. ExxonMobil's refining and chemical manufacturing operations are suitable for process costing analysis.

Background: ExxonMobil operates in over 200 countries and territories, with a diverse portfolio that includes exploration, production, refining, and marketing of oil and gas products. The company's refining and chemical manufacturing operations involve complex processes that require accurate cost allocation to determine the profitability of each product.

Process Costing at ExxonMobil: ExxonMobil uses a process costing system to allocate costs to its various products. The company's refining process involves the conversion of crude oil into various refined products, such as gasoline, diesel, and jet fuel. Similarly, its chemical manufacturing process produces a wide range of products, including plastics, solvents, and lubricants.

- **Cost Allocation:** ExxonMobil allocates costs to its products based on the direct materials, direct labor, and manufacturing overhead incurred in each process. Direct materials include the crude oil used in the refining process and the raw materials used in chemical manufacturing. Direct labor includes the wages and benefits of employees directly involved in the production process. Manufacturing overhead includes indirect costs such as utilities, maintenance, and depreciation of plant and equipment.
- **Cost Accumulation:** ExxonMobil accumulates costs in each production process by using cost drivers. For example, the amount of crude oil processed is used as a cost driver in the refining process, while the number of units produced is used as a cost driver in the chemical manufacturing process. By tracking these cost drivers, ExxonMobil can accurately allocate costs to each product.
- **Cost Calculation:** ExxonMobil calculates the cost per unit by dividing the total costs incurred in each process by the number of units produced. This cost per unit is then used to determine the selling price of each product. By accurately calculating the cost per unit, ExxonMobil can make informed decisions about pricing and profitability.

Conclusion: ExxonMobil's process costing system is an effective method for allocating costs and determining the profitability of its refining and chemical manufacturing operations. By accurately tracking cost drivers and calculating the cost per unit, the company can make informed decisions about pricing and optimize its production processes.

SUMMARY

Chapter 5 explore process costing which is a method used by companies to calculate the cost of producing goods or services in a continuous production process. It is commonly used in industries like manufacturing, chemical processing, and food processing. The total cost of production is divided by the total number of units produced to determine the cost per unit, allowing companies to make informed decisions regarding pricing and profitability. Key features of process costing include cost centers, work-in-progress (WIP), and the calculation of unfinished goods. It provides a detailed breakdown of costs at each stage of production, enabling businesses to identify areas for cost reduction, increase efficiency, and reduce waste. Process costing also plays a crucial role in resource allocation, ensuring efficient operations and promoting uniformity in reporting.

Process costing involves calculating equivalent units, which are the number of units that have been partially completed and expressed in terms of fully completed units. This is crucial for continuous manufacturing processes, as not all units are completed at the same time. To calculate equivalent units, companies must determine the number of fully completed units, partially completed units, and convert them into equivalent units. The total number of units produced during a month is then added to the equivalent units to get the total number of units produced.

Process costing also involves calculating applicable costs, which are the costs of producing a product or service in a continuous manufacturing process. For example, ABC Manufacturing Company can calculate the cost of goods completed and transferred out from different departments using the weighted average method.

The cost per unit is calculated by dividing the total cost by the total number of units. This information is crucial for decision-making, cost control, and pricing purposes.

Process costing involves allocating costs to both complete and incomplete products through steps such as identifying production departments and assigning unique cost centers. Weighted average costs and standard costs are common methods used in process costing. Weighted average costs divide the total costs incurred in each process by the total number of units produced, while standard costs are predetermined costs based on historical data, industry standards, and management's expectations. Understanding these processes is essential for businesses to make informed decisions about pricing, production, and financial reporting.

First-in, First-out (FIFO) is another cost allocation method that assigns costs to each stage of a production process, allowing for accurate decision-making and cost control. It is useful when multiple stages or departments are involved, as the costs of the earliest units produced are transferred first. For example, a company producing widgets would allocate costs to Stage A ($10,000) first, then Stage B ($5,000), and finally Stage C ($2,000). This method accurately allocates costs to each stage, providing valuable information for decision-making and cost control.

Process costing has pros such as cost allocation, cost control, pricing decisions, inventory valuation, performance evaluation, standardization, cost comparison, budgeting, cost reduction, and cost transparency. However, it also has cons like complexity, time-consumingness, lack of accuracy, limited flexibility, difficulty in cost control, overhead allocation, incomplete cost information, inefficiency identification, inaccurate pricing, and limited decision-making support. Understanding the cost flow in process costing is crucial for effective cost management and decision-making, helping identify bottlenecks, reduce costs, and improve overall efficiency.

MULTIPLE CHOICE QUESTIONS

1. What is process costing used for?

a. To calculate the cost of producing goods or services in a continuous production process.

b. To determine the profitability of products.

c. To allocate costs to different production departments.

d. All of the above.

2. What are the key features of process costing?

a. The use of cost centers and the calculation of the cost of unfinished goods.

b. The tracking of direct materials, direct labor, and overhead costs.

c. The ability to identify areas for improvement and reduce costs.

d. All of the above.

3. Why is process costing important for businesses?

a. It allows for better monitoring of profit margins.

b. It helps with inventory control and resource allocation.

c. It provides insights into the profitability of different products or services.

d. All of the above.

4. What is the first step in process costing?

a. Analyzing the inventory.

b. Calculating equivalent units.

c. Determining the number of units produced.

d. Allocating costs to complete and incomplete products.

5. How are equivalent units calculated in process costing?

a. By determining the number of units that are fully completed.

b. By converting partially completed units into equivalent units.

c. By adding fully completed units and equivalent units together.

d. All of the above.

6. What is the purpose of calculating applicable costs in process costing?

a. To determine the total cost of production.

b. To allocate costs to different production departments or processes.

c. To calculate the cost of goods completed and transferred out.
d. All of the above.

7. What is the importance of calculating the cost per unit in process costing?

a. It allows for accurate pricing decisions.
b. It helps with cost management and overall profitability.
c. It provides information for financial reporting and budgeting.
d. All of the above.

8. What is one of the common methods used in process costing?

a. Weighted Average Costs
b. Standard Costs
c. First-in, First-out (FIFO)
d. Cost Flow

9. How is the weighted average cost per unit determined?

a. By dividing the total costs incurred in a process by the total number of units produced in that process.
b. By adding up the total costs incurred in both processes and dividing it by the total number of units produced.
c. By multiplying the total costs incurred in a process by the total number of units produced in that process.
d. By subtracting the total costs incurred in a process from the total number of units produced in that process.

10. What are standard costs based on?

a. Historical data, industry standards, and management's expectations.
b. Actual costs incurred during a specific period.
c. Changes in material prices, labor inefficiencies, and overhead expenses.
d. The cost of finished goods.

11. What does the FIFO method assume?

a. The costs of the earliest units produced are the first to be assigned to the cost of goods sold or completed units.
b. The costs of the units that enter the process first are transferred to the next stage or department first.
c. The costs of the partially completed widgets in Stage A are transferred to Stage B first.
d. The costs of the final touches in Stage C are added to the total cost.

12. What is the purpose of understanding the cost flow in process costing?

a. Effective cost management and decision-making.
b. Allocating costs to each production department or process.

c. Determining the most cost-effective production methods.

d. Identifying bottlenecks, reducing costs, and improving overall efficiency.

13. How are costs allocated to the units produced in process costing?

a. Based on the number of units, or the amount of work done in each process.

b. Based on the total costs incurred in each process.

c. Based on historical data, industry standards, and management's expectations.

d. Based on the cost of finished goods.

Answers to Multiple Choice Questions

1. (d); 2. (d); 3. (d); 4. (a); 5. (d); 6. (d); 7. (d); 8. (a); 9. (a); 10. (a); 11. (a); 12. (a); 13. (a)

REFERENCES

1. Basu, T., (2020). Process Costing. 1-18
2. Drury, C., (2013). Costing: An Introduction. Springer.
3. Flow of Costs (Process Costing), (n.d.). Accounting for Managers. https://courses.lumenlearning.com/wm-accountingformanagers/chapter/flow-of-costs-in-a-process-costing-system/ (accessed on 04 April 2024).
4. Horngren, C. T., Bhimani, A., Datar, S. M., & Foster, G., (2002). Management and Cost Accounting. Harlow: Financial Times/Prentice Hall.
5. Parkinson, J., (2015). Teaching process cost accounting. International Journal of Education and Social Science, 2(3), 10–23.
6. Team, M. S., (2020). FIFO (First in First Out) – Definition, Importance & Example. MBA Skool. https://www.mbaskool.com/business-concepts/operations-logistics-supply-chain-terms/18084-fifo-first-in-first-out.html (accessed on 04 April 2024).

CHAPTER

6 Activity-Based Costing

LEARNING OBJECTIVES

After studying this chapter, you will be able to:

- To identify and understand various key components of designing an Activity-Based Costing system, including:
  - Identify activities;
  - Collecting activity data;
  - Cost allocation to activities;
  - Determine cost drivers;
  - Calculating activity rates;
  - Analyzing activity costs;
  - Analyzing the results of activity.
- To identify and understand various benefits and limitations of activity-based costing.

INTRODUCTORY EXAMPLE

Activity-based costing (ABC) is a method used by companies to allocate costs to their products or services based on the activities involved in producing them. This approach provides a more accurate understanding of the true costs involved in the production process.

To illustrate the concept of ABC, let's consider the case of Nippon Steel Corporation, a global leader in the steel industry. Nippon Steel produces a wide range of steel products, including flat steel, pipes, and bars.

Traditionally, Nippon Steel has used a simple cost allocation method based on direct labor hours. However, the company has realized that this approach doesn't accurately reflect the actual costs incurred in producing different products. For example, the cost of producing flat steel is significantly different from the cost of producing pipes or bars due to variations in the production process.

To address this issue, Nippon Steel has decided to implement ABC to gain a more precise understanding of their costs. They have identified several activities involved in the production process, such as material handling, machine setup, and quality control.

By analyzing these activities, Nippon Steel can determine the resources required for each activity and allocate costs accordingly. For example, they may find that material handling is a major cost driver for flat steel production, while machine setup is a significant cost driver for pipe production.

By allocating costs based on these activity drivers, Nippon Steel can accurately determine the cost of each product. This information is invaluable for pricing decisions, as well as identifying areas for cost reduction and process improvement.

In conclusion, ABC is a powerful tool that allows companies like Nippon Steel Corporation to gain a more accurate understanding of their costs. By analyzing the activities involved in production and allocating costs accordingly, companies can make informed decisions to improve their profitability and competitiveness in the market.

UNIT INTRODUCTION

Activity-Based Costing (ABC) is a method used by companies to allocate costs to their products or services based on the activities involved in producing them. Traditional costing methods often rely on simple cost drivers, such as direct labor hours or machine hours, to allocate costs. However, ABC takes a more detailed approach by identifying and assigning costs to specific activities that contribute to the production process (Gosselin, 2006).

The main purpose of ABC is to provide more accurate cost information for decision-making. By analyzing the activities that drive costs, companies can better understand the factors that influence their expenses and profitability. This information can help in various areas, such as pricing decisions, product mix analysis, and process improvement initiatives.

The ABC process involves several steps. First, the company identifies its activities, which can include tasks like machine setup, material handling, or quality control. Then, it determines the cost drivers for each activity, such as the number of setups or the number of units produced. These cost drivers are used to allocate the costs associated with each activity to the products or services.

To illustrate the differences between ABC and traditional costing, let's consider a manufacturing company that produces two products: Product A and Product B. The company has identified three activities that drive costs: machine setup, material handling, and quality control.

Under traditional costing, the company would allocate overhead costs based on a single cost driver, such as direct labor hours. If Product A requires more direct labor hours than Product B, Product A would be allocated a higher share of overhead costs, regardless of the actual activities driving those costs (Gosselin, 2006).

In contrast, ABC would allocate overhead costs based on the activities that drive them. For example, if Product A requires more machine setups and quality control checks than Product B, it would be allocated a higher share of the overhead costs associated with those activities.

By using ABC, companies can gain a more accurate understanding of the costs associated with each product or service. This information can help them make more informed decisions regarding pricing, product mix, and resource allocation.

According to Gosselin (2006), when designing an Activity-Based Costing (ABC) system, it is crucial to follow a step-by-step process to ensure accuracy and effectiveness. The following steps outline the key components of designing an ABC system:

1. Identify Activities: Begin by identifying all the activities within the organization. This includes both primary activities, such as production and customer service, and support activities, such as administration and maintenance.
2. Collecting Activity Data: Collecting activity data for ABC is to identify the

activities that consume resources within the organization. These activities can range from production processes to administrative tasks.

3. Cost Allocation to Activities: Once activities are identified, assign costs to each activity. This involves allocating direct costs, such as labor and materials, as well as indirect costs, such as overhead expenses.
4. Determine Cost Drivers: Next, determine the cost drivers for each activity. Cost drivers are the factors that cause costs to be incurred in relation to the activity. For example, the number of machine hours may be a cost driver for the activity of machine maintenance.
5. Calculating Activity Rates: Calculate the activity rates by dividing the total cost of each activity by its respective cost driver. This will provide a rate per unit of the cost driver.
6. Analyzing Activity Costs: Finally, analyze the results of the ABC system. This includes comparing the costs assigned to products or services under the ABC system to those assigned under a traditional costing system. This analysis can provide valuable insights into the true costs of products or services and help identify areas for cost reduction or process improvement.
7. Analyzing the Results of Activity-Based Costing: By analyzing the results of ABC, companies can gain valuable insights into their cost structure and make informed decisions to improve efficiency and profitability.

Did you know?

Activity-based costing (ABC) was first developed in the 1980s as an alternative to traditional costing methods, such as the traditional costing system or the direct costing system.

By following these steps, organizations can develop an accurate and effective ABC system that provides valuable information for decision-making and cost management.

6.1. IDENTIFYING ACTIVITIES

Learning Objectives

To learn and understand different types of activity-based costing activities, including:

- Unit-level activities;
- Batch-level activities;
- Product-level activities;
- Customer-level activities;
- Organization-level activities.

Following reviews given by Jalalabadi et al. (2018), analyzing and identifying the activities that contribute to the generation of costs, Activity-Based Costing allows companies to allocate expenses more precisely, improving decision-making processes and resource allocation. This method involves breaking down the various activities performed by different departments or units and assigning costs based on the resources consumed by each activity. By doing so, ABC provides a more accurate picture of the true costs associated with each product, service, or process. This information can then be used to identify areas of inefficiency, implement cost-saving measures, and ultimately improve overall profitability.

6.1.1. Types of Activity-Based Costing Activities

6.1.1.1. Unit-Level Activities

Unit-level activities are activities that are performed for each individual unit of a product or service. These activities directly affect the cost of producing each unit. These activities can include tasks such as assembling components, packaging finished products, and inspecting individual units for quality control. The costs associated with these activities are allocated to each unit based on the number of units produced. By using ABC, companies can gain a more accurate understanding of the costs associated with producing each unit. This can help them make more informed decisions regarding pricing, product mix, and resource allocation (Jalalabadi et al., 2018).

To illustrate this, let's consider a car manufacturing company that produces two types of cars: Sedans and SUVs. The company has identified the following unit-level activities and their associated costs:

Keyword

Quality Control – It is a crucial aspect of any production process that involves monitoring and inspecting products to ensure they meet the required standards before they are released to the market.

1. Assembling the Car: This activity involves putting together all the components of the car, such as the body, chassis, and interior. The cost of this activity is $500 per car.
2. Painting the Car: This activity involves applying the paint to the car's body. The cost of this activity is $300 per car.
3. Installing the Engine: This activity involves fitting the engine into the car. The cost of this activity is $800 per car.

By allocating these costs to each car produced, the company can determine the total cost of producing each type of car.

For example, if the company produces 100 sedans and 50 SUVs, the total cost of producing the sedans would be:

(100 sedans × $500 assembling cost) + (100 sedans × $300 painting cost) + (100 sedans × $800 engine installation cost) = $80,000

Similarly, the total cost of producing the SUVs would be:

(50 SUVs × $500 assembling cost) + (50 SUVs × $300 painting cost) + (50 SUVs × $800 engine installation cost) = $40,000

By using activity-based costing, the car manufacturing company can accurately determine the cost of producing each type of car, allowing them to make informed decisions regarding pricing, production volume, and resource allocation.

6.1.1.2. Batch-Level Activities

Activity-Based Costing (ABC) is particularly useful for companies that produce products in batches. Batch-level activities are activities that are performed for each batch of products produced. These activities include setting up the equipment, inspecting the products, and testing the products for quality.

By using ABC, companies can accurately determine the cost of each batch-level activity and allocate it to the corresponding batch of products. This allows companies to identify the true cost of producing each batch and make informed decisions about pricing and production quantities.

For example, let's say a company produces 100 batches of a product in a month:

- The cost of setting up the equipment for each batch is $100;
- The cost of inspecting each batch is $50;
- The cost of testing each batch is $75.

Using ABC, the company can determine that the total cost of batch-level activities for the month is $22,500 ($100 + $50 + $75 = $225 × 100 batches).

By accurately determining the cost of each batch-level activity, the company can make decisions about pricing and production quantities that will maximize profitability. They can also identify opportunities to reduce costs by streamlining or eliminating certain activities.

6.1.1.3. Product-Level Activities

Product-level activities are an important component of Activity-Based Costing (ABC). Product-level activities refer to the activities that are directly related to the production of a specific product. These activities can include product design, engineering, and testing. By identifying and allocating the costs of these activities to specific products, ABC provides a more accurate understanding of the true cost of producing each product. This information can be valuable for decision-making, pricing, and profitability analysis (Jalalabadi et al., 2018).

To better understand ABC, let's consider a hypothetical laptop company. The company produces two types of laptops: Basic and Premium. Each laptop goes through various activities before it is completed and ready for sale. The activities involved in the production of laptops include designing, assembling, testing, and packaging. Each activity requires different resources, such as labor, equipment, and materials. These resources have associated costs that need to be allocated to the products.

In the case of the laptop company, the Basic laptop requires less design and testing compared to the Premium laptop. However, the Premium laptop requires additional activities, such as customization and quality control, which the Basic laptop does not require. These additional activities result in higher costs for the Premium laptop.

By using ABC, the laptop company can allocate costs more accurately to each product. Instead of using a traditional costing method that simply divides costs based on the number of units produced, ABC takes into account the specific activities and resources utilized by each product.

For example;

If the design activity costs $10,000 and the company produces 1,000 Basic laptops and 500 Premium laptops, the ABC approach would allocate $6,667 to the Basic laptops and $3,333 to the Premium laptops. This allocation is based on the proportion of resources consumed by each product.

By implementing ABC, the laptop company can make more informed decisions regarding pricing, product development, and resource allocation. It provides a clearer picture of the costs associated with each product, allowing the company to better understand profitability and make strategic decisions accordingly.

6.1.1.4. Customer-Level Activities

Customer-level activities is another category of activities in ABC. These activities are performed for specific customers or groups of customers and are not directly related to the production of a product or service. Examples of customer-level activities include sales visits, customer support, and order processing.

To illustrate the concept of customer-level activities, let's consider a company that manufactures and sells customized furniture. The company has two types of customers: individual customers and corporate clients.

For individual customers, the company provides personalized design consultations, home visits for measurements, and product delivery. These activities are specific to each individual customer and are considered customer-level activities.

For corporate clients, the company offers on-site consultations, space planning, and bulk delivery. These activities are tailored to the needs of corporate clients and are also classified as customer-level activities.

By identifying and allocating the costs of customer-level activities, the company can gain a better understanding of the costs associated with serving different types of customers. This information can then be used to make informed decisions regarding pricing, marketing strategies, and resource allocation (Jalalabadi et al., 2018).

6.1.1.5. Organization-Level Activities

These are activities that support the overall operations of the organization. These activities cannot be directly traced to individual products or services. Instead, they benefit the organization as a whole. Examples of organization-level activities include facility maintenance, employee training, and general administrative tasks.

To illustrate the concept of organization-level activities, let's consider a manufacturing company that produces different types of furniture. The company has a facility where the furniture is manufactured, and it also has a showroom where customers can view and purchase the furniture.

In this example, the facility maintenance would be considered an organization-level activity. The cost of maintaining the facility, such as cleaning, repairs, and utilities, cannot be directly traced to a specific product. However, it is necessary for the overall operations of the company.

Similarly, the cost of employee training would also be classified as an organization-level activity. Training programs benefit all employees of the organization, regardless of their specific roles or the products they work on.

Finally, general administrative tasks, such as accounting and human resources, would also fall under organization-level activities. These tasks are essential for the smooth functioning of the organization as a whole.

By identifying and allocating costs to organization-level activities, ABC provides a more accurate picture of the true cost of producing products or services. This information can be used to make informed decisions regarding pricing, product mix, and resource allocation.

Did You Understand?

1. What is the main purpose of Activity-Based Costing (ABC)?
2. How does ABC allocate costs compared to traditional costing methods?
3. What are the key steps involved in designing an ABC system?

Answer 1: The primary objective of Activity-Based Costing, also known as ABC, is to precisely assign costs to particular activities and products on the basis of the resources that are actually consumed by those activities and products. This makes it possible to have a more accurate understanding of the actual costs that are associated with each activity and product, which in turn enables improvement in decision-making and the distribution of resources.

Answer 2: When it comes to allocating costs, traditional costing methods frequently rely on straightforward cost drivers, such as the number of hours that machines or direct laborers put in. ABC, on the other hand, takes a more comprehensive approach by determining and assigning costs to particular activities that are a part of the production process. Instead of focusing on a single cost driver, ABC prioritizes allocating costs according to the activities that are responsible for them. This allows for a more precise comprehension of the costs that are associated with each individual product or service.

Answer 3: The key steps in designing an ABC system include: identifying activities within the organization, collecting activity data to determine resource consumption, allocating costs to each activity, determining cost drivers for each activity, calculating activity rates, analyzing activity costs, and analyzing the results of ABC to gain insights into the cost structure and make informed decisions for efficiency and profitability improvement.

6.2. COLLECTING ACTIVITY DATA

Learning Objectives

- To learn and understand different Methods for collecting activity data, including direct observation, self-reporting, and technological methods.
- To learn and understand tips for ensuring data accuracy.

One of the key steps in implementing ABC is the collection of activity data. This involves identifying the various activities that take place within the organization and determining the resources, such as time and materials that are consumed by each activity.

To collect the necessary data, it is important to establish a system for tracking and recording the time and materials used for each activity. This can be done through the use of timesheets, expense reports, or other similar tools. It is also important to ensure that the data collected is accurate and reliable, as any errors or inconsistencies can lead to inaccurate cost allocations.

Once the data has been collected, it can be used to calculate the cost of each activity. This is typically done by assigning a cost driver to each activity, which is a factor that causes costs to be incurred. For example, in a manufacturing setting, the number of units produced may be used as a cost driver for production activities.

By accurately determining the cost of each activity, ABC provides valuable insights into the true costs of products and services. This information can then be used to make more informed decisions regarding pricing, resource allocation, and process improvement, ultimately leading to improved profitability and efficiency for the organization (Cokins, 2002).

6.2.1. Methods for Collecting Activity Data

There are several methods for collecting activity data:

1. Direct Observation: This involves physically observing employees as they perform their tasks and recording the time and resources used. Direct observation can provide accurate data, but it may not be practical for large organizations or activities that require a significant amount of time to complete.
2. Self-Reporting: In this method, employees themselves record their activities and

the resources used. Self-reporting can be efficient and cost-effective, especially if employees are provided with clear guidelines on how to accurately report their activities. However, it is essential to establish a system of checks and balances to verify the accuracy of the reported data.

3. Technological Methods: Technology can also play a significant role in collecting activity data. For example, organizations can use automated systems to track the time spent on different activities or the resources consumed. These systems can provide real-time data and reduce the risk of human error. However, it is crucial to ensure that the technology is reliable and regularly maintained to avoid any inaccuracies in the data.

To ensure the accuracy of activity data, organizations should establish clear guidelines and procedures for data collection. Employees should be trained on how to accurately record their activities and provided with ongoing support and feedback. Regular audits should also be conducted to verify the accuracy of the collected data and identify any potential issues or discrepancies.

6.2.2. Tips for Ensuring Data Accuracy

To obtain reliable results, it is crucial to ensure the accuracy of the data collected. Below are some helpful tips on how to achieve data accuracy when collecting activity data for ABC.

1. Clearly Define Activities: Before collecting data, it is essential to have a clear understanding of the activities that need to be measured. This involves breaking down complex tasks into smaller, more manageable activities. By clearly defining activities, you can avoid confusion and ensure that the collected data accurately reflects the costs associated with each activity.
2. Use Multiple Data Collection methods: To enhance data accuracy, it is advisable to use a combination of data collection methods. This can include direct observation, interviews with employees, and the use of technology such as sensors or software. By employing multiple methods, you can cross-verify the data and identify any inconsistencies or errors.
3. Train Data Collectors: Properly trained data collectors are essential for accurate data collection. Provide training to individuals responsible for gathering activity data, ensuring they understand the purpose of ABC and the specific activities they need to measure. This will help them collect data consistently and accurately.
4. Implement Data Validation Procedures: To ensure the accuracy of collected data, it is crucial to implement data validation procedures. This involves reviewing the collected data for completeness, consistency, and reasonableness. By conducting regular checks, you can identify and rectify any errors or anomalies in the data.
5. Regularly Update Activity Data: Activities within an organization can change over time. To maintain data accuracy, it is important to regularly update activity data. This

includes revisiting the defined activities, reviewing the data collection methods, and making necessary adjustments to ensure the data accurately reflects the current state of the organization.

6. Conduct Periodic Audits: Periodic audits of the collected data can help identify any discrepancies or inaccuracies. These audits should involve reviewing the data collection process, verifying the accuracy of the collected data, and addressing any issues or concerns. By conducting regular audits, you can ensure ongoing data accuracy and reliability.

Quick Fact

A study conducted by Smith and Johnson (2018) found that companies using ABC experienced a significant improvement in cost allocation accuracy. This accuracy allows for better decision-making regarding pricing, product mix, and resource allocation.

6.3. COST ALLOCATION TO ACTIVITIES

Learning Objectives

To understand cost allocation methods, including:

- Direct method.
- Step-down method.
- Reciprocal method.
- Activity-based costing with time-driven activity-based costing (TDABC).

Cokins (2002) states that, cost allocation is a crucial process in business management. It involves assigning costs to specific activities or resources within an organization. This helps in determining the true cost of producing goods or providing services.

To illustrate this concept, let's consider a manufacturing company that produces two products: Product A and Product B. The company incurs various costs, such as direct materials, direct labor, and factory overhead.

To allocate these costs to activities, the company uses cost drivers. A cost driver is a factor that causes costs to be incurred. For example, the number of units produced can be a cost driver for direct materials and direct labor costs.

The company calculates the total cost of each activity by multiplying the cost driver by the cost rate. The cost rate is the amount of cost incurred per unit of the cost driver.

For instance, if the cost rate for direct materials is $10 per unit and Product A requires 100 units of direct materials, the total cost of direct materials for Product A would be $1,000.

Once the total cost of each activity is determined, it can be allocated to the products based on their usage of the activity. In our example, if Product A requires 80% of the total direct labor hours, then 80% of the total direct labor cost would be allocated to Product A.

By allocating costs to activities, the company can accurately determine the cost of producing each product. This information is valuable for pricing decisions, cost control, and overall financial management.

6.3.1. Cost Allocation Methods

There are several different cost allocation methods used in ABC. These methods help to determine how costs should be allocated to different activities and ultimately to products or services. Here are a few commonly used methods:

1. Direct Method: This method allocates costs directly to activities based on a predetermined cost driver rate. The cost driver rate is calculated by dividing the total cost of an activity by the total quantity of the cost driver. This method is simple and straightforward, but it may not accurately reflect the actual cost drivers.
2. Step-Down Method: Also known as the sequential allocation method, this approach allocates costs in a sequential manner, starting with the activity that has the highest direct cost. It then allocates the remaining costs to subsequent activities based on a predetermined sequence. This method is useful when there are multiple cost drivers and activities that depend on each other.
3. Reciprocal Method: In situations where there is a high degree of interdependence between activities, the reciprocal method is used. This method takes into account the mutual services provided by activities to each other and allocates costs accordingly. It is a more complex method, but it provides a more accurate allocation of costs.
4. Activity-based Costing with Time-Driven Activity-based Costing (TDABC): It is a simplified version of ABC that uses time as the cost driver. It estimates the time required to perform an activity and assigns costs based on the time spent. This method is easier to implement and provides a more accurate allocation of costs compared to traditional ABC.

Each cost allocation method has its own advantages and disadvantages, and the choice of method depends on the specific needs and characteristics of the organization. It is important to carefully consider these methods to ensure accurate cost allocation and ultimately make informed business decisions (Cokins, 2002).

Did You Understand?

1. What are some methods for collecting activity data?
2. How can organizations ensure the accuracy of activity data?
3. What are some tips for ensuring data accuracy when collecting activity data for ABC?

Answer 1: Some methods for collecting activity data include direct observation, self-reporting, and technological methods.

Answer 2: Making sure that activity data is accurate is a key consideration for organizations. There are a number of ways to accomplish this. One strategy is to establish reliable methods of data collection, where information is gathered in a systematic and consistent manner. Another option for organizations looking to validate their data is to implement regular audits and checks. These will help to spot any inconsistencies or mistakes in the data. Organizations can also keep their activity data accurate by investing in dependable data management systems and technology. Organizations can improve the trustworthiness and accuracy of their data—essential for making smart choices and propelling success—by implementing these measures.

Answer 3: Some tips for ensuring data accuracy when collecting activity data for ABC include:

- It is crucial to have a clear understanding of the activities that need to be measured before collecting data. Breaking down complex tasks into smaller, more manageable activities is an essential step in the process. It is important to have a clear definition of activities in order to prevent any confusion and to ensure that the data collected accurately represents the costs associated with each activity.
- It is recommended to utilize a variety of data collection methods in order to improve the accuracy of the data. Various methods can be employed to gather information, such as direct observation, conducting interviews with employees, and utilizing technology like sensors or software. Utilizing various techniques allows for the cross-verification of data, enabling the detection of any inconsistencies or errors that may be present.
- Training data collectors is crucial in ensuring accurate data collection. Offer comprehensive training to individuals tasked with collecting activity data, ensuring a clear understanding of the significance of ABC and the specific activities that require measurement. This will help them collect data consistently and accurately.

6.4. DETERMINING COST DRIVERS

Learning Objectives

- To understand volume-based cost drivers;
- To understand non-volume-based cost drivers.

Cost drivers can be classified into two categories volume-based and non-volume-based. By identifying and analyzing cost drivers, ABC helps organizations gain a better understanding of the factors that drive costs. This allows for a more accurate allocation of costs to products or services, leading to better decision-making and cost control.

6.4.1. Volume-Based Cost Drivers

Going by reviews given by Granof, Platt, & Vaysman (2000), volume-based cost drivers are those that are directly related to the level of production or the quantity of goods or services provided. They are often referred to as activity-based cost drivers, as they measure the activities performed by a business that contribute to its costs. These drivers can vary in different industries, but some common examples include the number of units produced, the number of hours worked, or the number of customers served.

One of the key volume-based cost drivers is the number of units produced. As the production volume increases, the costs associated with producing each unit tend to decrease. This is due to economies of scale, which occur when fixed costs are spread over a larger number of units.

For example, a company that produces 100 units may have a higher cost per unit compared to a company that produces 1,000 units, as the fixed costs are spread out more effectively in the latter case.

Another volume-based cost driver is the number of hours worked. In industries where labor plays a significant role, such as manufacturing or service industries, the number of hours worked directly affects the costs incurred. As more hours are worked, the labor costs increase. This can be particularly relevant when considering overtime pay or hiring additional staff to meet increased demand.

Furthermore, the number of customers served can also be a volume-based cost driver. In industries such as retail or hospitality, the costs incurred are often directly related to the number of customers served. For example, a restaurant may need to hire more staff or purchase more ingredients to accommodate a higher number of customers. This can result in increased costs, but also increased revenue if the additional customers generate more sales.

Understanding volume-based cost drivers is crucial for businesses as it allows them to analyze their cost structure and make informed decisions. By identifying the key cost drivers, companies can focus on optimizing their operations to reduce costs and improve profitability. For example, a company may decide to invest in technology or automation to increase production volume and take advantage of economies of scale. Alternatively, they may choose to streamline their processes to reduce the number of hours worked or explore ways to increase customer satisfaction without incurring additional costs.

Keyword

Economies of Scale – It is the cost advantages that businesses can achieve when they increase their production levels.

It is important to note that while volume-based cost drivers are significant, they are not the only factors that influence costs. Other cost drivers, such as time-based or complexity-based drivers, should also be considered. Time-based cost drivers, for instance, are related to the time required to complete a task or deliver a service. Complexity-based cost drivers, on the other hand, are associated with the complexity or difficulty of a task. These drivers can have a significant impact on costs and should not be overlooked (Cokins, 2002).

6.4.2. Non-Volume-Based Cost Drivers

These are factors that influence the costs of a business that are not directly related to the volume of production or sales. These cost drivers can have a significant impact on a company's expenses and profitability.

One example of a non-volume-based cost driver is the complexity of a product or service. When a company offers a complex product or service, it often requires more resources and expertise to produce and deliver. This complexity can increase costs, as additional time and effort are needed to ensure the quality and functionality of the product or service. For example, a software company that develops intricate and sophisticated programs may require a team of highly skilled programmers and engineers, which can drive up labor costs.

Another non-volume-based cost driver is the level of customization required by customers. When customers demand personalized products or services, it often requires additional time and resources to meet their specific needs. This customization can increase costs, as companies may need to invest in specialized equipment or hire additional staff to accommodate these requests. For instance, a furniture manufacturer that offers custom-made pieces may need to purchase unique materials and employ skilled craftsmen to fulfill individual customer orders, resulting in higher production costs (Granof, Platt, & Vaysman, 2000).

Furthermore, the geographical location of a business can also be a non-volume-based cost driver. Companies operating in remote or challenging locations may face higher transportation costs, limited access to suppliers, or higher labor costs. For instance, a mining company that operates in a remote area may need to transport equipment and materials over long distances, incurring additional expenses for transportation and logistics.

Keyword

Compliance Costs – It is the expenses incurred by businesses in order to adhere to laws, regulations, and standards.

Additionally, technology can be a significant non-volume-based cost driver. Companies that rely heavily on technology may face high costs associated with equipment maintenance, software updates, and cyber-security measures. For example, a financial institution that relies on advanced computer systems to process transactions and secure customer data may need to invest in regular software updates and employ IT professionals to ensure the system's integrity, resulting in higher technology-related expenses.

Moreover, government regulations and compliance requirements can also be non-volume-based cost drivers. Companies operating in heavily regulated industries may need to invest in additional staff, training, and systems to ensure compliance with various laws and regulations. For instance, a pharmaceutical company that develops and manufactures drugs may need to comply with strict quality control standards and extensive documentation requirements, resulting in higher compliance costs.

Lastly, the level of competition in an industry can also be a non-volume-based cost driver. In highly competitive markets, companies may need to invest more in marketing and advertising to differentiate themselves from competitors. These promotional activities can increase costs, as companies may need to allocate resources to develop and implement effective marketing campaigns. For example, a smartphone manufacturer operating in a saturated market may need to spend significant amounts on advertising to attract customers and gain market share, resulting in higher marketing expenses (Granof, Platt, & Vaysman, 2000).

6.5. CALCULATING ACTIVITY RATES

Learning Objectives

- The main objective in this section is to learn and understand how to calculate activity rates in ABC.

Activity rates are the costs associated with each activity that is performed to produce a product or service. These rates are calculated by dividing the total cost of each activity by its corresponding cost driver.

To calculate activity rates in ABC, follow these steps:

1. Identify the Activities: Start by identifying all the activities that contribute to the production or delivery of a product or service. These activities can include setup, machine operation, quality control, and administrative tasks, among others.
2. Determine the Cost Drivers: Cost drivers are the factors that cause costs to be incurred in each activity. For example, the number of setups or machine hours could be cost drivers for the setup and machine operation activities, respectively.
3. Assign Costs to Activities: Once the cost drivers have been identified, assign the costs associated with each activity. This can include direct costs, such as labor and materials, as well as indirect costs, such as overhead expenses.
4. Calculate Activity Rates: To calculate the activity rates, divide the total cost of each activity by its respective cost driver. For example, if the total cost of setup activities is $10,000 and the number of setups is 100, the activity rate for setups would be $100 per setup.

By calculating activity rates in ABC, organizations can better understand the costs associated with each activity and make more informed decisions regarding resource allocation and pricing. This information can ultimately lead to improved efficiency and profitability.

Did You Understand?

1. What is volume-based cost drivers and why are they important?
2. Give an example of a volume-based cost driver and explain its impact on costs.
3. What is non-volume-based cost drivers and how do they influence costs?

Answer 1: Volume-based cost drivers are factors directly related to the level of production or the quantity of goods or services provided. They measure the activities performed by a business that contribute to its costs. Examples of volume-based cost drivers include the number of units produced, the number of hours worked, or the number of customers served. These cost drivers are important because they allow organizations to allocate costs accurately to products or services, leading to better decision-making and cost control.

Answer 2: One example of a volume-based cost driver is the number of units produced. As the production volume increases, the costs associated with producing each unit tend to decrease. This is due to economies of scale, where fixed costs are spread over a larger number of units. For instance, a company that produces 100 units may have a higher cost per unit compared to a company that produces 1,000 units because the fixed costs are spread out more effectively in the latter case.

Answer 3: Non-volume-based cost drivers are factors that influence the costs of a business that are not directly related to the volume of production or sales. Examples include the complexity of a product or service, the level of customization required by customers, the geographical location of a business, technology, government regulations and compliance requirements, and the level of competition in an industry. These cost drivers can significantly impact a company's expenses and profitability by increasing labor costs, transportation costs, technology-related expenses, compliance costs, and marketing expenses.

6.6. ANALYZING ACTIVITY COSTS

Learning Objectives

- To learn and understand how to analyze activity costs.
- To learn techniques used to effectively analyze activity costs in ABC.

According to Kennedy and Affleck-Graves (2001) remarks, to effectively manage costs, it is crucial to analyze activity costs. This involves examining the expenses associated with each activity performed within a business. By understanding the costs of individual activities, businesses can identify areas where costs can be reduced or eliminated.

To begin analyzing activity costs, businesses should first identify the activities that contribute to the production of goods or services. This can be done by breaking down the production process into its individual activities. For example, in a manufacturing business, activities may include purchasing raw materials, processing materials, assembling products, and packaging finished goods.

Once the activities have been identified, businesses can then determine the costs associated with each activity. This includes both direct costs, which can be easily traced to a specific activity, and indirect costs, which are more difficult to allocate to a specific activity. Direct costs may include labor costs, material costs, and equipment costs, while indirect costs may include overhead expenses such as rent, utilities, and administrative costs.

After determining the costs of each activity, businesses can analyze the data to identify areas of inefficiency or excessive spending. This may involve comparing the costs of similar activities across different departments or benchmarking against industry standards. By identifying areas of high costs, businesses can implement strategies to reduce or eliminate these expenses.

In addition to identifying areas of inefficiency, analyzing activity costs can also help businesses make more informed decisions regarding resource allocation. By understanding the costs associated with each activity, businesses can prioritize activities that provide the most value and allocate resources accordingly. This can help businesses optimize their operations and improve overall profitability (Granof, Platt, & Vaysman, 2000).

6.6.1. Techniques Used to Effectively Analyze Activity Costs in ABC

1. Cost Pool Identification: The first step in analyzing activity costs is to identify the cost pools. Cost pools are groups of costs that are associated with specific activities. By categorizing costs into different pools, it becomes easier to allocate them to the appropriate activities.
2. Cost Driver Selection: Once the cost pools have been identified, the next step is to select appropriate cost drivers. Cost drivers are factors that determine the amount of resources consumed by an activity. For example, in a manufacturing company, the number of machine hours may be used as a cost driver for the activity of machine maintenance.
3. Data Collection: Accurate and reliable data is crucial for analyzing activity costs. It is important to collect data on both the costs incurred and the activities performed. This can be done through various methods such as interviews, surveys, and direct observation.
4. Cost Allocation: After collecting the necessary data, the next step is to allocate costs to specific activities. This can be done by using cost drivers to determine the proportion of costs that should be assigned to each activity. The more accurately costs are allocated, the more meaningful the analysis will be.
5. Cost Analysis: Once costs have been allocated to activities, it is important to analyze the results. This involves comparing the costs of different activities and identifying any variations or inefficiencies. By analyzing activity costs, businesses can make informed decisions about resource allocation and process improvement.
6. Continuous Monitoring: Activity-based costing is an ongoing process. It is important to continuously monitor activity costs and make adjustments, as necessary. By regularly analyzing activity costs, businesses can identify trends and make proactive changes to improve efficiency and reduce costs.

6.7. ANALYZING THE RESULTS OF ACTIVITY-BASED COSTING

Learning Objectives

- To learn and understand how to analyze the results of activity-based costing.

By analyzing the results of ABC, companies can gain valuable insights into their operations and make informed decisions to improve efficiency and profitability.

One of the key benefits of ABC is its ability to provide a more accurate picture of the costs associated with each activity. Traditional costing methods often allocate costs based on volume or direct labor hours, which can lead to distorted cost information. ABC, on the other hand, takes into account the various activities that consume resources and assigns costs accordingly. This helps companies identify the true drivers of costs and make more informed decisions about pricing, product mix, and resource allocation (Kennedy & Affleck-Graves, 2001).

When analyzing the results of ABC, it is important to focus on the cost drivers and their impact on overall costs. Cost drivers are the activities or factors that cause costs to be incurred. By identifying and analyzing the cost drivers, companies can better understand the relationship between activities and costs. This information can be used to optimize processes, eliminate non-value-added activities, and reduce costs.

Another aspect to consider when analyzing ABC results is the accuracy of the cost allocations. ABC relies on assigning costs to specific activities based on their consumption of resources. It is important to ensure that the cost allocations are accurate and reflect the actual resource usage. This can be achieved through regular monitoring and review of the cost allocation process. Furthermore, analyzing the results of ABC can help companies identify opportunities for process improvement. By understanding the costs associated with each activity, companies can identify bottlenecks, inefficiencies, and areas for improvement. This can lead to process redesign, automation, or other initiatives to streamline operations and reduce costs.

6.8. BENEFITS AND LIMITATIONS OF ACTIVITY-BASED COSTING

Learning Objectives

- To identify various benefits and limitations of activity-based costing.

Activity-based costing is an approach that provides a more accurate reflection of the true costs associated with producing goods or providing services, compared to traditional costing methods that rely on arbitrary allocation bases such as direct labor hours or machine hours.

One of the main benefits of ABC is that it provides a more accurate understanding of the costs of different activities within an organization. By identifying and analyzing the various activities involved in the production process, ABC allows managers to determine the true cost drivers of these activities. This information can then be used to make more informed decisions regarding resource allocation and process improvement. For example, by identifying activities that consume a significant amount of resources but do not add much value to the final product, managers can focus on reducing or eliminating these activities, thereby reducing costs, and improving overall efficiency (Kennedy & Affleck-Graves, 2001).

Another benefit of ABC is that it helps in identifying and managing overhead costs. Traditional costing methods often allocate overhead costs based on a single allocation base, such as direct labor hours. This approach can lead to inaccurate cost assignments, as different products or services may consume overhead resources in different ways. ABC, on the other hand, assigns overhead costs to activities based on their consumption of resources, providing a more accurate reflection of the true costs associated with each activity. This allows managers to better understand the cost structure of their organization and make more informed decisions regarding pricing, product mix, and resource allocation.

Furthermore, ABC can help in improving the accuracy of product costing. Traditional costing methods often rely on arbitrary allocation bases, such as direct labor hours or machine hours, to assign costs to products. This approach can lead to inaccurate cost assignments, especially in organizations where overhead costs constitute a significant portion of the total costs. ABC, by assigning costs to activities based on their consumption of resources, provides a more accurate reflection of the costs associated with producing each product. This information can be used to make more informed decisions regarding pricing, product profitability, and resource allocation.

However, despite its benefits, ABC also has some limitations. One of the main limitations of ABC is the cost and time involved in implementing and maintaining the system. ABC requires a significant amount of data collection and analysis, as well as the development of cost drivers and activity cost pools. This can be a time-consuming and costly process, especially for organizations with complex operations or limited resources. Additionally, maintaining the accuracy of the system requires ongoing monitoring and updating of cost drivers and activity cost pools, which can be a challenging task (Kennedy & Affleck-Graves, 2001).

Another limitation of ABC is the subjectivity involved in assigning costs to activities. The allocation of costs to activities often requires judgment calls and estimations, which can introduce bias and inaccuracies into the costing process. Different managers or accountants may have different opinions on how costs should be assigned, leading to inconsistencies and potential disputes. This subjectivity can also make it difficult to compare costs across different organizations or industries, as the cost assignments may not be consistent or comparable.

Did You Understand?

1. What are the steps involved in analyzing activity costs?
2. What techniques can be used to effectively analyze activity costs in ABC?
3. What are the benefits and limitations of Activity-Based Costing (ABC)?

Answer 1: The steps involved in analyzing activity costs are as follows:

- Identify the activities that contribute to the production of goods or services.
- Determine the costs associated with each activity, including direct and indirect costs.
- Analyze the data to identify areas of inefficiency or excessive spending.
- Make informed decisions regarding resource allocation based on the costs associated with each activity.
- Continuously monitor activity costs and make adjustments, as necessary.

Answer 2: Some techniques that can be used to effectively analyze activity costs in ABC are:

- Cost pool identification: Categorizing costs into different pools to allocate them to the appropriate activities.
- Cost driver selection: Selecting appropriate factors that determine the amount of resources consumed by an activity.

- Data collection: Collecting accurate and reliable data on both costs and activities performed.
- Cost allocation: Allocating costs to specific activities using cost drivers to determine the proportion of costs assigned to each activity.
- Cost analysis: Comparing the costs of different activities and identifying variations or inefficiencies.
- Continuous monitoring: Regularly analyzing activity costs, identifying trends, and making proactive changes to improve efficiency and reduce costs.

Answer 3: The benefits of ABC include:

- Providing a more accurate understanding of the costs of different activities within an organization.
- Identifying and managing overhead costs more effectively.
- Improving the accuracy of product costing.
- Making more informed decisions regarding resource allocation, process improvement, pricing, and product mix.
- The limitations of ABC include:
- The cost and time involved in implementing and maintaining the system.
- The subjectivity involved in assigning costs to activities, which can introduce bias and inaccuracies.
- Difficulty comparing costs across different organizations or industries due to inconsistencies in cost assignments.

CASE STUDY

- **Introduction:** This case study focuses on the implementation of Activity-Based Costing (ABC) in Savencia SA, a global dairy company. ABC is a cost accounting method that aims to allocate costs to products or services based on the activities that drive those costs. This approach provides more accurate cost information compared to traditional cost allocation methods, such as direct labor or machine hours. Savencia SA decided to adopt ABC to better understand their product costs and make informed decisions.
- **Background:** Savencia SA operates in the dairy industry, producing a wide range of dairy products, including cheese, butter, and yogurt. The company faced challenges in accurately determining the costs associated with each product. Traditional cost allocation methods did not provide a clear picture of the true costs, as they relied heavily on direct labor and machine hours. This led to inaccurate pricing decisions and difficulty in identifying profitable products.
- **Implementation of ABC:** To address these challenges, Savencia SA implemented ABC. The first step was to identify the activities that consumed resources and drove costs. These activities included production setup, machine maintenance, quality control, and packaging. The next step was to determine the cost drivers for each activity. For example, the number of setups was identified as the cost driver for production setup activity, while machine hours were identified as the cost driver for machine maintenance activity.

Once the activities and cost drivers were identified, Savencia SA collected data on the resources consumed by each activity and the corresponding cost drivers. This data was used to calculate the cost rates for each activity. The cost rates were then applied to the cost drivers to allocate costs to the products.

- **Results and Benefits:** The implementation of ABC provided Savencia SA with more accurate product costs. It revealed that some products were overpriced, while others were underpriced. This information allowed the company to adjust the prices, accordingly, resulting in increased profitability. ABC also helped in identifying non-value-added activities, which were then eliminated or reduced, further reducing costs.

Furthermore, ABC provided insights into the profitability of different products and customers. Savencia SA was able to identify high-profit products and customers, allowing them to focus their resources on those areas. This strategic decision-making based on accurate cost information led to improved overall performance and competitiveness.

- **Conclusion:** The implementation of Activity-Based Costing in Savencia SA proved to be beneficial in providing accurate cost information and guiding decision-making. It allowed the company to better understand their product costs, adjust prices accordingly, and identify areas for cost reduction. ABC also provided insights into the profitability of different products and customers, enabling the company to focus on high-profit areas. Overall, ABC played a crucial role in improving the performance and competitiveness of Savencia SA in the dairy industry.

SUMMARY

Chapter 6 discusses Activity-Based Costing (ABC), which is a method used by companies to allocate costs to their products or services based on the activities involved in producing them. It involves identifying activities, determining cost drivers for each activity, allocating costs to activities, calculating activity rates, and analyzing the results. ABC provides more accurate cost information for decision-making and helps companies understand factors that influence expenses and profitability. It can be used for pricing decisions, product mix analysis, and process improvement initiatives.

Following a step-by-step process is crucial for designing an effective ABC system. ABC allows companies to allocate expenses more accurately by analyzing the activities that contribute to costs. This method involves breaking down activities performed by different departments or units and assigning costs based on the resources consumed. ABC provides a more accurate understanding of the true costs associated with each product, service, or process, which can be used to identify inefficiencies, implement cost-saving measures, and improve profitability. Collecting activity data is a key step in implementing ABC. It involves identifying activities within the organization and determining the resources consumed by each activity. To collect the necessary data, a system for tracking and recording time and materials used is established. Accuracy and reliability of the data are important to avoid inaccurate cost allocations. Cost allocation is the process of assigning costs to specific activities or resources within an organization. This helps determine the true cost of producing goods or providing services. Cost drivers, such as the number of units produced, are used to calculate the total cost of each activity. Once the total cost of each activity is determined, it can be allocated to products based on their usage of the activity. Cost drivers can be classified into two categories: volume-based and non-volume-based. Volume-based cost drivers are directly related to the level of production, or the quantity of goods or services provided. Non-volume-based cost drivers, on the other hand, are factors that influence costs but are not directly related to production or sales volume. Activity rates are calculated by dividing the total cost of each activity by its corresponding cost driver. Analyzing activity costs involves examining the expenses associated with each activity performed within a business. This helps identify areas where costs can be reduced or eliminated. The process includes identifying activities, determining costs, analyzing data, and making informed decisions regarding resource allocation. Analyzing the results of ABC provides valuable insights into operations and helps make informed decisions to improve efficiency and profitability. The benefits of ABC include a more accurate understanding of costs, better management of overhead costs, and improved accuracy of product costing. However, implementing and maintaining ABC can be costly and time-consuming, and there may be subjectivity involved in assigning costs to activities.

MULTIPLE CHOICE QUESTION

1. **What is the main purpose of Activity-Based Costing (ABC)?**
   a. To allocate costs based on direct labor hours
   b. To identify and assign costs to specific activities
   c. To analyze the factors that influence expenses and profitability
   d. To allocate costs based on machine hours
2. **What are the cost drivers used in ABC?**
   a. Direct labor hours and machine hours
   b. Number of setups and number of units produced
   c. Material handling and quality control checks
   d. Machine setups and direct labor hours
3. **How does ABC allocate overhead costs compared to traditional costing?**
   a. Based on direct labor hours
   b. Based on machine hours
   c. Based on the activities that drive costs
   d. Based on the number of units produced
4. **What is the direct method of cost allocation?**
   a. Allocates costs directly to activities based on a predetermined cost driver rate.
   b. Allocates costs sequentially starting with the activity that has the highest direct cost.
   c. Takes into account the mutual services provided by activities to each other and allocates costs accordingly.
   d. Uses time as the cost driver and assigns costs based on the time spent.
5. **What is the step-down method of cost allocation?**
   a. Allocates costs directly to activities based on a predetermined cost driver rate.
   b. Allocates costs sequentially starting with the activity that has the highest direct cost.
   c. Takes into account the mutual services provided by activities to each other and allocates costs accordingly.
   d. Uses time as the cost driver and assigns costs based on the time spent.
6. **What is the reciprocal method of cost allocation?**
   a. Allocates costs directly to activities based on a predetermined cost driver rate.
   b. Allocates costs sequentially starting with the activity that has the highest direct cost.
   c. Takes into account the mutual services provided by activities to each other and allocates costs accordingly.
   d. Uses time as the cost driver and assigns costs based on the time spent.

7. **What is the activity-based costing with time-driven activity-based costing (TDABC)?**
   a. Allocates costs directly to activities based on a predetermined cost driver rate.
   b. Allocates costs sequentially starting with the activity that has the highest direct cost.
   c. Takes into account the mutual services provided by activities to each other and allocates costs accordingly.
   d. Uses time as the cost driver and assigns costs based on the time spent.
8. **Why is it important to carefully consider cost allocation methods?**
   a. To accurately determine the cost of producing each product.
   b. To make informed business decisions.
   c. To optimize operations and reduce costs.
   d. All of the above.
9. **What are activity rates in Activity-Based Costing (ABC) calculated by?**
   a. Dividing the total cost of each activity by its corresponding cost driver.
   b. Dividing the total cost of each activity by the number of setups.
   c. Dividing the total cost of each activity by the number of machine hours.
   d. Dividing the total cost of each activity by the total cost of all activities.
10. **What is the first step in calculating activity rates in ABC?**
   a. Determine the cost drivers.
   b. Assign costs to activities.
   c. Identify the activities.
   d. Calculate the activity rates.
11. **What is the purpose of analyzing activity costs in ABC?**
   a. To identify areas of inefficiency or excessive spending.
   b. To determine the cost drivers of each activity.
   c. To allocate costs to specific activities.
   d. To calculate the activity rates.
12. **What is the first step in effectively analyzing activity costs in ABC?**
   a. Cost Pool Identification.
   b. Cost Driver Selection.
   c. Data Collection.
   d. Cost Allocation.
13. **What is one of the limitations of Activity-Based Costing (ABC)?**
   a. The subjectivity involved in assigning costs to activities.
   b. The accuracy of the cost allocations.
   c. The cost and time involved in implementing and maintaining the system.
   d. The ability to provide a more accurate reflection of costs.

Answers to Multiple Choice Questions

1. (c); 2. (b); 3. (c); 4. (a); 5. (b); 6. (c); 7. (d); 8. (d); 9. (a); 10. (c); 11. (a); 12. (a); 13. (c)

REFERENCES

1. Cokins, G., (2002). Activity-Based Cost Management: An Executive's Guide. John Wiley & Sons.
2. Gosselin, M., (2006). A review of activity-based costing: Technique, implementation, and consequences. Handbooks of Management Accounting Research, 2, 641–671.
3. Granof, M. H., Platt, D. E., & Vaysman, I., (2000). Using Activity-Based Costing to Manage More Effectively. PricewaterhouseCoopers Endowment for the Business of Government.
4. Jalalabadi, F., Milewicz, A. L., Shah, S. R., Hollier, Jr. L. H., & Reece, E. M., (2018). Activity-based costing. In: Seminars in Plastic Surgery (Vol. 32, No. 4, pp. 182–186). Thieme Medical Publishers.
5. Kennedy, T., & Affleck-Graves, J., (2001). The impact of activity-based costing techniques on firm performance. Journal of Management Accounting Research, 13(1), 19–45.

CHAPTER 7

Budgeting and Forecasting

LEARNING OBJECTIVES

After studying this chapter, you will be able to:

- Types of budgets;
- Budgeting process;
- Forecasting methods;
- Budgeting techniques;
- Budget monitoring and control;
- Budgeting software and tools.

INTRODUCTORY EXAMPLE

Ameer Dairy Pvt. is a leading dairy company that specializes in producing and distributing high-quality dairy products. As a growing business, Ameer Dairy recognizes the importance of effective budgeting and forecasting to ensure financial stability and growth.

Budgeting is the process of creating a detailed plan that outlines the company's financial goals and objectives for a specific period. By setting clear targets and allocating resources accordingly, Ameer Dairy can effectively manage its expenses and maximize its profitability.

Forecasting, on the other hand, involves predicting future financial outcomes based on historical data and market trends. By analyzing past performance and market conditions, Ameer Dairy can make informed decisions regarding its future investments, production levels, and pricing strategies.

Both budgeting and forecasting play a crucial role in Ameer Dairy's overall financial management. By creating a realistic budget and accurately forecasting its financial performance, the company can identify potential risks and opportunities, allowing it to make proactive adjustments to its operations.

Furthermore, budgeting and forecasting enable Ameer Dairy to monitor its progress towards its financial goals. By regularly comparing actual financial results to the budgeted figures and forecasts, the company can identify any deviations and take corrective actions to stay on track.

In conclusion, budgeting and forecasting are essential tools for Ameer Dairy Pvt. in achieving financial stability and growth. By effectively managing its finances and making informed decisions, the company can ensure its long-term success in the competitive dairy industry.

UNIT INTRODUCTION

Budgeting and forecasting are fundamental concepts in financial management that play crucial roles in the success and sustainability of any organization. To start with, budgeting is the process of creating a detailed plan that outlines an organization's financial goals and objectives for a specific period, typically a year. It involves estimating and allocating resources to different activities and functions within the organization to ensure the efficient utilization of funds. On the other hand, forecasting is the process of predicting future financial outcomes based on historical data, market trends, and other relevant factors. It helps organizations anticipate potential challenges and opportunities, allowing them to make informed decisions and take proactive measures to achieve their financial goals (Nugus, 2009).

One of the key benefits of budgeting is that it provides a roadmap for financial decision-making. By setting clear financial targets and allocating resources accordingly, organizations can prioritize their spending, control costs, and ensure that funds are allocated to areas that will generate the highest returns. Budgeting also promotes accountability and transparency within an organization. It allows management to monitor actual performance against the budgeted targets, identify any deviations, and take corrective actions, as necessary. This ensures that financial resources are used effectively and efficiently, minimizing wastage, and maximizing value creation.

Forecasting, on the other hand, helps organizations anticipate and plan for the future. By analyzing past performance and market trends, organizations can make informed predictions about future revenues, expenses, and cash flows. This enables them to identify potential risks and opportunities, adjust their strategies accordingly, and make proactive decisions to mitigate risks and capitalize on opportunities.

In addition to these benefits, budgeting and forecasting also play crucial roles in financial planning. They provide a basis for evaluating investment opportunities, assessing the feasibility of new projects, and determining the financial resources required to achieve strategic objectives. They also facilitate effective communication and coordination among different departments and stakeholders, ensuring that everyone is aligned with the organization's financial goals and objectives (Nugus, 2009).

7.1. TYPES OF BUDGETS

Learning Objectives

1. **To Understand Various Types of Budgets in Business:** There are several types of budgets that businesses use to manage their finances effectively. These budgets help businesses plan and allocate resources, set financial goals, and track their performance. Here are some common types of business budgets:

i. **Operating Budget:** This budget outlines the company's projected expenses and revenues for a specific period, such as a year. It includes costs like:

- Salaries;
- Rent;
- Utilities;
- Marketing expenses.

ii. **Cash Flow Budget:** This budget focuses on tracking the inflow and outflow of cash within a company. It helps to ensure that there is sufficient cash available to cover expenses and investments. For example, a business may use a cash flow budget to plan for purchasing new equipment while maintaining enough cash reserves for day-to-day operations.

iii. **Financial Budget:** This budget provides an overview of the company's financial goals and objectives. It includes financial statements, such as:

- The balance sheet;
- Income statement;
- Cash flow statement.

The financial budget helps in analyzing the company's financial health and making strategic decisions.

iv. **Sales Budget:** This budget projects the company's sales revenue for a specific period. It considers factors like market demand, pricing strategies, and sales targets. For instance, a business may set a sales budget to estimate the revenue it expects to generate from its products or services.

v. **Production Budget:** This budget determines the quantity of goods or services that a company plans to produce within a given timeframe. It considers factors like customer demand, production capacity, and inventory levels. A manufacturing company may use a production budget to plan the number of units it needs to produce to meet market demand.

vi. **Labor Budget:** This budget focuses on the company's labor costs, including salaries, wages, and benefits. It helps in managing workforce requirements, scheduling, and cost control. For example, a retail store may create a labor budget to ensure that it has enough staff during peak hours while optimizing labor costs during slower periods.

vii. **Capital Budget:** This budget outlines the company's long-term investment plans, such as purchasing new assets or expanding facilities. It considers factors like return on investment, project timelines, and funding sources. A construction company may create a capital budget to estimate the costs and benefits of building a new office building.

viii. **Static Budget:** This budget sets fixed targets for revenues and expenses based on a specific level of activity. It is not adjusted for changes in actual sales or production levels. For instance, a static budget may set a fixed amount for marketing expenses regardless of the actual sales achieved.

ix. **Overhead Budget:** This budget estimates the indirect costs of running a business, such as: rent, utilities, and administrative expenses. It helps in planning and controlling overhead costs. An office-based company may create an overhead budget to allocate funds for rent, utilities, and office supplies.

x. **Master Budget:** This budget consolidates all the individual budgets mentioned above into a comprehensive financial plan for the entire organization. It provides a holistic view of the company's financial performance and guides decision-making. A company may use a master budget to align its various budgets and ensure they are consistent and achievable.

Did You Understand?

1. What is budgeting?
2. What is forecasting?

Answer 1: Budgeting is the process of creating a detailed plan that outlines an organization's financial goals and objectives for a specific period, typically a year. It involves estimating and allocating resources to different activities and functions within the organization to ensure the efficient utilization of funds.

Answer 2: Forecasting is the process of predicting future financial outcomes based on historical data, market trends, and other relevant factors. It helps organizations anticipate potential challenges and opportunities, allowing them to make informed decisions and take proactive measures to achieve their financial goals.

7.2. BUDGETING PROCESS

Learning Objectives

- To understand a step-by-step process on how to create a budget in business.
- To learn and understand various techniques used to ensure a smooth and effective budgeting process.

Creating a budget is an essential task for any business. It helps in planning and managing finances effectively. To ensure a successful budget, it is important to follow a step-by-step process.

7.2.1. A Step-by-Step Process on How to Create a Budget in Business

1. **Set Financial Goals:** Start by defining your financial objectives. What do you want to achieve with your budget? It could be increasing profits, reducing costs, or expanding your business. Clearly outline your goals to guide your budgeting process.
2. **Gather Financial Data:** Collect all relevant financial information from various sources. This includes sales records, expense reports, invoices, and bank statements. Ensure that you have accurate and up-to-date data to base your budget on.
3. **Analyse Past Performance:** Review your previous financial performance to identify trends and patterns. Look for areas where you have overspent or areas where you can cut costs. This analysis will help you make informed decisions when creating your budget.
4. **Estimate Future Revenue:** Based on your sales records and market trends, project your future revenue. Consider any factors that may impact your sales, such as seasonality or economic conditions. Be realistic in your estimations to avoid overestimating your income.
5. **Determine Fixed and Variable Costs:** Categorize your expenses into fixed and variable costs. Fixed costs are expenses that remain constant, such as rent or salaries. Variable costs fluctuate with your business activities, such as raw materials or advertising. Understanding these cost categories will help you allocate your budget effectively.
6. **Allocate Funds:** Distribute your budget across different departments or cost centers. Consider the needs and priorities of each area. Allocate sufficient funds to support essential operations and invest in areas that contribute to your financial goals.

7. **Monitor and Adjust:** Regularly review your budget to track your progress. Compare your actual expenses and revenue against your budgeted amounts. Identify any discrepancies and make necessary adjustments. This ongoing monitoring will help you stay on track and make informed financial decisions.

Remember, creating a budget is not a one-time task. It requires continuous evaluation and adaptation to meet changing business needs. By following this step-by-step process, you can develop a well-planned budget that supports your financial goals and helps your business thrive (Passoja, 2015).

7.2.2. Techniques to Ensure a Smooth and Effective Budgeting Process

Although budgeting is a critical aspect of running a successful business, it can be complex and challenging, especially if you are not familiar with the best practices. To help you navigate this process smoothly, here are some practical tips and techniques to consider:

1. **Start with a Clear Understanding of Your Financial Goals:** Before you begin budgeting, it is essential to have a clear understanding of your financial objectives. Identify your revenue targets, cost-saving goals, and any other financial milestones you wish to achieve. This clarity will guide your budgeting decisions and help you stay focused on your objectives.
2. **Involve Key Stakeholders:** Budgeting should not be a one-person job. Involve key stakeholders, such as department heads and finance professionals, in the process. Their input and expertise will provide valuable insights and ensure that the budget reflects the needs and priorities of the entire organization.
3. **Review Historical Data:** Analyzing past financial data is crucial for creating an accurate budget. Review your previous financial statements, including income statements, balance sheets, and cash flow statements. This analysis will help you identify trends, patterns, and areas where you can make improvements.
4. **Use Budgeting Software:** Consider investing in budgeting software to streamline the process. These tools can automate calculations, generate reports, and provide real-time insights into your financial performance. They also allow for collaboration and easy updating of budget information.
5. **Break Down Your Budget into Manageable Chunks:** Instead of creating one large budget, break it down into smaller, manageable parts. This approach will make it easier to track and manage expenses. Consider creating budgets for individual departments or projects, allowing for better control and accountability.
6. **Be Realistic:** When setting budget targets, be realistic and avoid overestimating revenues or underestimating expenses. It is better to be conservative and have room for unexpected costs rather than facing financial difficulties later on.
7. **Monitor and Adjust Regularly:** A budget is not a static document. Continuously monitor your actual financial performance against your budgeted targets. If you notice any significant variances, investigate the reasons behind them and make

necessary adjustments to your budget. Regular reviews and updates will help you stay on track and make informed decisions.

8. **Communicate and Educate:** Ensure that everyone in your organization understands the budget and their role in achieving its objectives. Communicate the budgeting process, goals, and expectations clearly to all employees. Provide training and resources to help them understand how their actions impact the budget and overall financial health of the business.

By following these practical tips and techniques, you can ensure a smooth and effective budgeting process in your business. Remember, budgeting is not just about numbers; it is a strategic tool that can help drive your business towards success (Passoja, 2015).

Did You Understand?

1. What is the importance of creating a budget for a business?
2. What are some techniques to ensure a smooth and effective budgeting process?

Answer 1: Creating a budget is important for a business because it helps in planning and managing finances effectively. It allows businesses to set financial goals, analyze past performance, estimate future revenue, allocate funds, and monitor and adjust their financial activities. Overall, a budget provides a roadmap for businesses to achieve their financial objectives and thrive.

Answer 2: Some techniques to ensure a smooth and effective budgeting process include starting with a clear understanding of financial goals, involving key stakeholders, reviewing historical data, using budgeting software, breaking down the budget into manageable parts, being realistic with targets, monitoring and adjusting regularly, and communicating and educating employees about the budget and its objectives. These techniques help businesses navigate the complexity of budgeting and make informed financial decisions.

7.3. FORECASTING METHODS

Learning Objectives

- To understand various different forecasting methods.

According to Evans (2003), forecasting plays a crucial role in decision-making and planning for businesses, as it enables them to anticipate future trends and make informed choices. By examining these methods, we will gain a comprehensive understanding of how businesses can effectively predict future outcomes (Hoshmand, 2009).

1. **Qualitative Forecasting:** This approach relies on expert opinions and judgments to predict future trends. It is particularly useful when historical data is limited or unreliable. Experts provide their insights based on their knowledge and experience, allowing businesses to make informed decisions.
2. **Time Series Analysis:** This method utilizes historical data to identify patterns and make predictions. By analyzing past trends and patterns, businesses can forecast future outcomes. Time series analysis is commonly used in sales forecasting, allowing businesses to estimate future sales based on historical data.
3. **Causal Forecasting:** Focuses on cause-and-effect relationships. By examining the impact of various factors on a particular outcome, businesses can make predictions. For example, a company may analyze the impact of advertising expenditure on sales to forecast future sales based on their marketing efforts.
4. **Regression Analysis:** This statistical technique examines the relationship between two or more variables to predict future outcomes. By identifying the correlation between variables, businesses can forecast future trends. Regression analysis is widely used in financial forecasting, where variables such as interest rates and stock prices are analyzed to predict future financial performance.
5. **Econometric Modelling:** This method combines economic theory and statistical analysis to forecast future outcomes. By incorporating economic factors such as inflation rates and GDP growth, businesses can make predictions about future market conditions.
6. **Scenario Analysis:** This approach involves creating various scenarios or hypothetical situations to predict future outcomes. By considering different possibilities, businesses can prepare for different scenarios and make informed decisions.

7. **Simulation Modeling:** This method involves creating a computerized model that simulates real-world scenarios. By inputting various variables and parameters, businesses can analyze different scenarios and predict future outcomes. Simulation modeling is commonly used in operations management to optimize processes and predict future performance.
8. **Trend Analysis:** This method examines historical data to identify and predict long-term trends. By analyzing past trends, businesses can forecast future market conditions and adapt their strategies accordingly.
9. **Delphi Method:** This approach involves gathering opinions from a panel of experts through a series of questionnaires. By aggregating and analyzing these opinions, businesses can make predictions. The Delphi method is particularly useful when dealing with complex and uncertain situations.
10. **Market Research:** This method involves collecting data through surveys, interviews, and observations to understand consumer preferences and predict future market trends. By analyzing market research data, businesses can anticipate changes in consumer behavior and adjust their strategies accordingly.

7.4. BUDGETING TECHNIQUES

Learning Objectives

To learn and understand various budgeting techniques, including:

- Activity-based budgeting;
- Incremental budgeting;
- Imposed budgeting;
- Value proposition budgeting;
- Flexible budgeting;
- Participatory budgeting;
- Rolling budgeting.

There are several different methods that businesses can use to create and maintain a budget. We will explore some of the most popular budgeting methods and discuss their advantages and disadvantages.

7.4.1. Activity-Based Budgeting

Activity-based budgeting is a budgeting approach that focuses on the activities that drive costs within an organization. It is a method that seeks to align the budget with the organization's strategic goals and objectives. The process involves identifying the key activities that contribute to costs, estimating the cost drivers associated with each activity, and allocating resources accordingly. By doing so, activity-based budgeting provides a more accurate and detailed picture of an organization's financial situation, allowing for better decision-making and resource allocation. This approach also encourages accountability and transparency, as it requires managers to justify their resource requests based on the activities, they are responsible for (Shim, Siegel, & Shim, 2011).

In this case, we will use a bakery business as an example to illustrate how activity-based budgeting works.

1. The first step in activity-based budgeting is to identify the different activities that the bakery business engages in. These activities may include:
   - Baking bread;
   - Making pastries;

- Decorating cakes;
- Delivering orders.

By identifying these activities, the bakery can gain a better understanding of the costs associated with each one.

2. Next, the bakery needs to determine the cost drivers for each activity. Cost drivers are the factors that directly influence the cost of an activity. For example:
   - The cost of baking bread may be driven by the amount of flour and yeast used, while the cost of decorating cakes may be driven by the amount of time spent on each cake.
3. Once the cost drivers have been identified, the bakery can allocate its costs to each activity. This involves determining how much of each cost is associated with each activity. For example:
   - The bakery may allocate the cost of flour and yeast to the activity of baking bread based on the amount used for each loaf.
4. After allocating costs to each activity, the bakery can then determine the cost of each unit of output. This involves dividing the total cost of each activity by the number of units produced. For example:
   - If the bakery bakes 100 loaves of bread and the total cost of baking bread is $500, the cost per loaf would be $5.

Using this information, the bakery can then create a budget for each activity. This budget will outline the expected costs and revenues for each activity. By focusing on the specific activities that generate revenue, the bakery can make more informed decisions about resource allocation and pricing.

7.4.2. Incremental Budgeting

Incremental budgeting is a budgeting method that involves making small adjustments to the previous budget. It is a common approach used by many organizations, including businesses and government agencies.

The process of incremental budgeting begins by taking the previous year's budget as a starting point. From there, adjustments are made based on changes in the organization's needs and goals. These adjustments are typically made on a line-item basis, meaning that each individual expense or revenue category is examined and adjusted, as necessary.

For example, let's say a company's previous year's budget allocated $100,000 for marketing expenses. During the budgeting process for the upcoming year, the company's marketing team may request an increase in their budget to $120,000. This increase could be justified by new marketing initiatives or a desire to capture a larger market share. The budget decision-makers would then review this request and decide whether or not to approve the increase (Shim, Siegel, & Shim, 2011).

Incremental budgeting is often criticized for its lack of flexibility and tendency to perpetuate inefficiencies. Since it is based on the previous year's budget, it can be difficult to make significant changes or allocate resources to new initiatives. However, it is also seen as a relatively simple and straightforward approach that provides stability and predictability.

7.4.3. Imposed Budgeting

Imposed budgeting refers to a situation where a budget is set by an external entity, such as a government agency or a board of directors and is then enforced upon the individuals or departments responsible for managing the funds. This method is commonly employed in situations where there is a need for strict financial discipline or when there is a lack of trust in the ability of individuals to make sound financial decisions.

To better understand imposed budgeting, let's consider an example. Imagine a local government facing a financial crisis due to mismanagement and overspending. In order to regain control of the situation, the central government decides to impose a budget on the local government. This means that the local government will no longer have the freedom to allocate funds as they see fit. Instead, they will be required to follow a predetermined budget, which outlines the amount of money that can be allocated to each department or project (Shim, Siegel, & Shim, 2011).

The imposed budget will typically include specific guidelines and restrictions on spending. For instance, it may limit the amount that can be spent on salaries, infrastructure development, or public services. This ensures that the local government adheres to the financial constraints imposed upon them and prevents any further financial mismanagement.

While imposed budgeting can be effective in controlling spending and restoring financial stability, it can also have its drawbacks. One major disadvantage is the potential lack of flexibility. Since the budget is predetermined and enforced, it may not allow for adjustments or unforeseen circumstances. This rigidity can hinder the ability to respond to changing needs or emergencies.

7.4.4. Value Proposition Budgeting

Value proposition budgeting is an essential aspect of financial planning for any business. It involves allocating resources to support the creation and delivery of a compelling value proposition to customers (Shim, Siegel, & Shim, 2011).

To better understand this concept, let's consider an example. Imagine you own a bakery and want to introduce a new line of gluten-free products. You believe this will appeal to a niche market and differentiate your bakery from competitors.

First, you need to determine the costs associated with developing and producing these gluten-free products. This includes expenses such as research and development, sourcing ingredients, and modifying your production processes. By accurately estimating these costs, you can ensure that your budget adequately covers all necessary expenses.

Next, you must evaluate the potential revenue generated by these gluten-free products. This involves analyzing market demand, pricing strategies, and sales projections. By conducting thorough market research, you can make informed decisions about pricing and estimate the potential revenue from this new product line.

Once you have a clear understanding of both the costs and potential revenue, you can determine the value proposition budget. This budget should account for all expenses related to the creation and delivery of the gluten-free products, while also considering the expected revenue generated.

For example, let's say the estimated costs for developing and producing the gluten-free products amount to $10,000. Based on market research, you project that the revenue from these products will be $15,000 in the first year. In this case, your value proposition budget should allocate $10,000 for costs and leave a $5,000 surplus from the projected revenue.

By effectively budgeting for your value proposition, you can ensure that your business remains financially sustainable while delivering a unique and compelling offering to your customers.

7.4.5. Flexible Budgeting

Flexible budgeting is a method used by businesses to create a budget that can be adjusted based on changes in activity levels. It allows for more accurate financial planning and analysis by taking into account the fluctuations in revenue and expenses that occur as a result of changes in production or sales volume (Nugus, 2009).

To understand how flexible budgeting works, let's consider an example. Imagine a manufacturing company that produces and sells widgets. The company's budget is based on the assumption that it will produce and sell 10,000 widgets. However, due to an increase in demand, the company ends up producing and selling 12,000 widgets.

With a flexible budget, the company can adjust its revenue and expense projections to reflect this change in activity level. For example, if the company originally budgeted for a selling price of $10 per widget, it could now adjust its revenue projection to account for the additional 2,000 widgets sold at this price. Similarly, the company can adjust its expense projections to reflect the increase in production and sales volume.

By using a flexible budget, the company can compare its actual performance to its budgeted performance and analyze the reasons for any variances. This allows for better decision-making and the ability to make adjustments as necessary to meet financial goals.

7.4.6. Participatory Budgeting

Participatory budgeting is a democratic process that allows community members to directly decide how to allocate a portion of a public budget. It gives citizens the opportunity to have a say in the financial decisions that affect their lives.

To illustrate this concept, let's consider an example. Imagine a city with a population of 100,000 residents. The city has a budget of $10 million for infrastructure projects, such as road repairs, park renovations, and public transportation improvements.

In a traditional budgeting process, city officials and experts would make decisions on how to allocate the $10 million based on their own priorities and expertise. However, with participatory budgeting, the process is more inclusive and transparent.

In this example, the city decides to allocate $1 million of the budget through participatory budgeting. They invite residents to propose and vote on projects that they believe will benefit the community the most. These projects could include building a new community center, creating bike lanes, or enhancing public spaces.

Residents are encouraged to attend public meetings, where they can learn about the proposed projects and discuss their merits. They can also submit project proposals themselves, providing detailed information on the estimated costs and potential benefits.

Once the proposals are collected, they are reviewed by city officials and experts to ensure feasibility and alignment with the city's goals. The approved proposals are then presented to the community for a voting process.

Residents are given the opportunity to vote on the projects they support the most. The voting can take place through various methods, such as in-person voting booths, online platforms, or mail-in ballots. The projects with the highest number of votes are funded using the allocated $1 million.

Participatory budgeting allows citizens to have a direct impact on their community by deciding how public funds are spent. It promotes transparency, accountability, and civic engagement (Nugus, 2009).

7.4.7. Rolling Budgeting

Rolling budgeting is a flexible budgeting approach that allows businesses to continuously update and adjust their budgets throughout the year. This method is particularly useful for organizations operating in dynamic and unpredictable environments.

Traditional budgeting methods typically involve creating an annual budget at the beginning of the fiscal year and strictly adhering to it. However, this approach can be problematic when circumstances change, as it may require significant revisions or render the budget irrelevant.

In contrast, rolling budgeting allows businesses to adapt their budgets as new information becomes available or when unexpected events occur. By regularly reviewing and revising the budget, companies can make more accurate forecasts and better respond to changes in the market.

To illustrate this concept, let's consider an example. ABC Company operates in the retail industry and is in the process of creating its budget for the upcoming year. Instead of creating a static budget for the entire year, ABC Company decides to implement rolling budgeting.

At the beginning of the year, ABC Company establishes its initial budget based on its best estimates and market conditions at that time. However, as the year progresses, the company continually revisits and adjusts the budget based on actual sales figures, market trends, and other relevant factors.

For instance, let's say ABC Company initially budgets $100,000 for marketing expenses for the year. After three months, the company reviews its sales performance and realizes that its marketing efforts have been particularly effective, resulting in higher-than-expected sales. As a result, ABC Company decides to increase its marketing budget to $120,000 for the remainder of the year to capitalize on this success.

On the other hand, if ABC Company experiences a decline in sales or faces unexpected expenses, it can reduce its budget accordingly to ensure it remains aligned with its financial goals.

By implementing rolling budgeting, ABC Company can make more informed decisions and allocate resources more effectively. This approach allows for greater flexibility and responsiveness, enabling the company to adapt to changing circumstances and improve its overall financial performance (Nugus, 2009).

Did You Understand?

1. What is qualitative forecasting?
2. How does time series analysis work?
3. What is regression analysis?
4. What is participatory budgeting?

Answer 1: Qualitative forecasting is an approach that relies on expert opinions and judgments to predict future trends. It is useful when historical data is limited or unreliable. Experts provide insights based on their knowledge and experience, allowing businesses to make informed decisions.

Answer 2: Time series analysis utilizes historical data to identify patterns and make predictions. By analyzing past trends and patterns, businesses can forecast future outcomes. It is commonly used in sales forecasting to estimate future sales based on historical data.

Answer 3: Regression analysis is a statistical technique that examines the relationship between two or more variables to predict future outcomes. By identifying the correlation between variables, businesses can forecast future trends. It is widely used in financial forecasting, analyzing variables such as interest rates and stock prices to predict future financial performance.

Answer 4: Participatory budgeting is a democratic process that allows community members to directly decide how to allocate a portion of a public budget. It gives citizens the opportunity to have a say in the financial decisions that affect their lives. Residents propose and vote on projects they believe will benefit the community, and the projects with the highest number of votes are funded using the allocated budget.

7.5. BUDGET MONITORING AND CONTROL

Learning Objectives

To learn and understand various concepts used in budget monitoring and control, including:

- Budget variance analysis;
- Budget report;
- Corrective actions.

Following the reviews given by Nugus (2009), budget monitoring and control is a crucial process in financial management. It involves tracking and managing expenses to ensure that they align with the approved budget. By monitoring the budget regularly, organizations can identify any variances or deviations and take necessary actions to address them.

One of the primary objectives of budget monitoring and control is to prevent overspending. By closely monitoring expenses, organizations can identify areas where costs are exceeding the budgeted amounts. This allows them to take corrective measures, such as reducing spending or reallocating resources, to bring the budget back on track.

Another important aspect of budget monitoring and control is to ensure that funds are being used effectively and efficiently. By analyzing the budget and expenditure data, organizations can identify areas where resources are being underutilized or wasted. This enables them to make informed decisions and reallocate funds to areas that require more investment.

Budget monitoring and control also helps organizations in making strategic decisions. By having accurate and up-to-date information on budget performance, organizations can evaluate the impact of their financial decisions. This allows them to make necessary adjustments and align their spending with their overall goals and objectives. To effectively monitor and control the budget, organizations need to establish a robust system. This includes setting clear guidelines and procedures for budget monitoring, as well as assigning responsibilities to individuals or teams. Regular reporting and analysis of budget data are also essential to ensure that any deviations are identified and addressed promptly (Passoja, 2015).

7.5.1. Budget Variance Analysis

Budget variance analysis is a crucial aspect of financial management. It involves comparing actual financial results with the budgeted amounts to assess the organization's financial performance.

To illustrate this concept, let's consider an example. Imagine a company that manufactures and sells widgets. The company's budget for the year projected the sales revenue to be $1 million. However, at the end of the year, the actual sales revenue amounted to $900,000.

To perform budget variance analysis, the company would calculate the variance between the budgeted sales revenue and the actual sales revenue. In this case, the variance would be $100,000 ($1 million – $900,000). By analyzing this variance, the company can identify the reasons for the deviation from the budgeted amount.

There are various factors that could contribute to this variance. For instance, the company may have experienced lower-than-expected demand for its widgets due to changes in market conditions or increased competition. Alternatively, the company may have faced production issues that resulted in lower sales volumes.

By identifying the causes of the budget variance, the company can take appropriate actions to address the issues. For example, the company might focus on improving marketing strategies to boost sales or implement measures to enhance production efficiency.Budget Monitoring and Control is an ongoing process that enables organizations to track their financial performance and make informed decisions. By regularly analyzing budget variances, companies can identify areas of concern and take proactive steps to achieve their financial goals.

7.5.2. Budget Report

According to Passoja (2015), a budget report is a crucial tool for businesses to track and manage their finances effectively. It provides a comprehensive overview of the company's financial situation, including income, expenses, and overall profitability. In this article, we will explore a budget report example to understand its components and how it can help businesses make informed decisions (Passoja, 2015).

Components of a budget report:

1. **Income:** This section of the report outlines all sources of revenue for the business. It includes sales figures, investment income, and any other income streams. By analyzing this data, businesses can identify their primary sources of income and make adjustments accordingly.
2. **Expenses:** The expenses section details all the costs incurred by the business. It includes fixed expenses like rent, salaries, and utilities, as well as variable expenses such as raw materials and marketing expenses. By reviewing this section, businesses can identify areas where cost-cutting measures can be implemented.
3. **Profitability:** The profitability section provides an overview of the company's financial performance. It calculates the net profit by subtracting total expenses from total income. This section helps businesses determine their profitability and make necessary adjustments to improve their financial position.
4. **Budget Variance Analysis:** The budget variance analysis compares the actual figures with the

budgeted amounts. It highlights any deviations from the planned budget, allowing businesses to identify areas where they have over- or underperformed. This analysis helps in making informed decisions and taking corrective actions.

Example budget report:

XYZ Company Budget Report

Period: January 2022

Income:

- **Sales Revenue:** $100,000
- **Investment Income:** $5,000
- **Total Income:** $105,000

Expenses:

- **Rent:** $10,000
- **Salaries:** $40,000
- **Utilities:** $2,000
- **Raw Materials:** $30,000
- **Marketing Expenses:** $10,000
- **Total Expenses:** $92,000

Profitability:

- **Net Profit:** $13,000

Budget Variance Analysis:

- **Sales Revenue:** +5% variance
- **Rent:** –10% variance
- **Salaries:** +2% variance
- **Utilities:** +5% variance
- **Raw Materials:** –3% variance
- **Marketing Expenses:** –8% variance

7.5.3. Corrective Actions

In the world of business, budgets play a crucial role in determining the financial health and success of an organization. However, even with careful planning and analysis, unforeseen circumstances can arise that require corrective actions to be taken. Corrective actions are steps taken to rectify any deviations or issues that may arise in a budget. These actions are necessary to ensure that the budget remains on track and aligned with the organization's goals and objectives (Passoja, 2015).

One example of a corrective action in a business budget is when there is an unexpected increase in expenses. Let's say a company budgeted a certain amount for marketing expenses, but due to unforeseen circumstances, such as the need for additional advertising or a sudden increase in marketing costs, the actual expenses exceed the budgeted amount. In this case, the company would need to take corrective actions to address this deviation.

The first step in this corrective action would be to identify the cause of the increase in expenses. This could involve reviewing invoices, analyzing spending patterns, or conducting meetings with relevant stakeholders. Once the cause is identified, the company can then devise a plan to address the issue.

In this example, the company could explore various options to reduce marketing expenses without compromising the effectiveness of their campaigns. This could involve renegotiating contracts with advertising agencies, exploring more cost-effective marketing channels, or reallocating funds from other areas of the budget.

Implementing the chosen corrective actions requires effective communication and coordination among the relevant departments and stakeholders. It is essential to ensure that everyone is aware of the changes and understands their roles and responsibilities in implementing them (Passoja, 2015).

7.6. BUDGETING SOFTWARE AND TOOLS

To streamline budgeting process, businesses can utilize various software and tools. Here are some of the key examples:

1. **QuickBooks:** It is a widely used accounting software that offers budgeting features. It allows businesses to create budgets, track expenses, and generate financial reports. With its user-friendly interface, even those without accounting expertise can easily navigate and utilize its budgeting capabilities.
2. **Excel:** It is a versatile tool that can be used for budgeting purposes. Its spreadsheet functionality enables businesses to organize and analyze their financial data effectively. With built-in formulas and functions, Excel can perform calculations and generate reports, making it a popular choice for budgeting.
3. **Mint:** It is a free online tool that helps businesses manage their budgets. It allows users to link their bank accounts, credit cards, and other financial accounts to track expenses automatically. Mint also provides budgeting recommendations based on spending patterns, making it a convenient option for businesses looking for automated budgeting assistance.

3\. **Zoho Books:** It is an accounting software that offers budgeting capabilities. It allows businesses to create budgets, track expenses, and generate financial reports. Zoho Books also integrates with other Zoho applications, making it a comprehensive solution for budgeting and financial management.

4\. **YNAB (You Need a Budget):** It is a budgeting software that focuses on helping businesses gain control over their finances. It offers features like goal tracking, debt management, and expense tracking. YNAB's emphasis on budgeting principles and financial education sets it apart from other budgeting tools.

Did You Understand?

1. What is the purpose of budget monitoring and control?
2. What is budget variance analysis?
3. What are the components of a budget report?
4. What are corrective actions in budgeting?

Answer 1: The purpose of budget monitoring and control is to ensure that expenses align with the approved budget and to prevent overspending. It also helps organizations use funds effectively and make strategic decisions.

Answer 2: Budget variance analysis involves comparing actual financial results with the budgeted amounts to assess the organization's financial performance. It helps identify reasons for deviations from the budgeted amount.

Answer 3: The components of a budget report include income, expenses, profitability, and budget variance analysis. The income section outlines sources of revenue, the expenses section details costs incurred, the profitability section calculates net profit, and the budget variance analysis compares actual figures with the budgeted amounts.

Answer 4: Corrective actions are steps taken to rectify deviations or issues that arise in a budget. They are necessary to keep the budget on track and aligned with the organization's goals. Corrective actions involve identifying the cause of the deviation and implementing a plan to address it.

CASE STUDY

- **Introduction:** This case study focuses on the budgeting and forecasting practices of Japfa Ltd., a leading agri-food company based in Singapore. The study aims to analyze the company's budgeting and forecasting processes, identify any issues or challenges faced, and propose recommendations for improvement.
- **Background:** Japfa Ltd. operates in the agri-food industry, with a diverse portfolio that includes animal protein production, animal feed, and consumer food products. The company has a global presence, with operations in various countries across Asia and beyond. As a publicly listed company, Japfa Ltd. faces the challenge of meeting the expectations of its shareholders while also ensuring sustainable growth and profitability.
- **Budgeting Process:** Japfa Ltd. follows a comprehensive budgeting process that involves multiple stakeholders and departments. The process begins with the identification of key business objectives and goals, which are then translated into financial targets. The budgeting team collaborates with various departments to gather necessary data and insights for accurate forecasting. The budget is then prepared based on these inputs and undergoes a rigorous review and approval process.
- **Forecasting Process:** Japfa Ltd. recognizes the importance of accurate forecasting in its decision-making process. The company uses both qualitative and quantitative techniques to forecast future financial performance. These techniques include trend analysis, market research, and expert opinions. The forecasting team works closely with the budgeting team to ensure alignment between the budget and forecast.
- **Challenges Faced:** While Japfa Ltd. has a well-defined budgeting and forecasting process, there are several challenges that the company faces. One of the main challenges is the volatility of the agri-food industry, which makes it difficult to accurately forecast demand and pricing. Additionally, the company operates in multiple countries with varying economic conditions, further complicating the forecasting process. Another challenge is the coordination and collaboration required between different departments and stakeholders, which can sometimes result in delays and inefficiencies.
- **Recommendations:** To address these challenges and improve the budgeting and forecasting process, Japfa Ltd. can consider the following recommendations:

1. **Enhance Data Collection and Analysis:** The company should invest in advanced data analytics tools and technologies to gather and analyze data more efficiently. This will enable better forecasting accuracy and reduce reliance on manual processes.
2. **Improve Communication and Collaboration:** Japfa Ltd. should foster a culture of open communication and collaboration among departments and stakeholders involved in the budgeting and forecasting process. Regular meetings and updates should be conducted to ensure everyone is aligned and informed.

3. **Develop Scenario Planning Capabilities:** Given the volatility of the agri-food industry, Japfa Ltd. should develop scenario planning capabilities to assess the impact of various market conditions on its financial performance. This will enable the company to make more informed decisions and mitigate risks.

- **Conclusion:** In conclusion, Japfa Ltd. has a robust budgeting and forecasting process in place, but there are challenges that need to be addressed to improve accuracy and efficiency. By implementing the recommended strategies, the company can enhance its budgeting and forecasting capabilities and drive sustainable growth in the agri-food industry.

SUMMARY

Chapter 7 discusses budgeting and forecasting, which are crucial concepts in financial management that are essential for the success and sustainability of organizations. Budgeting involves creating a detailed plan that outlines an organization's financial goals and objectives, while forecasting predicts future financial outcomes based on historical data and market trends.

Budgeting provides a roadmap for financial decision-making by setting clear targets and allocating resources efficiently. It promotes accountability and transparency by monitoring actual performance against budgeted targets. Forecasting helps organizations anticipate potential challenges and opportunities, enabling them to make informed decisions and take proactive measures. It also plays a crucial role in financial planning, evaluating investment opportunities, and assessing the feasibility of new projects.

There are several types of budgets that businesses use, including operating budgets, cash flow budgets, financial budgets, sales budgets, production budgets, labor budgets, capital budgets, static budgets, overhead budgets, and master budgets. Each type serves a specific purpose in managing finances effectively.

Creating a budget involves a step-by-step process that includes setting financial goals, gathering financial data, analyzing past performance, estimating future revenue, determining fixed and variable costs, allocating funds, and monitoring and adjusting the budget regularly. To ensure a smooth and effective budgeting process, it is important to have a clear understanding of financial goals, involve key stakeholders, review historical data, use budgeting software, break down the budget into manageable parts, be realistic in setting targets, monitor and adjust regularly, and communicate and educate everyone in the organization about the budget.

Forecasting methods are crucial for businesses to make informed decisions and anticipate future trends. Qualitative forecasting relies on expert opinions and judgments, while time series analysis uses historical data to identify patterns. Causal forecasting examines cause-and-effect relationships, regression analysis analyzes the relationship between variables, and econometric modeling combines economic theory and statistical analysis. Scenario analysis involves creating hypothetical situations, simulation modeling uses computerized models, and trend analysis examines long-term trends. The Delphi method gathers opinions from experts, and market research collects data to understand consumer preferences.

Budgeting techniques include activity-based budgeting, incremental budgeting, imposed budgeting, and value proposition budgeting. Flexible budgeting allows for adjustments based on changes in activity levels, participatory budgeting involves community members in decision-making, and rolling budgeting allows for continuous updates and adjustments throughout the year.

Budget monitoring and control involve tracking and managing expenses to ensure they align with the approved budget. Budget variance analysis compares actual financial results with the budgeted amounts to assess the organization's financial performance.

Corrective actions are taken to address deviations or issues in the budget, such as renegotiating contracts or reallocating funds.

Businesses can streamline the budgeting process by using software and tools like QuickBooks, Excel, Mint, Zoho Books, and YNAB, which offer features such as budget creation, expense tracking, and financial reporting. These tools help businesses effectively manage their finances and make informed decisions.

MULTIPLE CHOICE QUESTIONS

1. **What is budgeting?**
   a. The process of predicting future financial outcomes
   b. The process of creating a detailed plan for financial goals and objectives
   c. The process of allocating resources to different activities within an organization
   d. The process of monitoring actual performance against budgeted targets
2. **What is the benefit of budgeting?**
   a. It provides a roadmap for financial decision-making
   b. It promotes accountability and transparency within an organization
   c. It helps organizations anticipate potential challenges and opportunities
   d. All of the above
3. **What is forecasting?**
   a. The process of predicting future financial outcomes
   b. The process of creating a detailed plan for financial goals and objectives
   c. The process of allocating resources to different activities within an organization
   d. The process of monitoring actual performance against budgeted targets
4. **What is the purpose of a sales budget?**
   a. To estimate the revenue generated from products or services
   b. To determine the quantity of goods or services to produce
   c. To allocate funds for rent, utilities, and office supplies
   d. To outline long-term investment plans
5. **What is the purpose of a production budget?**
   a. To estimate the revenue generated from products or services
   b. To determine the quantity of goods or services to produce
   c. To allocate funds for rent, utilities, and office supplies
   d. To outline long-term investment plans
6. **What is the purpose of a capital budget?**
   a. To estimate the revenue generated from products or services
   b. To determine the quantity of goods or services to produce

   c. To allocate funds for rent, utilities, and office supplies
   d. To outline long-term investment plans

7. **What is the purpose of a master budget?**
   a. To estimate the revenue generated from products or services
   b. To determine the quantity of goods or services to produce
   c. To allocate funds for rent, utilities, and office supplies
   d. To consolidate all individual budgets into a comprehensive financial plan

8. **What is activity-based budgeting?**
   a. A budgeting approach that focuses on the activities that drive costs within an organization.
   b. A budgeting approach that focuses on the overall financial situation of an organization.
   c. A budgeting approach that allocates resources based on previous year's budget.
   d. A budgeting approach that allows community members to decide how to allocate a public budget.

9. **What is the disadvantage of incremental budgeting?**
   a. Lack of flexibility and perpetuation of inefficiencies.
   b. Difficulty in making significant changes or allocating resources to new initiatives.
   c. Limited ability to respond to changing needs or emergencies.
   d. All of the above.

10. **What is imposed budgeting?**
    a. A budgeting method that involves making small adjustments to the previous budget.
    b. A budgeting method where a budget is set by an external entity and enforced upon the responsible individuals or departments.
    c. A budgeting method that involves allocating resources to support the creation and delivery of a value proposition.
    d. A budgeting method that allows community members to directly decide how to allocate a portion of a public budget.

11. **What is value proposition budgeting?**
    a. A budgeting approach that focuses on the activities that drive costs within an organization.
    b. A budgeting approach that allows community members to decide how to allocate a public budget.
    c. A budgeting method that involves allocating resources to support the creation and delivery of a compelling value proposition to customers.
    d. A budgeting method that allows businesses to continuously update and adjust their budgets throughout the year.

12. **What is rolling budgeting?**
    a. A budgeting approach that focuses on the activities that drive costs within an organization.
    b. A budgeting method where a budget is set by an external entity and enforced upon the responsible individuals or departments.
    c. A budgeting method that involves allocating resources to support the creation and delivery of a compelling value proposition to customers.
    d. A flexible budgeting approach that allows businesses to continuously update and adjust their budgets throughout the year.
13. **What is the primary objective of budget monitoring and control?**
    a. To prevent overspending
    b. To increase profitability
    c. To allocate resources effectively
    d. To make strategic decisions
14. **Why is budget variance analysis important?**
    a. To track financial performance
    b. To identify areas of concern
    c. To make informed decisions
    d. All of the above
15. **What does a budget report provide?**
    a. An overview of income and expenses
    b. Analysis of profitability
    c. Budget variance analysis
    d. All of the above
16. **What are corrective actions in budgeting?**
    a. Steps taken to rectify deviations
    b. Measures to improve financial position
    c. Actions to address budget issues
    d. All of the above
17. **What are some examples of budgeting software and tools?**
    a. QuickBooks
    b. Excel
    c. Mint
    d. All of the above

Answers to Multiple Choice Questions

1. (b); 2. (d); 3. (a); 4. (a); 5. (b); 6. (d); 7. (d); 8. (a); 9. (d); 10. (b); 11. (c); 12. (d); 13. (a); 14. (d); 15. (d); 16. (d); 17. (d)

REFERENCES

1. Evans, M. K., (2003). *Practical Business Forecasting*. Blackwell (Malden).
2. Hoshmand, A. R., (2009). *Business Forecasting: A Practical Approach*. Routledge.
3. Nugus, S., (2009). *Financial Planning Using Excel: Forecasting, Planning, and Budgeting Techniques*. Butterworth-Heinemann.
4. Passoja, P., (2015). *Budgeting and Forecasting Application Development: An Evaluation*. Master's thesis (80 pages)
5. Shim, J. K., Siegel, J. G., & Shim, A. I., (2011). *Budgeting Basics and Beyond* (Vol. 574). John Wiley & Sons.

CHAPTER

8 Standard Costing and Variance Analysis

LEARNING OBJECTIVES

After studying this chapter, you will be able to:

- To understand setting standard costs.
- To learn and understand how to calculate and interpret of variances.
- To understand the causes of variances.
- To learn and understand the importance of variance analysis in performance evaluation.
- To learn and understand the importance of standard costing and variance analysis in budgeting and forecasting.

INTRODUCTORY EXAMPLE

Standard costing and variance analysis are essential tools used by companies like Danone to manage and control their costs. By establishing standard costs for materials, labor, and overhead, companies can compare their actual costs to the expected costs and identify any deviations or variances.

Danone, a multinational food company, utilizes standard costing and variance analysis to monitor and manage its costs effectively. By establishing standard costs for its products, Danone can evaluate the efficiency of its operations and identify areas where costs can be reduced or controlled.

For example, if the standard cost for a particular product is $10 per unit, but the actual cost turns out to be $12 per unit, Danone can investigate the reasons behind the $2 variance. It may find that the cost of raw materials has increased or that there were inefficiencies in the production process. By identifying these issues, Danone can take corrective actions to address them and bring the costs back in line with the standards.

Furthermore, variance analysis helps Danone in budgeting and forecasting. By understanding the reasons behind the variances, the company can make more accurate predictions about future costs and plan its resources accordingly. This allows Danone to make informed decisions and allocate its resources effectively.

In conclusion, standard costing and variance analysis play a crucial role in managing costs and improving profitability for companies like Danone. By establishing standard costs and analyzing variances, companies can identify areas for improvement, control costs, and make informed decisions to achieve their financial goals.

UNIT INTRODUCTION

Standard costing is a management accounting technique that helps organizations evaluate and control their costs. It involves establishing predetermined standards for various cost elements, such as materials, labor, machine, and overhead, and then comparing the actual costs incurred with these standards. By doing so, organizations can identify areas of inefficiency and take appropriate corrective actions (Badem, Ergin, & Drury, 2013) (Figure 8.1).

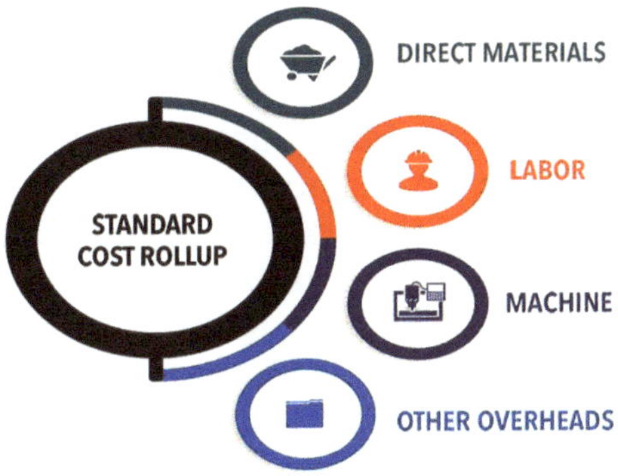

Figure 8.1. *Various elements in standard cost system.*

Source: What Is Standard Costing – Define | Meaning | Objectives (2022).

Variance analysis, on the other hand, is the process of analyzing the differences between the standard costs and the actual costs. It helps organizations understand the reasons behind these variances and enables them to make informed decisions. Variances can be favorable or unfavorable, depending on whether the actual costs are lower or higher than the standard costs. Through variance analysis, organizations can identify the root causes of these variances and take necessary steps to improve performance (Gelman, 2006).

Both standard costing and variance analysis play a crucial role in the decision-making process of an organization. They provide valuable insights into cost control, performance evaluation, and budgeting. By comparing actual costs with predetermined standards, organizations can identify cost-saving opportunities and make adjustments to their operations. This helps in improving efficiency and profitability.

Moreover, standard costing and variance analysis facilitate the evaluation of individual departments or units within an organization. By analyzing the variances, management can identify areas that are performing well and those that require improvement. This information can be used to allocate resources effectively and reward high-performing departments.

To understand standard costing and variance analysis better, it is essential to be familiar with some basic concepts and terminology. The standard cost. It is the predetermined cost per unit of a product or service, based on the expected level of efficiency and utilization of resources. Standard costs are determined through a combination of historical data, industry benchmarks, and management's expectations.

Remember

Standard costing is not a one-size-fits-all solution and may not be suitable for every organization. It is important to consider the specific needs and characteristics of the business before implementing standard costing as a management accounting technique.

The standard cost is composed of various elements, including direct materials, direct labor, and overhead. Direct materials refer to the materials that can be directly traced to the production of a product or service. Direct labor, on the other hand, includes the wages and benefits of the employees directly involved in the production process. Overhead costs encompass all the other indirect costs, such as rent, utilities, and administrative expenses (Badem, Ergin, & Drury, 2013).

Once the standard costs are established, organizations can compare them with the actual costs incurred. The difference between the standard costs and the actual costs is known as a variance. There are different types of variances, such as material price variance, material usage variance, labor rate variance, and labor efficiency variance. These variances help in identifying the specific areas where costs deviate from the standards.

8.1. SETTING STANDARD COSTS

Learning Objectives

- To understand the methods used to determine standard costs.

According to Ngozi (2013), setting standard costs is a crucial aspect of cost accounting. It involves establishing predetermined costs for materials, labor, and overhead that are expected to be incurred during the production process. These predetermined costs serve as benchmarks against which actual costs can be compared. By comparing actual costs to standard costs, businesses can evaluate their performance, identify areas of inefficiency, and make informed decisions regarding pricing, budgeting, and cost control.

8.1.1. Methods Used to Determine Standard Costs

8.1.1.1. Historical Data Analysis

This method involves analyzing past cost data to identify trends and patterns that can be used to predict future costs. By examining historical data, businesses can gain insights into factors such as inflation rates, labor productivity, and material price fluctuations. This information can then be used to establish standard costs that reflect expected future conditions.

Now, let's consider an example to further clarify this process. Suppose a company, XYZ Manufacturing, wants to determine the standard cost for producing a widget. They gather historical data for the past year, including:

- Material costs.
- Labor hours.
- Overhead expenses.

After analyzing the data, XYZ Manufacturing identifies that material costs have been consistently averaging $10 per unit. Labor hours have varied between 2 and 3 hours per unit, with an average of 2.5 hours. Overhead expenses have fluctuated due to changes in production volume.

Based on this analysis, XYZ Manufacturing sets the standard cost for producing a widget as follows:

- $10 for materials.
- 2.5 labor hours.
- An estimated overhead expense based on average production volume.

By using historical data analysis to determine standard costs, companies like XYZ Manufacturing can make informed decisions about pricing, budgeting, and performance evaluation. This process provides a foundation for effective cost management and enhances overall financial performance.

8.1.1.2. Engineering Estimates

This approach involves analyzing the specifications and requirements of a product or process to estimate the costs associated with its production. Engineering estimates take into account factors such as material quantities, labor hours, and machine usage. By carefully assessing these factors, businesses can develop accurate estimates of the costs involved in producing a product or providing a service (Iliemena & Amedu, 2019).

The first step in the engineering estimate method is to break down the product into its various components. This requires a thorough understanding of the product and its manufacturing process. Each component is then analyzed to determine the materials, labor, and overhead costs associated with its production.

Once the costs of each component are determined, they are added together to obtain the total cost of the product. This total cost is then divided by the number of units produced to obtain the standard cost per unit.

The engineering estimate method is beneficial for several reasons. Firstly, it provides a detailed breakdown of the costs associated with each component, allowing for better cost control and analysis. Secondly, it allows for the identification of cost-saving opportunities by comparing the estimated costs with the actual costs incurred during production (Badem, Ergin, & Drury, 2013).

However, it is important to note that the engineering estimate method has its limitations. It relies on estimates and assumptions, which may not always accurately reflect the actual costs. Additionally, it does not take into account external factors such as market conditions or changes in raw material prices, which can impact the actual costs of production.

While setting standard costs is essential, it is not without its challenges and considerations. One challenge is the dynamic nature of business environments. External factors such as changes in market conditions, technology advancements, and regulatory requirements can all impact costs. Therefore, it is crucial for businesses to regularly review and update their standard costs to ensure they remain relevant and accurate.

Additionally, setting accurate standard costs requires careful consideration of various factors. For instance, businesses must consider the level of detail at which standard costs are established. Setting costs at a high level of detail can provide more accurate information but may also increase the complexity and cost of the process. On the other hand, setting costs at a lower level of detail may simplify the process but may result in less accurate information.

Another consideration is the balance between cost control and motivation. Standard costs are often used as performance measures and can influence employee behavior. If standard costs are set too low, employees may feel overwhelmed or demotivated, leading to decreased productivity. Conversely, if standard costs are set too high, employees may become complacent or engage in wasteful practices. Therefore, businesses must strike a balance that encourages efficiency and motivation while maintaining cost control.

Did You Understand?

1. What is standard costing and variance analysis?
2. How do standard costing and variance analysis benefit organizations?
3. How are standard costs determined?

Answer 1: Concepts like variance analysis and standard costing play a significant role in financial management and accounting. Companies use standard costing when they have an idea of how much money they will need to make a product or provide a service. However, in order to find any discrepancies, variance analysis compares the actual costs with the standard costs. Businesses can learn a lot about their cost performance and how to make smart decisions to boost efficiency and profits by looking at these differences.

Answer 2: Organizations can gain a lot from standard costing and variance analysis. They provide insightful information about performance assessment and cost management, enabling businesses to pinpoint problem areas and take well-informed decisions. Organizations can identify deviations and take corrective action to improve efficiency and profitability by comparing actual costs to standard costs. Variance analysis also aids in the creation of realistic forecasts and budgets, facilitating improved resource allocation and financial planning. All things considered, these instruments are essential for raising organizational effectiveness and promoting ongoing development.

Answer 3: Standard costs are determined through a combination of historical data, industry benchmarks, and management's expectations. Historical data analysis involves analyzing past cost data to identify trends and patterns that can be used to predict future costs. Engineering estimates, on the other hand, involve analyzing the specifications and requirements of a product or process to estimate the costs associated with its production. Each method has its advantages and limitations, and businesses must carefully consider various factors when setting accurate standard costs. Regular review and updates are also necessary to ensure that standard costs remain relevant and accurate in dynamic business environments. Additionally, businesses must strike a balance between cost control and motivation when setting standard costs, considering the level of detail at which costs are established.

8.2. CALCULATION AND INTERPRETATION OF VARIANCES

Learning Objectives

- To learn and understand the calculation and interpretation of variances.

To calculate variances, we need to understand the components of standard costs. These include the standard quantity or hours required for production, the standard price or rate for each component, and the actual quantity or hours used, as well as the actual price or rate paid. By comparing these figures, we can identify the causes of variances.

The formula for calculating variance is as follows:

Variance = Actual Value – Planned Value

To perform a thorough analysis, it is important to break down the variances into their respective components. This can be done by using sub-formulas, such as price variance and quantity variance.

Price Variance = (Actual Price – Planned Price) × Actual Quantity

Quantity Variance = (Actual Quantity – Planned Quantity) × Planned Price

By analyzing these sub-variances, one can gain insights into the specific reasons behind the overall variance. This information can then be used to make informed decisions and take appropriate actions to address any issues or capitalize on opportunities (Figure 8.2).

Let's take a look at an example. Suppose a company sets a standard cost of $10 for each unit of raw material, and it expects to use 100 units for a particular product. However, due to an increase in raw material prices, the company ends up paying $12 per unit, resulting in a price variance of $200 ([$12 – $10] × 100). This variance indicates that the company paid more than expected for the raw material.

A General Model for Variance Analysis

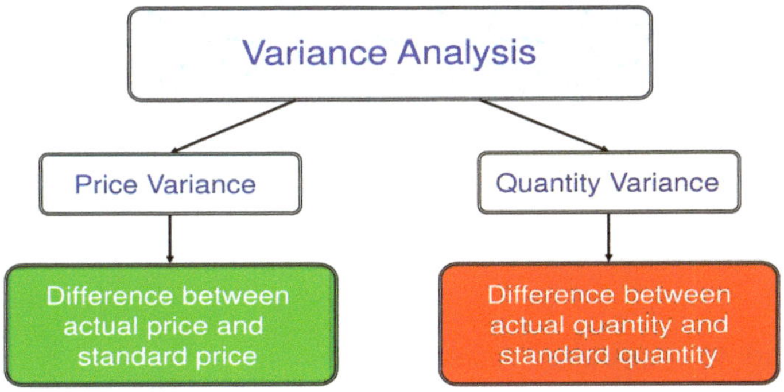

Figure 8.2. *A general model for variance analysis.*

Source: Trait (2014).

> **Remember**
>
> Variance analysis should not be seen as a one-time exercise. It is an ongoing process that requires regular monitoring and analysis. By continuously reviewing variances, businesses can stay proactive and make timely adjustments to achieve their goals.

Similarly, if the company actually used 90 units of raw material instead of the expected 100 units, it would result in a usage variance of $100 ([$10 – $12] × 90). This variance suggests that the company used less raw material than anticipated.

Once we have calculated the variances, the next step is to interpret them. Variances can be classified as favorable or unfavorable, depending on whether they have a positive or negative impact on profitability. In our example, the price variance of $200 is unfavorable because it increased the cost of production. On the other hand, the usage variance of $100 is favorable because it reduced the amount of raw material used.

It is important to note that variances should not be viewed in isolation. Instead, they should be analyzed in conjunction with other relevant information to gain a complete understanding of the situation. For instance, a favorable usage variance may be due to improved efficiency or better-quality control, while an unfavorable price variance may be a result of inflation or changes in supplier prices.

Furthermore, variances should be investigated to determine their root causes. This involves identifying the responsible individuals or departments and examining the underlying factors that contributed to the variances. By doing so, management can take appropriate corrective actions to address the issues and improve future performance.

8.3. CAUSES OF VARIANCES

Learning Objectives

- To learn and understand the causes of variances.

Variance Analysis helps managers identify areas where costs are deviating from expectations and provides insights into the reasons behind these deviations. By understanding the causes of variances, managers can take appropriate actions to improve performance and control costs.

There are several factors that can lead to variances in standard costing. One common factor is price changes. Fluctuations in the prices of raw materials or other inputs can directly impact costs. For example, if the price of a key raw material increases, it will result in a higher cost of production, leading to a negative variance. Similarly, if there is a decrease in prices, it can result in a positive variance (Gelman, 2006).

Efficiency issues can also contribute to variances. These issues can arise from factors such as poor production planning, inadequate training, or inefficient use of resources. For instance, if employees are not properly trained or if there are bottlenecks in the production process, it can result in lower productivity and higher costs. This will be reflected in negative variances.

Another factor that can cause variances is changes in production volume. When the actual production volume differs from the planned volume, it can impact costs. For example, if the actual production volume is lower than planned, fixed costs will be spread over a smaller number of units, resulting in higher costs per unit. This will lead to a negative variance. On the other hand, if the actual production volume is higher than planned, fixed costs will be spread over a larger number of units, resulting in lower costs per unit and a positive variance.

To identify the root causes of variances, managers can use various strategies. One approach is to conduct a detailed analysis of the factors contributing to each variance. This can involve reviewing purchase records, production reports, and employee performance data. By examining these records, managers can pinpoint the specific areas where deviations are occurring. Another strategy is to implement a system of regular monitoring and reporting. By continuously tracking and analyzing costs, managers can quickly identify any significant variances and take timely corrective actions. This can involve setting up alerts or dashboards that provide real-time updates on cost performance.

Additionally, managers can consider conducting a variance analysis at different levels of the organization. By breaking down variances by department or product line, managers can gain a deeper understanding of the specific areas that need attention. This can help in allocating resources and implementing targeted improvement initiatives.

Once the root causes of variances are identified, managers can take appropriate actions to address them. This may involve renegotiating supplier contracts to mitigate price fluctuations, providing additional training to employees to improve efficiency, or revising production plans to better align with actual demand. By addressing the root causes, managers can prevent future variances and improve overall cost performance (Gelman, 2006).

Did You Understand?

1. What are the components of standard costs that are needed to calculate variances?
2. Can you provide an example of how variances are calculated and interpreted?
3. What strategies can managers use to identify the root causes of variances?

Answer 1: To calculate variances, we need to understand the standard quantity or hours required for production, the standard price or rate for each component, and the actual quantity or hours used, as well as the actual price or rate paid.

Answer 2: Suppose a company sets a standard cost of $10 for each unit of raw material and expects to use 100 units for a particular product. As a result of the rise in raw material costs, the company is now paying $12 per unit, leading to a price variance of $200 ([$12 - $10] × 100). Based on the data, it can be observed that the company's expenditure on the raw material exceeded the initial expectations. In a scenario where the company utilized 90 units of raw material instead of the anticipated 100 units, a usage variance of $100 would arise. This calculation is derived from multiplying the difference between the expected cost per unit and the actual cost per unit ($10 - $12) by the actual quantity used (90 units). Based on the variance, it appears that the company utilized a lower amount of raw material than initially expected.

Answer 3: Managers can use various strategies to identify the root causes of variances. One approach is to conduct a detailed analysis of the factors contributing to each variance by reviewing purchase records, production reports, and employee performance data. Another strategy is to implement a system of regular monitoring and reporting to quickly identify significant variances and take timely corrective actions. Managers can also consider conducting a variance analysis at different levels of the organization, breaking down variances by department or product line, to gain a deeper understanding of specific areas that need attention.

8.4. IMPORTANCE OF VARIANCE ANALYSIS IN PERFORMANCE EVALUATION

Learning Objectives

- To understand the importance of variance analysis in performance evaluation.

Variance analysis is a significant tool in performance evaluation as it allows organizations to compare actual results with expected or budgeted results. By analyzing the variances, organizations can identify areas of success or areas that need improvement. Variances can be calculated for various aspects of performance, such as sales, costs, and profits.

When assessing the performance of individuals, variances can provide valuable insights. For example, if an individual's sales performance exceeds the budgeted sales, a favorable variance is observed. This indicates that the individual has performed exceptionally well in generating sales. On the other hand, an unfavorable variance suggests that the individual's sales performance has fallen short of expectations. By analyzing these variances, organizations can reward outstanding performers and provide additional training or support to those who need improvement.

Similarly, variances can be used to evaluate the performance of departments within an organization. For instance, if the production department consistently achieves favorable variances in terms of cost savings, it demonstrates their efficiency in managing resources. Conversely, unfavorable variances may indicate inefficiencies or wastage within the department. By monitoring these variances, organizations can identify areas for improvement and implement strategies to enhance departmental performance (Gelman, 2006).

Furthermore, variance analysis can be applied to assess the overall performance of the organization. By analyzing the variances across various departments and functions, organizations can gain a holistic understanding of their performance. This allows them to identify strengths and weaknesses at the organizational level. For example, if the organization consistently achieves favorable variances in terms of profitability, it indicates effective overall performance. Conversely, unfavorable variances may highlight areas where the organization is underperforming. By closely examining these variances, organizations can make informed decisions to enhance their overall performance.

Despite its usefulness, variance analysis has certain limitations. Firstly, it relies heavily on accurate and reliable data. If the data used for calculating variances is flawed or incomplete, the analysis may provide misleading results. Additionally, variance analysis assumes that the budgeted figures are realistic and achievable. However, in dynamic and uncertain business environments, these assumptions may not always hold true. Furthermore, variance analysis focuses solely on the differences between actual and budgeted figures, without providing insights into the underlying causes. Therefore, organizations may need to supplement variance analysis with other performance evaluation methods to gain a comprehensive understanding of their performance.

In light of these limitations, alternative methods for performance evaluation can be considered. One such method is the use of key performance indicators (KPIs). KPIs are specific metrics that measure the performance of individuals, departments, and the organization as a whole. Unlike variance analysis, KPIs provide a more comprehensive and balanced view of performance by considering multiple factors. For example, a sales department may use KPIs such as customer satisfaction, sales growth, and market share to evaluate their performance. By focusing on these broader indicators, organizations can gain a deeper understanding of their performance and identify areas for improvement (Gelman, 2006).

8.5. THE IMPORTANCE OF STANDARD COSTING AND VARIANCE ANALYSIS IN BUDGETING AND FORECASTING

Learning Objectives

- To understand the importance of standard costing and variance analysis in budgeting and forecasting.

Standard costing and variance analysis play a crucial role in budgeting and forecasting. Standard costing involves setting predetermined costs for materials, labor, and overheads based on historical data and industry standards. These predetermined costs are then compared to actual costs to identify variances. Variance analysis, on the other hand, involves analyzing these variances to understand their causes and implications.

By incorporating standard costs and variances into the budgeting process, organizations can improve accuracy. Standard costs provide a benchmark against which actual costs can be measured, allowing for better cost control and performance evaluation. Variances, when analyzed, provide insights into the reasons behind deviations from standard costs, enabling managers to take corrective actions and make informed decisions.

Moreover, standard costing and variance analysis facilitate decision-making. By identifying the causes of variances, managers can determine whether they are due to controllable factors, such as inefficient processes or poor resource allocation, or uncontrollable factors, such as external market conditions. This information helps in making decisions regarding process improvements, resource reallocation, or pricing strategies (Badem, Ergin, & Drury, 2013).

However, using standard costing for budgeting purposes comes with its own set of challenges and considerations. Firstly, setting accurate standard costs can be difficult, as it requires a thorough understanding of the organization's operations and industry standards. Inaccurate standard costs can lead to misleading variances and ineffective decision-making.

Secondly, standard costing assumes a static environment, where costs remain constant regardless of changes in production levels or other factors. In reality, costs fluctuate due to factors like inflation, changes in demand, or technological advancements. This can result in variances that may not accurately reflect the performance of the organization.

Furthermore, standard costing may focus primarily on cost control, neglecting other important aspects like quality, customer satisfaction, or innovation. Relying solely on cost-based variances may lead to suboptimal decision-making, as it fails to consider the broader organizational objectives.

Another consideration is the time and resources required for implementing and maintaining a standard costing system. Developing accurate standard costs, collecting, and analyzing data, and training staff can be time-consuming and costly. Small organizations may find it challenging to allocate sufficient resources for this purpose (Ngozi, 2013).

Keyword

Inflation – It is a term used to describe the general increase in prices of goods and services in an economy over a period of time.

Did You Understand?

1. How can variance analysis be used in performance evaluation?
2. How do standard costing and variance analysis contribute to budgeting and forecasting?

Answer 1: Variance analysis can be used to compare actual results with expected or budgeted results. By analyzing the variances, organizations can identify areas of success or areas that need improvement.

Answer 2: Standard costing and variance analysis improve accuracy in budgeting and forecasting. Standard costs provide a benchmark against which actual costs can be measured, allowing for better cost control and performance evaluation. Variances, when analyzed, provide insights into the reasons behind deviations from standard costs, enabling managers to take corrective actions and make informed decisions.

CASE STUDY

- **Introduction:** This case study examines the implementation of standard costing and variance analysis at Novamex, a manufacturing company. Standard costing is a widely used accounting technique that helps companies determine the expected costs of producing products or services. Variance analysis, on the other hand, is a tool used to compare the actual costs with the standard costs and identify the reasons for any deviations. By analyzing the variances, companies can take appropriate actions to control costs and improve their overall financial performance.
- **Background:** Novamex is a company that produces and sells consumer goods. They have a wide range of products, including food and beverages. To effectively manage their costs, Novamex decided to implement standard costing and variance analysis. The main objective was to have a better understanding of their cost structure and identify areas where costs could be controlled.
- **Implementation of Standard Costing:** To implement standard costing, Novamex first determined the standard costs for their products. These standard costs included direct materials, direct labor, and overhead costs. Direct materials costs were determined by analyzing the quantity and price of materials used in production. Direct labor costs were determined by analyzing the labor hours required and the labor rate. Overhead costs were determined by analyzing the indirect costs associated with production.

Once the standard costs were determined, Novamex used them as a benchmark to compare with the actual costs. Any deviations between the standard costs and the actual costs were analyzed to identify the reasons for the variances. Novamex used variance analysis to categorize the variances into different types, such as material price variance, material quantity variance, labor rate variance, and labor efficiency variance. This helped them pinpoint the specific areas where costs were deviating from the standards.

- **Benefits of Standard Costing and Variance Analysis:** By implementing standard costing and variance analysis, Novamex gained several benefits. Firstly, they were able to identify the reasons for cost deviations and take appropriate actions to control costs. For example, if they found that the material price variance was unfavorable, they could negotiate better prices with their suppliers or find alternative suppliers. Secondly, they were able to compare their performance with industry standards and identify areas where they were lagging behind. This helped them set performance targets and improve their overall efficiency. Lastly, standard costing and variance analysis provided Novamex with a better understanding of their cost structure, enabling them to make more informed decisions regarding pricing and product profitability.
- **Conclusion:** Standard costing and variance analysis have proven to be valuable tools for Novamex in managing their costs and improving their financial performance. By implementing these techniques, they were able to identify cost deviations, take appropriate actions to control costs, and improve their overall efficiency. This case study highlights the importance of standard costing and variance analysis in helping companies make informed decisions and achieve their financial goals.

SUMMARY

Chapter 8 discusses standard costing and variance analysis, two crucial management accounting techniques. Standard costing helps organizations evaluate and control their costs by establishing predetermined standards for various cost elements and comparing them to actual costs. Variance analysis is the process of analyzing the differences between standard costs and actual costs to understand the reasons behind these variances. Both standard costing and variance analysis are crucial for cost control, performance evaluation, and budgeting. They help identify areas of inefficiency, allocate resources effectively, and reward high-performing departments. Standard costs are determined through historical data analysis and engineering estimates, taking into account factors such as material costs, labor hours, and overhead expenses. However, setting accurate standard costs can be challenging due to the dynamic nature of business environments and the need to balance cost control and motivation.

Variance analysis is a method used to calculate and interpret the differences between actual and expected results in terms of costs, sales, and profits. It involves comparing standard costs with actual costs to identify the causes of variances. Variances can be classified as favorable or unfavorable depending on their impact on profitability. Factors such as price changes, efficiency issues, and changes in production volume can contribute to variances. To identify the root causes of variances, managers can conduct detailed analyzes, implement monitoring systems, and break down variances by department or product line. Once the root causes are identified, appropriate actions can be taken to address them and improve performance. Variance analysis is also important in performance evaluation as it allows organizations to compare actual results with expected results. Variances can be used to assess the performance of individuals, departments, and the organization as a whole. However, variance analysis has limitations and may need to be supplemented with other performance evaluation methods, such as key performance indicators (KPIs), to gain a comprehensive understanding of performance.

Standard costing and variance analysis are important tools in budgeting and forecasting. Standard costing involves setting predetermined costs based on historical data and industry standards, which are then compared to actual costs to identify variances. Variance analysis helps understand the causes and implications of these variances. By incorporating standard costs and variances into the budgeting process, organizations can improve accuracy, cost control, and performance evaluation. It also facilitates decision-making by identifying controllable and uncontrollable factors affecting variances. However, there are challenges in setting accurate standard costs, as well as limitations in assuming a static environment and focusing solely on cost control. Implementing and maintaining a standard costing system can also be time-consuming and costly for small organizations.

MULTIPLE CHOICE QUESTIONS

1. **What is the purpose of setting standard costs in cost accounting?**
   a. To establish benchmarks for comparing actual costs
   b. To evaluate performance and identify areas of inefficiency
   c. To make informed decisions regarding pricing, budgeting, and cost control
   d. All of the above
2. **Which method involves analyzing past cost data to predict future costs?**
   a. Historical data analysis
   b. Engineering estimates
   c. Variance analysis
   d. Key performance indicators
3. **What factors are considered when using historical data analysis to determine standard costs?**
   a. Inflation rates, labor productivity, and material price fluctuations
   b. Market conditions and changes in raw material prices
   c. Material quantities, labor hours, and machine usage
   d. Purchase records, production reports, and employee performance data
4. **What is the benefit of using engineering estimates to determine standard costs?**
   a. Provides a detailed breakdown of costs for better cost control and analysis
   b. Allows for the identification of cost-saving opportunities
   c. Takes into account external factors such as market conditions
   d. All of the above
5. **What are some limitations of the engineering estimate method?**
   a. Relies on estimates and assumptions that may not accurately reflect actual costs
   b. Does not consider external factors such as market conditions or changes in raw material prices
   c. May result in less accurate information if costs are set at a lower level of detail
   d. All of the above
6. **Why is it important to regularly review and update standard costs?**
   a. External factors can impact costs, such as changes in market conditions or technology advancements
   b. Ensures that standard costs remain relevant and accurate
   c. Allows for effective cost management and enhances overall financial performance
   d. All of the above

7. **What is the balance that businesses must strike when setting standard costs?**
   a. Encouraging efficiency and motivation while maintaining cost control
   b. Setting costs at a high level of detail for more accurate information
   c. Setting costs at a lower level of detail to simplify the process
   d. All of the above
8. **What components are needed to calculate variances?**
   a. Standard quantity or hours, standard price or rate, actual quantity or hours, actual price, or rate
   b. Sales, costs, profits
   c. Key performance indicators
   d. None of the above
9. **How can variances be classified?**
   a. Favorable or unfavorable, depending on their impact on profitability
   b. Positive or negative, depending on their impact on performance
   c. High or low, depending on their magnitude
   d. All of the above
10. **What should be considered when interpreting variances?**
    a. Other relevant information to gain a complete understanding of the situation
    b. The underlying causes of the variances
    c. The responsible individuals or departments
    d. All of the above
11. **What is the next step after calculating variances?**
    a. Identifying the root causes of the variances
    b. Taking appropriate corrective actions
    c. Improving future performance
    d. All of the above
12. **What factor can directly impact costs and lead to variances?**
    a. Price changes
    b. Efficiency issues
    c. Changes in production volume
    d. All of the above
13. **How can managers identify the root causes of variances?**
    a. Conducting a detailed analysis of the factors contributing to each variance
    b. Implementing a system of regular monitoring and reporting
    c. Conducting a variance analysis at different levels of the organization
    d. All of the above

14. What can managers do once the root causes of variances are identified?

a. Take appropriate actions to address the issues

b. Improve future performance

c. Prevent future variances

d. All of the above

Answers to Multiple Choice Questions

1. (d); 2. (a); 3. (a); 4. (d); 5. (d); 6. (d); 7. (a); 8. (a); 9. (a); 10. (d); 11. (d); 12. (d); 13. (d); 14. (d)

REFERENCES

1. Badem, A. C., Ergin, E., & Drury, C., (2013). Is standard costing still used? Evidence from Turkish automotive industry. *International Business Research*, *6*(7), 79.
2. Gelman, A., (2006). Analysis of variance. *New Palgrave Dictionary of Economics*.
3. Iliemena, R. O., & Amedu, J. M. A., (2019). Effect of standard costing on profitability of manufacturing companies: Study of Edo State Nigeria. *Journal of Resources Development and Management*, *53*(3), 28–34.
4. Ngozi, O. V., (2013). *Effects of Standard Costing on The Profitability of Manufacturing Companies 2-5*
5. Trait., (2014). *PPT – Variance Analysis PowerPoint Presentation, Free Download – ID:2745593*. SlideServe. https://www.slideserve.com/tait/variance-analysis (accessed on 04 April 2024).
6. *What is Standard Costing – Define, Meaning, Objectives*, (2022). Parag Gupta Classes. https://www.paraggupta.com/standard-costing/ (accessed on 04 April 2024).

CHAPTER

9

Performance Measurement and Balanced Scorecard

LEARNING OBJECTIVES

After studying this chapter, you will be able to:

- Key performance indicators (KPIs);
- The balanced scorecard framework;
- Designing a balanced scorecard;
- Implementing a balanced scorecard;
- Performance measurement and organizational learning;
- Evaluating and improving performance measurement systems.

INTRODUCTORY EXAMPLE

Performance measurement is a crucial aspect of evaluating the success and effectiveness of a company. It provides valuable insights into various aspects of the business, allowing management to make informed decisions and improve overall performance. One popular tool used for performance measurement is the Balanced Scorecard, which provides a comprehensive view of a company's performance by considering multiple dimensions.

Toyota Motor, a renowned automobile manufacturer, is a prime example of a company that effectively utilizes performance measurement and the Balanced Scorecard. By implementing this tool, Toyota is able to assess its performance in four key areas: financial, customer, internal processes, and learning and growth.

In terms of financial performance, Toyota evaluates its profitability, revenue growth, and cost management. This helps the company identify areas of improvement and make necessary adjustments to achieve financial targets.

Customer satisfaction is another crucial aspect of performance measurement for Toyota. By analyzing customer feedback, conducting surveys, and monitoring customer loyalty, Toyota ensures that it is meeting customer expectations and continuously improving its products and services.

Internal processes are also evaluated by Toyota to identify areas of inefficiency or bottlenecks. By streamlining processes and improving operational efficiency, Toyota aims to deliver high-quality products and services in a timely manner.

Lastly, Toyota focuses on learning and growth as a means of continuous improvement. By investing in employee training and development, fostering a culture of innovation, and promoting knowledge sharing, Toyota ensures that it remains competitive and adapts to changing market demands.

In conclusion, performance measurement and the Balanced Scorecard are essential tools for evaluating and improving company performance. Toyota Motor serves as a prime example of a company that effectively utilizes these tools to assess its performance in various areas and drive continuous improvement.

UNIT INTRODUCTION

Performance measurement plays a crucial role in organizations as it enables them to evaluate their progress towards achieving their goals and objectives. It provides a structured approach to assess the effectiveness and efficiency of processes, systems, and individuals. Moreover, performance measurement allows organizations to identify areas of improvement and take appropriate actions to enhance their performance (Zin et al., 2013). One of the key benefits of performance measurement is that it facilitates informed decision-making. By measuring performance, organizations can gather data and information that can be used to make strategic decisions. This data-driven approach ensures that decisions are based on objective analysis rather than subjective opinions or assumptions.

Performance measurement also promotes accountability within organizations. By setting clear performance targets and measuring progress towards those targets, organizations can hold individuals and teams accountable for their performance. This fosters a culture of responsibility and encourages employees to strive for excellence in their work. Furthermore, performance measurement enables organizations to identify best practices and benchmark their performance against industry standards. By comparing their performance to that of competitors or industry leaders, organizations can identify areas where they excel and areas where they need improvement. This benchmarking process helps organizations to set realistic targets and continuously improve their performance.

There are various frameworks and models that organizations can use to assess and monitor their performance. One commonly used framework is the Balanced Scorecard (BSC). The BSC provides a holistic view of organizational performance by considering four key perspectives:

- Financial;
- Customer;
- Internal processes;
- Learning and growth.

By measuring performance across these perspectives, organizations can ensure a balanced approach to performance measurement.

Another popular model is the Key Performance Indicator (KPI) model. KPIs are specific metrics that organizations use to measure progress towards their goals. KPIs can be used at various levels within an organization, from individual performance to departmental or organizational performance. By selecting relevant and meaningful KPIs, organizations can effectively measure and monitor their performance (Zin et al., 2013). Additionally, organizations can utilize the Performance Prism framework, which focuses on stakeholders and their expectations. This framework helps organizations to identify the key stakeholders and their desired outcomes. By aligning performance measurement with stakeholder expectations, organizations can ensure that they are meeting the needs of their stakeholders and achieving their desired outcomes.

9.1. KEY PERFORMANCE INDICATORS (KPIS)

Learning Objectives

- To learn and understand the concept of Key Performance Indicators (KPIs) and their significance in measuring organizational performance.

Key Performance Indicators, or KPIs, are measurable values that indicate how effectively an organization is achieving its goals and objectives. They provide a way to track progress and measure success. KPIs can be financial, such as revenue or profit margins, or non-financial, such as customer satisfaction or employee productivity.

Selecting the right KPIs is crucial for accurately assessing organizational performance. The chosen KPIs should directly align with the organization's strategic objectives and reflect its unique goals. It is important to consider both short-term and long-term objectives when selecting KPIs. Additionally, KPIs should be specific, measurable, attainable, relevant, and time-bound (SMART). This ensures that they provide meaningful insights and can be effectively tracked and measured.

Aligning KPIs with organizational goals and objectives is essential for driving performance and success. KPIs should be directly linked to the desired outcomes of the organization and should reflect the areas that are most critical to its success. By aligning KPIs with organizational goals, employees are able to clearly understand their role in achieving these goals and can focus their efforts accordingly. This alignment also enables leaders to monitor progress and make informed decisions based on the data provided by the KPIs.

Developing and using KPIs effectively requires following best practices. Firstly, it is important to involve key stakeholders in the development process. This ensures that the KPIs chosen are relevant and meaningful to those who will be using them. Additionally, KPIs should be regularly reviewed and updated to reflect changes in the organization's goals and objectives. This allows for flexibility and ensures that the KPIs remain relevant and aligned with the organization's evolving needs.

Furthermore, it is crucial to communicate the purpose and importance of KPIs to all employees. This fosters a shared understanding of the organization's goals and objectives and encourages a collective effort towards achieving them. Regular communication and feedback on KPI performance can also help to motivate employees and drive continuous improvement (Zin et al., 2013).

9.2. THE BALANCED SCORECARD FRAMEWORK

Learning Objectives

- To learn and understand the Balanced Scorecard framework and its role in performance measurement.

The Balanced Scorecard is a strategic management tool that assists organizations in measuring and managing their performance effectively. It provides a comprehensive view by considering not only financial aspects but also other critical factors that contribute to success. The framework consists of four perspectives, each representing a different aspect of the organization's performance (Figure 9.1).

Figure 9.1. An illustration of a balanced scorecard framework.

Source: Staff (2023).

1. Financial Perspective: This focuses on financial indicators that demonstrate the organization's success in achieving its financial objectives. These indicators may include revenue growth, profitability, return on investment, and cost reduction. By evaluating these financial metrics, organizations can assess their financial health and make informed decisions to improve their financial performance.
2. Customer Perspective: It centers around understanding and meeting customer needs and expectations. This perspective examines customer satisfaction, loyalty, and retention rates. By monitoring these indicators, organizations can identify areas for improvement and develop strategies to enhance customer satisfaction

and loyalty. For example, a hotel chain may use customer feedback surveys to measure guest satisfaction and use the results to improve their services and amenities.

3. Internal Processes Perspective: It focuses on the internal operations and processes that drive organizational success. It involves identifying key processes and measuring their efficiency, quality, and effectiveness. By monitoring these indicators, organizations can identify bottlenecks and areas for improvement in their operations. For instance, a manufacturing company may measure its production cycle time to identify opportunities for streamlining processes and reducing costs.
4. Learning and Growth Perspective: It emphasizes the importance of continuous learning and development within the organization. It examines factors such as employee training, skill development, and employee satisfaction. By investing in employee development, organizations can enhance their capabilities and foster a culture of innovation and improvement. For example, a technology company may provide regular training sessions to its employees to ensure they stay updated with the latest industry trends and technologies.

Keyword

Performance Prism framework – It is a performance measurement tool that allows organizations to assess and evaluate their performance from multiple perspectives.

To illustrate the implementation of the Balanced Scorecard, let's consider a case study of a retail company. The company decided to implement the Balanced Scorecard framework to improve its overall performance. They began by identifying key performance indicators (KPIs) for each perspective.

Quick Fact

According to a study conducted by Harvard Business Review, companies that effectively use KPIs are more likely to achieve their strategic goals. The study found that organizations that align their KPIs with their overall objectives have a higher chance of success.

In the financial perspective, the company focused on revenue growth and profitability. They set targets for increasing sales and reducing costs. By monitoring these KPIs, they were able to identify strategies to improve their financial performance, such as implementing cost-saving measures and launching marketing campaigns to drive sales.

In the customer perspective, the company measured customer satisfaction and loyalty. They conducted regular surveys to gather feedback from customers and used the results to identify areas for improvement. For instance, if customers expressed dissatisfaction with the company's customer service, they would invest in training programs to enhance employee communication and problem-solving skills.

In the internal processes' perspective, the company measured key processes such as inventory management and order fulfillment. They aimed to reduce lead times and improve efficiency. By analyzing these metrics, they were able to identify process bottlenecks and implement changes to streamline operations, resulting in faster order processing and improved customer satisfaction.

the learning and growth perspective, the company focused on employee training and development. They provided regular training sessions to enhance employee skills and knowledge. Additionally, they implemented employee satisfaction surveys to gauge employee engagement and satisfaction levels. By investing in employee development, the company was able to foster a culture of continuous improvement and innovation (Franco-Santos et al., 2007).

Did you know?

The concept of the Balanced Scorecard was first introduced by Robert Kaplan and David Norton in the early 1990s.

9.3. DESIGNING A BALANCED SCORECARD

Learning Objectives:

- To learn and understand the process of designing a Balanced Scorecard for their organization.

The first step in designing a Balanced Scorecard is defining strategic objectives. This involves identifying the organization's long-term goals and determining how they align with its mission and vision. Strategic objectives should be specific, measurable, achievable, relevant, and time-bound (SMART). Examples of strategic objectives could include increasing market share, improving customer satisfaction, or reducing costs.

Once strategic objectives have been established, the next step is to identify performance measures. Performance measures are metrics that track progress towards achieving strategic objectives. They provide objective data that can be used to assess performance and make informed decisions. It is important to select performance measures that are relevant to the strategic objectives and align with the organization's values and culture. Examples of performance measures could include sales revenue, customer retention rate, or employee satisfaction.

After identifying performance measures, the next step is to set targets. Targets are specific goals that define what level of performance is expected. They provide a benchmark against which actual performance can be compared. Targets should be challenging yet achievable and should motivate employees to strive for excellence. When setting targets, it is important to consider historical performance, industry benchmarks, and external factors that may impact performance.

Finally, once targets have been set, the last step is to establish initiatives. Initiatives are the actions and projects that will be implemented to achieve the strategic objectives. They outline the specific steps that need to be taken and the resources required. Initiatives should be aligned with the strategic objectives and should be assigned to specific individuals or teams who are responsible for their implementation. It is important to regularly review and update initiatives to ensure they remain relevant and effective (Franco-Santos et al., 2007).

Successfully implementing a Balanced Scorecard requires careful planning and communication. Here are some tips and recommendations:

1. Gain Buy-in from Top Management: It is crucial to have support from senior leaders who can champion the Balanced Scorecard and allocate necessary resources.
2. Involve Employees: Engage employees at all levels in the design and implementation process. This will increase ownership and commitment to the Balanced Scorecard.
3. Communicate the Purpose and Benefits: Clearly explain why the Balanced Scorecard is being implemented and how it will benefit the organization and its employees. This will help overcome resistance and foster understanding.
4. Provide Training and Support: Ensure that employees have the necessary skills and knowledge to use the Balanced Scorecard effectively. Offer training sessions and provide ongoing support to address any questions or concerns.

Keyword

Systematic Risk – It refers to the potential for losses in an investment portfolio that are caused by factors that affect the overall market and cannot be diversified away.

5. Monitor and Evaluate Performance: Regularly review performance against targets and make adjustments as needed. This will help identify areas for improvement and ensure that the Balanced Scorecard remains relevant and effective.

Did You Understand?

1. What is the purpose of performance measurement in organizations?
2. What are the benefits of using Key Performance Indicators (KPIs) in performance measurement?
3. What are the four perspectives of the Balanced Scorecard framework and how do they contribute to organizational performance?

Answer 1: Performance measurement is crucial in organizations as it allows them to evaluate their progress towards goals, assess effectiveness and efficiency, identify areas of improvement, and make informed decisions based on objective analysis.

Answer 2: Using KPIs allows organizations to track progress and measure success, align performance with organizational goals, involve key stakeholders in the development process, regularly review and update KPIs, communicate the purpose and importance of KPIs to employees, and drive continuous improvement.

Answer 3: The four perspectives of the Balanced Scorecard framework are financial, customer, internal processes, and learning and growth. The financial perspective focuses on financial indicators to assess the organization's financial health. The customer perspective centers around meeting customer needs and enhancing satisfaction. The internal processes perspective examines key processes for efficiency and improvement. The learning and growth perspective emphasizes continuous learning and development to foster innovation and improvement. Together, these perspectives provide a comprehensive view of organizational performance.

9.4. IMPLEMENTING A BALANCED SCORECARD

Learning Objectives:

- To discuss the challenges and considerations involved in implementing a Balanced Scorecard.

According to Papenhausen and Einstein (2006), implementing a Balanced Scorecard can be a complex task for organizations. Without a well-defined strategy, it becomes difficult to develop meaningful performance measures and targets. Therefore, it is crucial for organizations to have a robust strategic planning process in place before embarking on the implementation of a Balanced Scorecard.

Another consideration is the selection of appropriate performance measures. It is important to choose measures that align with the organization's strategic objectives and provide a comprehensive view of performance across various dimensions, such as financial, customer, internal processes, and learning and growth. This requires careful consideration and consultation with key stakeholders to ensure that the selected measures are relevant and meaningful.

During the implementation process, organizations may encounter several obstacles. One common obstacle is resistance to change. Employees may be resistant to adopting a new performance measurement system, especially if they perceive it as a threat to their current ways of working. To overcome this obstacle, organizations should focus on effective change management strategies, including clear communication, employee involvement, and training programs. By involving employees in the design and implementation of the Balanced Scorecard, organizations can address their concerns and build a sense of ownership and commitment.

Another challenge is the lack of data availability and quality. Organizations may face difficulties in obtaining accurate and timely data for measuring performance against the selected indicators. To address this challenge, organizations should invest in data collection and management systems, as well as establish processes for data validation and verification. Additionally, organizations should ensure that employees responsible for data collection and reporting receive proper training and support.

Communication plays a vital role in the successful adoption of the Balanced Scorecard. It is important for organizations to effectively communicate the purpose, benefits, and expectations of the Balanced Scorecard to all employees. This can be achieved through regular communication channels, such as company-wide meetings, newsletters, and intranets. By keeping employees informed and engaged, organizations can foster a shared understanding of the Balanced Scorecard and its role in driving organizational performance (Papenhausen & Einstein, 2006).

Employee engagement is another critical factor in the successful implementation of the Balanced Scorecard. Organizations should involve employees in the development and refinement of performance measures, targets, and initiatives. This can be done through workshops, focus groups, and cross-functional teams. By involving employees in the process, organizations can tap into their knowledge and expertise, as well as enhance their commitment and motivation to achieve the desired outcomes.

Did you know?

Many leading organizations, including IBM, Coca-Cola, and General Electric, have successfully implemented the Balanced Scorecard to drive performance improvement.

9.5. PERFORMANCE MEASUREMENT AND ORGANIZATIONAL LEARNING

Learning Objectives:

- To examine the relationship between performance measurement and organizational learning.

Performance measurement plays a crucial role in organizational learning. It allows organizations to evaluate their performance against set goals and objectives, providing insights into areas that require improvement. By measuring performance, organizations can identify gaps and weaknesses, enabling them to take corrective actions and make necessary improvements. This process of measurement and evaluation encourages continuous learning and improvement within the organization (Zin et al., 2013).

Data analysis is a vital component of the learning process. It involves collecting, organizing, and interpreting data to gain insights and make informed decisions. Through data analysis, organizations can identify patterns, trends, and correlations that can inform their learning initiatives. For example, analyzing customer feedback data can provide valuable insights into customer preferences and expectations, allowing organizations to adapt their strategies accordingly. Moreover, data analysis helps organizations identify areas of improvement and measure the effectiveness of their learning initiatives.

Feedback also plays a significant role in the learning process. It provides organizations with valuable information on their performance, allowing them to identify strengths and weaknesses. Feedback can come from various sources, such as employees, customers, and stakeholders. Organizations should actively seek feedback and create channels for open communication. This feedback can then be used to guide decision-making and improve organizational processes. For instance, feedback from employees can highlight areas where training and development initiatives are needed, leading to improved performance, and learning outcomes (Figure 9.2).

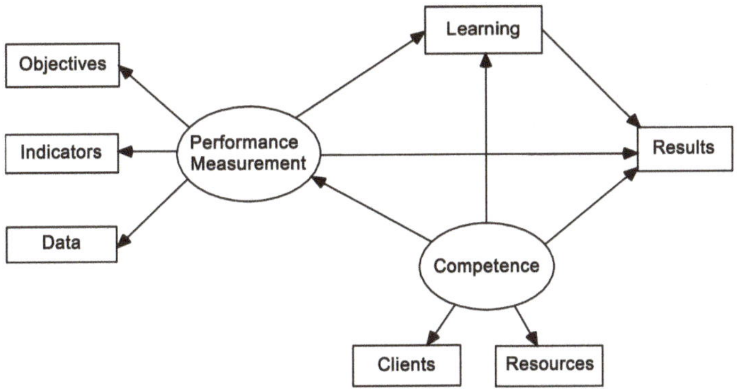

Figure 9.2. Model of performance measurement and organizational learning.

Source: Mausolff & Spence (2008).

To create a culture of learning within an organization, several recommendations can be implemented. Firstly, organizations should promote a growth mindset among employees. This involves fostering an environment where mistakes are seen as opportunities for learning and improvement rather than as failures. Encouraging employees to take risks and learn from their experiences can contribute to a culture of continuous learning (Zin et al., 2013).

Secondly, organizations should provide resources and support for learning initiatives. This includes investing in training programs, workshops, and other learning opportunities. By providing employees with the necessary tools and resources, organizations can empower them to enhance their skills and knowledge, ultimately contributing to organizational learning.

Thirdly, organizations should promote a culture of collaboration and knowledge sharing. Encouraging employees to share their insights, experiences, and best practices can foster a learning culture where knowledge is openly exchanged. This can be facilitated through regular team meetings, cross-functional projects, and knowledge-sharing platforms.

Lastly, organizations should establish mechanisms for measuring and evaluating learning outcomes. This involves setting clear learning objectives, tracking progress, and evaluating the impact of learning initiatives. By regularly measuring and evaluating learning outcomes, organizations can ensure that their efforts are effective and aligned with their goals.

9.6. EVALUATING AND IMPROVING PERFORMANCE MEASUREMENT SYSTEMS

Learning Objectives:

- To discuss methods for evaluating and improving performance measurement systems.

Performance measurement systems play a crucial role in assessing the performance of individuals, teams, and organizations. They provide valuable insights into the achievement of goals and objectives, as well as the identification of areas that require improvement. However, it is essential to regularly evaluate and improve these systems to ensure their accuracy and effectiveness.

One method for evaluating performance measurement systems is conducting a comprehensive review of the system's design and implementation. This involves examining the system's objectives, metrics, data collection methods, and reporting processes. By assessing these aspects, organizations can determine if the system aligns with their strategic goals and if the metrics used accurately reflect performance.

Another approach to evaluating the effectiveness of performance measurement systems is gathering feedback from stakeholders. This includes soliciting input from employees, managers, and customers who interact with the system. Their perspectives can provide valuable insights into the system's strengths and weaknesses, as well as identify areas for improvement.

Additionally, organizations can use benchmarking as a method to evaluate performance measurement systems. By comparing their system to industry best practices and standards, organizations can identify areas where their system falls short and develop strategies for improvement. Benchmarking also allows organizations to learn from others who have successfully implemented performance measurement systems (Franco-Santos et al., 2007).

Once the evaluation process is complete, organizations can identify areas for improvement. This may involve revising the system's objectives, metrics, or data collection methods to ensure they align with the organization's goals and accurately reflect performance. It may also involve improving the system's reporting processes to enhance the clarity and usefulness of the information provided. Regular review and refinement of performance measurement systems are vital to their continued relevance and effectiveness. As organizations evolve and adapt to changing circumstances, their goals and objectives may change. Therefore, it is crucial to regularly assess if the performance measurement system still aligns with these changing goals and objectives.

Moreover, the business environment is dynamic, and new challenges and opportunities arise over time. By regularly reviewing the performance measurement system, organizations can identify emerging trends and adjust their metrics and data collection methods accordingly. This ensures that the system remains up-to-date and provides accurate and relevant information (Franco-Santos et al., 2007).

Keyword

Benchmarking – It is a process that involves comparing a company's performance with that of its competitors or industry standards.

Did You Understand?

1. What are some considerations organizations should keep in mind when implementing a Balanced Scorecard?
2. How does performance measurement contribute to organizational learning?
3. How can organizations evaluate and improve their performance measurement systems?

Answer 1:

- Organizations should have a well-defined strategy in place before implementing a Balanced Scorecard.
- They should carefully select performance measures that align with their strategic objectives.
- They should address resistance to change by implementing effective change management strategies.
- They should invest in data collection and management systems and ensure employees receive proper training and support.

Answer 2:

- Performance measurement allows organizations to evaluate their performance against set goals and identify areas for improvement.
- Data analysis helps organizations identify patterns and trends that can inform learning initiatives.
- Feedback from employees, customers, and stakeholders provides valuable information for decision-making and process improvement.
- Creating a culture of learning involves promoting a growth mindset, providing resources and support for learning, promoting collaboration and knowledge sharing, and measuring and evaluating learning outcomes.

Answer 3:

- Organizations can conduct a comprehensive review of the system's design and implementation.
- They can gather feedback from stakeholders to identify strengths, weaknesses, and areas for improvement.
- Benchmarking can be used to compare the system to industry best practices and standards.
- Areas for improvement may involve revising objectives, metrics, or data collection methods, and improving reporting processes.
- Regular review and refinement of performance measurement systems are important to ensure their continued relevance and effectiveness.

CASE STUDY

- **Introduction:** This case study examines the implementation of performance measurement and the balanced scorecard at Kellanova, a manufacturing company. The purpose is to evaluate the effectiveness of these tools in improving organizational performance.
- **Background:** Kellanova, a leading manufacturer of consumer electronics, faced challenges in managing its performance. The company lacked a comprehensive performance measurement system, resulting in difficulties in monitoring and evaluating its performance. Additionally, Kellanova struggled to align its strategic objectives with its day-to-day operations.
- **Implementation of the Balanced Scorecard:** To address these challenges, Kellanova implemented the balanced scorecard framework. The balanced scorecard is a performance measurement tool that provides a holistic view of an organization's performance by considering financial and non-financial aspects. Kellanova developed four perspectives: financial, customer, internal processes, and learning and growth. These perspectives allowed the company to align its strategic objectives with its performance measures.
- **Results and Benefits:** The implementation of the balanced scorecard at Kellanova yielded several benefits. Firstly, it provided a clear framework for measuring and monitoring performance. This allowed the company to identify areas of improvement and take corrective actions. Secondly, the balanced scorecard facilitated communication and alignment of goals across different departments. It helped employees understand how their individual objectives contributed to the overall organizational goals. Lastly, the balanced scorecard improved decision-making by providing timely and accurate performance information.
- **Conclusion:** The case study demonstrates the effectiveness of performance measurement and the balanced scorecard in improving organizational performance. Kellanova's implementation of the balanced scorecard resulted in better performance monitoring, goal alignment, and decision-making. These benefits highlight the importance of implementing a comprehensive performance measurement system in organizations.

SUMMARY

Chapter 9 discusses the importance of performance measurement in organizations. Performance measurement is crucial for organizations as it allows them to evaluate their progress and make informed decisions. It promotes accountability, identifies best practices, and enables benchmarking. Key frameworks and models for performance measurement include the Balanced Scorecard, Key Performance Indicators (KPIs), and the Performance Prism. KPIs are measurable values that indicate organizational effectiveness and should be aligned with strategic objectives. The Balanced Scorecard framework considers financial, customer, internal processes, and learning and growth perspectives. A case study of a retail company implementing the Balanced Scorecard is provided as an example.

The first step in designing a Balanced Scorecard is defining strategic objectives, which should be specific, measurable, achievable, relevant, and time-bound (SMART). Performance measures are then identified to track progress towards these objectives, and targets are set as specific goals to define expected performance levels. Initiatives are established as the actions and projects to achieve the objectives. Tips for successful implementation include gaining buy-in from top management, involving employees, communicating the purpose and benefits, providing training and support, and regularly monitoring and evaluating performance. Implementing a Balanced Scorecard requires a well-defined strategy, appropriate performance measures, overcoming resistance to change, addressing data availability and quality challenges, effective communication, and employee engagement.

Performance measurement is important for organizational learning as it allows organizations to evaluate their performance and identify areas for improvement. Data analysis is crucial in this process as it helps organizations gain insights and make informed decisions. Feedback from employees, customers, and stakeholders also plays a significant role in the learning process. To create a culture of learning, organizations should promote a growth mindset, provide resources and support for learning initiatives, promote collaboration and knowledge sharing, and establish mechanisms for measuring and evaluating learning outcomes. It is important to regularly evaluate and improve performance measurement systems by reviewing their design and implementation, gathering feedback from stakeholders, and benchmarking against industry best practices. This ensures that the systems align with organizational goals and accurately reflect performance. Regular review and refinement of performance measurement systems are necessary to adapt to changing circumstances and ensure the systems remain relevant and effective.

MULTIPLE CHOICE QUESTIONS

1. What is the purpose of performance measurement in organizations?

a. To evaluate progress towards goals and objectives

b. To promote accountability within organizations

c. To identify areas of improvement
d. All of the above

2. Which framework provides a holistic view of organizational performance?

a. Key Performance Indicator (KPI) model
b. Performance Prism framework
c. Balanced Scorecard (BSC)
d. Financial perspective

3. What does the financial perspective of the Balanced Scorecard focus on?

a. Customer satisfaction
b. Internal processes
c. Learning and growth
d. Financial indicators

4. What are Key Performance Indicators (KPIs)?

a. Goals and objectives of an organization
b. Measures of progress towards goals and objectives
c. Financial metrics
d. Customer satisfaction surveys

5. What is the importance of aligning KPIs with organizational goals?

a. It helps employees understand their role in achieving goals
b. It allows leaders to monitor progress
c. It ensures that KPIs are meaningful and relevant
d. All of the above

6. What is the first step in designing a Balanced Scorecard?

a. Defining strategic objectives
b. Identifying performance measures
c. Setting targets
d. Establishing initiatives

7. What is an obstacle organization may face during the implementation of a Balanced Scorecard?

a. Lack of data availability and quality
b. Resistance to change
c. Communication challenges
d. All of the above

8. How can organizations create a culture of learning?

a. Promote a growth mindset
b. Provide resources and support for learning initiatives

c. Promote collaboration and knowledge sharing

d. All of the above

9. What is the purpose of evaluating and improving performance measurement systems?

a. To ensure accuracy and effectiveness

b. To align with changing goals and objectives

c. To address emerging trends and challenges

d. All of the above

10. Why is regular review and refinement of performance measurement systems important?

a. Goals and objectives may change over time

b. The business environment is dynamic

c. To provide accurate and relevant information

d. All of the above

Answers to Multiple Choice Questions

1. (d); 2. (c); 3. (d); 4. (b); 5. (d); 6. (a); 7. (d); 8. (d); 9. (d); 10. (d)

REFERENCES

1. Franco-Santos, M., Kennerley, M., Micheli, P., Martinez, V., Mason, S., Marr, B., & Neely, A., (2007). Towards a definition of a business performance measurement system. International Journal of Operations & Production Management, 27(8), 784–801.
2. Ghosh, S., & Mukherjee, S., (2006). Measurement of Corporate Performance Through Balanced Scorecard: An Overview. Vol. 11, 60-66
3. Mausolff, C., & Spence, J. C., (2008). Performance measurement and program effectiveness: A structural equation modeling approach. International Journal of Public Administration. https://doi.org/10.1080/01900690701640929.
4. Papenhausen, C., & Einstein, W., (2006). Implementing the balanced scorecard at a college of business. Measuring Business Excellence, 10(3), 15–22.
5. Staff, I., (2023). Why a Balanced Scorecard is Essential for Every Business. isixsigma.com. https://www.isixsigma.com/dictionary/balanced-scorecard/ (accessed on 04 April 2024).
6. Zin, N. M., Sulaiman, S., Ramli, A., & Nawawi, A., (2013). Performance measurement and balanced scorecard implementation: Case evidence of a government-linked company. Procedia Economics and Finance, 7, 197–204.

CHAPTER 10

Capital Budgeting and Decision Analysis

LEARNING OBJECTIVES

After studying this chapter, you will be able to:

- Time value of money;
- Cost of capital;
- Cash flow estimation;
- Capital budgeting techniques;
- Risk analysis in capital budgeting;
- Capital rationing;
- Real options analysis;
- Decision trees.

INTRODUCTORY EXAMPLE

Bouygues, a French multinational company, provides an introductory example on capital budgeting and decision analysis. This example involves a project to build a new factory that will produce construction materials.

To begin, the project's initial cost is estimated at €10 million. The factory is expected to generate an annual cash flow of €2 million for the next 10 years. Additionally, at the end of the project's life, the factory is expected to be sold for €1 million.

In order to evaluate the project's profitability, Bouygues uses several financial metrics. One of these metrics is the payback period, which measures the time it takes for the project to recover its initial investment. In this case, the payback period is calculated by dividing the initial cost of €10 million by the annual cash flow of €2 million, resulting in a payback period of 5 years.

Another metric used is the net present value (NPV), which takes into account the time value of money. Bouygues calculates the NPV by discounting the project's future cash flows to their present value and subtracting the initial investment. In this example, assuming a discount rate of 10%, the NPV is calculated as follows:

$$NPV = (€2 \text{ million} / (1 + 0.10)^1) + (€2 \text{ million} / (1 + 0.10)^2) + \ldots + (€2 \text{ million} / (1 + 0.10)^{10}) - €10 \text{ million}$$

By calculating the NPV, Bouygues can determine whether the project is expected to generate a positive or negative return. A positive NPV indicates that the project is expected to generate more cash inflows than outflows, making it a profitable investment. Conversely, a negative NPV suggests that the project is not expected to generate sufficient cash inflows to cover its costs, making it an unprofitable investment.

In conclusion, Bouygues uses capital budgeting and decision analysis to assess the profitability of projects, such as the construction of a new factory. By using financial metrics like the payback period and net present value, Bouygues can make informed investment decisions that align with their financial goals.

UNIT INTRODUCTION

Capital budgeting refers to the process of planning and managing long-term investments in a business. It involves assessing potential projects or investments, determining their viability, and allocating financial resources accordingly. This process is crucial in strategic planning as it helps organizations make informed decisions regarding the allocation of their financial resources (Bennouna, Meredith, & Marchant, 2010).

One method commonly used in capital budgeting is the Payback Period. This method calculates the time required for an investment to generate enough cash flows to recover the initial investment. The shorter the payback period, the more attractive the investment opportunity may be. However, this method does not consider the time value of money and fails to account for cash flows beyond the payback period.

Another method is the Net Present Value (NPV) analysis. This technique involves discounting future cash flows to their present value and subtracting the initial investment. If the NPV is positive, the investment is considered profitable. NPV takes into account the time value of money, making it a more comprehensive evaluation method. However, it relies heavily on accurate cash flow projections and an appropriate discount rate.

The Internal Rate of Return (IRR) is another widely used method. It calculates the discount rate at which the NPV of an investment becomes zero. If the IRR is higher than the required rate of return, the investment is deemed acceptable. However, IRR can sometimes lead to ambiguous results when cash flows change direction multiple times.

Sensitivity analysis is a technique used to assess the impact of changes in key variables on the profitability of an investment. By altering variables such as sales volume or production costs, organizations can evaluate the sensitivity of the investment's returns. This analysis provides valuable insights into the potential risks associated with an investment.

Risk analysis is also an essential component of capital budgeting. By evaluating the potential risks associated with an investment, organizations can make more informed decisions. Some common risks include market risk, technological risk, and financial risk. Market risk refers to the uncertainty in demand or the competitive landscape. Technological risk relates to the possibility of obsolescence due to technological advancements. Financial risk involves the potential impact of changes in interest rates or exchange rates.

To mitigate these risks, organizations can employ various strategies. Diversification, for example, involves investing in a range of projects to reduce the impact of any single investment's failure. Sensitivity analysis, as mentioned earlier, can also help identify potential risks and their impact on returns. Additionally, organizations can use risk-adjusted discount rates to account for the level of risk associated with an investment.

10.1. TIME VALUE OF MONEY

Learning Objectives

- To understand time value of money formula.
- To learn the effect of compounding periods on future value.
- To learn and understand discounting future cash flows to their present value.

The time value of money is a fundamental concept in finance that recognizes the idea that money available in the present is worth more than the same amount of money in the future. This concept is based on the premise that money can earn interest or be invested to generate returns over time. Therefore, a dollar received today is worth more than a dollar received in the future (Figure 10.1).

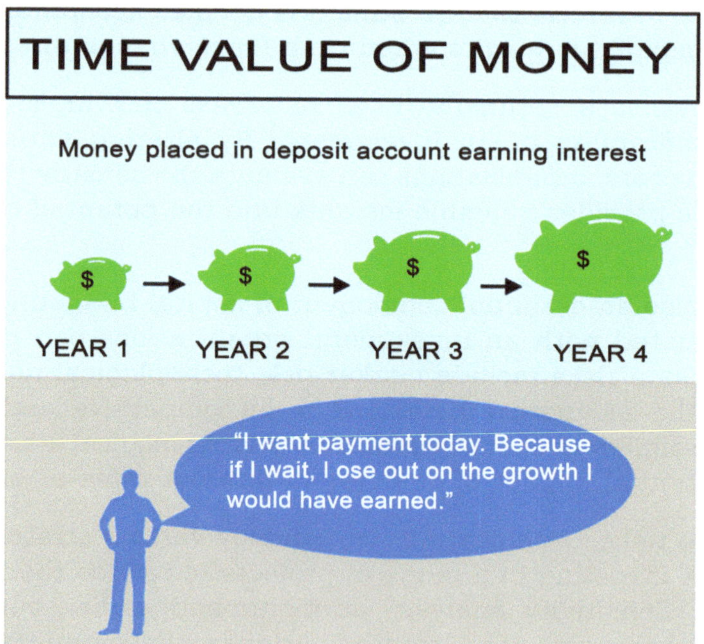

Figure 10.1. *A simple illustration of time value of money concept.*

Source: Nordqvist (2024).

One of the main reasons why the time value of money is essential in capital budgeting is because it helps in comparing cash flows occurring at different points in time. By discounting future cash flows to their present value, businesses can make meaningful comparisons and determine the most profitable investment option. This is done by applying a discount rate, which reflects the opportunity cost of investing in a particular project.

Discounting future cash flows also takes into account the risk associated with the investment. The time value of money recognizes that there is a level of uncertainty in future cash flows, and by discounting them, businesses can factor in this risk. By considering the time value of money, businesses can assess the potential profitability of an investment and make informed decisions.

10.1.1. Time Value of Money Formula

The time value of money formula is a mathematical equation used to determine the present value of future cash flows. It takes into account the concept that money received in the future is worth less than money received today due to factors such as inflation and the potential to earn interest on invested funds.

The formula is as follows:

$$PV = FV / (1 + r)^n$$

where; PV is the present value; FV is the future value; r is the interest rate; and n is the number of periods.

To calculate the present value, you divide the future value by 1 plus the interest rate raised to the power of the number of periods. This accounts for the fact that the value of money decreases over time.

Let's consider a hypothetical example to illustrate this formula. Suppose you have $1,000 that you want to invest for five years at an annual interest rate of 5%. By using the time value of money formula, we can determine the future value of this investment.

$$FV = \$1,000 \times (1 + 0.05)^5$$

$$FV = \$1,000 \times (1.05)^5$$

$$FV = \$1,000 \times 1.2763$$

$$FV = \$1,276.30$$

Therefore, after five years, your $1,000 investment will grow to $1,276.30.

Understanding the time value of money is crucial in making informed financial decisions. By applying this formula, you can evaluate the potential returns and make informed choices about investments or loans (Bennouna, Meredith, & Marchant, 2010).

10.1.2. Effect of Compounding Periods on Future Value

In finance, the compounding period refers to the frequency at which interest is added to an investment. Common compounding periods include annually, semi-annually, quarterly, monthly, and daily. The more frequent the compounding period, the faster the investment grows due to the compounding effect.

Hypothetical example:

Let's consider an investment of $10,000 with an annual interest rate of 5%. We will compare the future value of this investment over different compounding periods: annually, semi-annually, quarterly, monthly, and daily.

1. **Annually:** If the investment compounds annually, the future value after one year can be calculated using the formula:

Future Value = Principal × (1 + Interest Rate)^Number of Years.
In this case, the future value would be $10,000 × $(1 + 0.05)^{1}$ = $10,500.

2. **Semi-Annually:** If the investment compounds semi-annually, the future value after one year can be calculated using the formula:

Future Value = Principal × (1 + (Interest Rate/2))^Number of Compounding Periods.
In this case, the future value would be $10,000 × $(1 + (0.05/2))^{2}$ = $10,512.50.

3. **Quarterly:** If the investment compounds quarterly, the future value after one year can be calculated using the formula:

Future Value = Principal × (1 + (Interest Rate/4))^Number of Compounding Periods.
In this case, the future value would be $10,000 × $(1 + (0.05/4))^{4}$ = $10,515.64.

4. **Monthly:** If the investment compounds monthly, the future value after one year can be calculated using the formula:

Future Value = Principal × (1 + (Interest Rate/12))^Number of Compounding Periods.
In this case, the future value would be $10,000 × $(1 + (0.05/12))^{12}$ = $10,518.52.

5. **Daily:** If the investment compounds daily, the future value after one year can be calculated using the formula:

Future Value = Principal × (1 + (Interest Rate/365))^Number of Compounding Periods.
In this case, the future value would be $10,000 × $(1 + (0.05/365))^{365}$ = $10,519.62.

As demonstrated by the hypothetical example, the compounding period has a significant impact on the future value of an investment. The more frequent the compounding period, the higher the future value. Therefore, investors should carefully consider the compounding period when making investment decisions to maximize their returns (Figure 10.2).

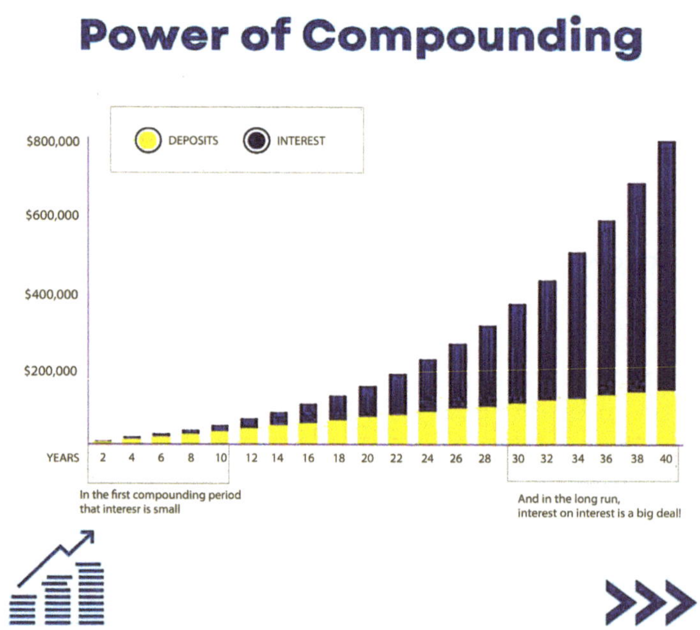

Figure 10.2. *Power of compounding in investment.*

Source: M. (2022).

10.1.3. Discounting Future Cash Flows to Their Present Value

Discounting future cash flows to their present value is a common financial practice. It involves calculating the current worth of future cash flows by applying a discount rate. This process is important for making informed investment decisions. To better understand this concept, let's consider a hypothetical example. Suppose you are considering investing in a project that is expected to generate cash flows of $10,000 per year for the next five years. However, due to the time value of money, the value of these future cash flows is not equal to $50,000 (i.e., $10,000 × 5 years).

To accurately assess the present value of these cash flows, you need to discount them using an appropriate discount rate. The discount rate is typically determined based on factors such as the riskiness of the investment, market conditions, and the opportunity cost of capital (Bennouna, Meredith, & Marchant, 2010). Let's say the discount rate for this project is 8%. To calculate the present value of the cash flows, you would divide each cash flow by (1 + discount rate) raised to the power of the respective year. Here's how the calculation would look:

Year 1: \$10,000 / $(1 + 0.08)^1$ = \$9,259.26

Year 2: \$10,000 / $(1 + 0.08)^2$ = \$8,561.80

Year 3: \$10,000 / $(1 + 0.08)^3$ = \$7,924.07

Year 4: \$10,000 / $(1 + 0.08)^4$ = \$7,340.08

Year 5: \$10,000 / $(1 + 0.08)^5$ = \$6,804.69

By discounting the future cash flows, you can determine that the present value of the project is $39,889.90. This means that the project is worth $39,889.90 in today's dollars. Discounting future cash flows to their present value is a crucial step in financial analysis. It allows investors to compare the value of different investment opportunities and assess their profitability. By considering the time value of money, investors can make more informed decisions and maximize their returns.

Did You Understand?

1. What is the time value of money and why is it important in capital budgeting?
2. How does the compounding period affect the future value of an investment?

Answer 1: The time value of money recognizes that money available in the present is worth more than the same amount of money in the future. It is important in capital budgeting because it helps in comparing cash flows occurring at different points in time, allowing businesses to determine the most profitable investment option and factor in the risk associated with the investment.

Answer 2: The compounding period refers to the frequency at which interest is added to an investment. The more frequent the compounding period, the faster the investment grows due to the compounding effect. As demonstrated by the hypothetical example, the compounding period has a significant impact on the future value of an investment. The more frequent the compounding period, the higher the future value. Therefore, investors should carefully consider the compounding period when making investment decisions to maximize their returns.

10.2. COST OF CAPITAL

Learning Objectives

- To learn and understand various methods for calculating the cost of capital including:
  - Dividend growth model (DGM);
  - Capital asset pricing model (CAPM);
  - Weighted average cost of capital (WACC).
- To understand the sources of capital and methods used to estimate their costs.

The cost of capital is a crucial factor to consider when making decisions regarding investments. It is the rate of return that must be earned on an investment project to satisfy the expectations of investors and lenders.

The cost of capital is determined by a variety of factors, including:

- The risk associated with the investment project;
- The prevailing interest rates;
- The company's own cost of borrowing.

The riskier the investment project, the higher the cost of capital will be. This is because investors and lenders will require a higher return to compensate for the additional risk they are taking on.

Interest rates also play a significant role in determining the cost of capital. When interest rates are high, the cost of capital will also be high. This is because investors and lenders have alternative investment opportunities that offer higher returns. Therefore, to attract investors and lenders, companies must offer a higher return on their investment projects.

The company's own cost of borrowing is another factor that affects the cost of capital. If a company has a high cost of borrowing, it will need to earn a higher return on its investment projects to cover the cost of borrowing. On the other hand, if a company has a low cost of borrowing, it may be able to offer a lower return on its investment projects.

10.2.1. Methods for Calculating the Cost of Capital

There are several methods for calculating the cost of capital, each with its own strengths and weaknesses.

1. **Dividend Growth Model (DGM):** This method calculates the cost of equity by estimating the future dividends that shareholders expect to receive and discounting them back to the present value. The advantage of this method is that it is relatively simple and easy to understand. However, it relies on accurate dividend forecasts, which can be difficult to obtain.

To illustrate how the DGM works, let's consider a hypothetical example.

Suppose a company, ABC Corp, is expected to pay a dividend of $2 per share next year. The growth rate of the dividends is projected to be 5% per year. The required rate of return for investors in ABC Corp is 10%.

Using the DGM formula, we can calculate the cost of capital for ABC Corp as follows:

Cost of Capital = Dividend / Price + Growth Rate

In this case, the dividend is $2, the price is unknown, and the growth rate is 5%. Plugging these values into the formula, we get:

Cost of Capital = $2 / Price + 5%

To solve for the price, we rearrange the formula:

Price = $2 / (Cost of Capital – 5%)

Let's assume the calculated cost of capital is 12%. Plugging this value into the formula, we can find the price:

Price = $2 / (12% – 5%)

Simplifying the equation, we get:

Price = $2 / 7%

Therefore, the estimated price of ABC Corp's stock is $28.57.

2. **Capital Asset Pricing Model (CAPM):** This method calculates the cost of equity by taking into account the risk-free rate of return, the expected market return, and the beta of the company's stock. The advantage of this method is that it considers the **systematic risk** of the investment, which is important for determining the required rate of return. However, it relies on accurate estimates of the beta, which can be subject to volatility (Bennouna, Meredith, & Marchant, 2010).

Keyword

Systematic Risk – It refers to the potential for losses in an investment portfolio that are caused by factors that affect the overall market and cannot be diversified away.

The formula for CAPM is as follows:

Expected Return = Risk-Free Rate + Beta × (Market Return – Risk-Free Rate)

To understand how this formula works, let's consider a hypothetical example.

Suppose an investor is considering investing in a stock with a beta of 1.2. The risk-free rate is 2% and the market return is 8%. Using the CAPM formula, we can calculate the expected return on this investment as follows:

Expected Return = 2% + 1.2 × (8% – 2%)

Expected Return = 2% + 1.2 × 6%

Expected Return = 2% + 7.2%

Expected Return = 9.2%

Therefore, based on the CAPM formula, the investor can expect a return of 9.2% on this investment. This expected return takes into account the risk associated with the investment and the potential return of the overall market.

It's important to note that CAPM is a theoretical model and there are limitations to its accuracy. However, it provides a useful framework for investors to make informed decisions about their investments.

3. **Weighted Average Cost of Capital (WACC):** This method calculates the overall cost of capital by taking into account the proportion of debt and equity in a company's capital structure. It considers both the cost of equity and the cost of debt, weighted by their respective proportions. The advantage of this method is that it reflects the company's actual financing structure. However, it assumes that the company's capital structure remains constant, which may not always be the case (Baker & English, 2011).

The formula for calculating WACC is as follows:

WACC = (E/V) × Re + (D/V) × Rd × (1 – Tc)

where; 'E' represents the market value of equity; 'V' represents the total market value of equity and debt; 'Re' represents the cost of equity; 'D' represents the market value of debt; 'Rd' represents the cost of debt; and 'Tc' represents the corporate tax rate.

To illustrate the calculation, let's consider a hypothetical company called XYZ Corp. XYZ Corp has a market value of equity (E) of $10 million and a market value of debt (D) of $5 million. The total market value of equity and debt (V) is $15 million. The cost of equity (Re) is 10% and the cost of debt (Rd) is 5%. The corporate tax rate (Tc) is 20%.

Using the WACC formula, we can calculate XYZ Corp's WACC as follows:

WACC = (10/15) × 0.10 + (5/15) × 0.05 × (1 – 0.20)

= 0.6667 × 0.10 + 0.3333 × 0.05 × 0.80

= 0.0667 + 0.0133

= 0.08

Therefore, XYZ Corp's WACC is 8%.

By calculating the WACC, companies can determine the minimum return they need to generate on their investments to satisfy their investors and lenders. It is an important metric for decision-making and evaluating the financial health of a company.

Once the cost of capital has been determined, it can be used to evaluate investment projects. Companies can compare the expected return on an investment project to the cost of capital to determine whether the project is worth pursuing. If the expected return is higher than the cost of capital, the project may be considered a good investment. However, if the expected return is lower than the cost of capital, the project may not be worth pursuing.

This method calculates the cost of equity by estimating the future dividends that shareholders expect to receive and discounting them back to the present value. The advantage of this method is that it is relatively simple and easy to understand. However, it relies on accurate dividend forecasts, which can be difficult to obtain.

10.2.2. Sources of Capital and Methods Used to Estimate Their Costs

Sources of capital are crucial aspects of financial management. It is important for businesses to understand the different sources of capital available to them and how to determine the costs associated with each source.

There are various sources of capital that businesses can utilize, such as:

- Equity financing;
- Debt financing;
- Retained earnings.

Equity financing involves raising capital by selling shares of ownership in the company, while debt financing involves borrowing money from external sources. Retained earnings, on the other hand, refer to the profits that a company keeps and reinvests in the business.

Estimating the costs of these capital sources is essential for making informed financial decisions. The cost of equity is typically estimated using methods like the dividend discount model or the capital asset pricing model. These methods take into account factors such as the expected dividends or the risk associated with investing in the company's stock.

The cost of debt, on the other hand, is determined by factors such as the interest rate on the borrowed funds and any associated fees. It is important to consider both the explicit and implicit costs of debt when estimating its overall cost.

By understanding the different sources of capital and the methods used to estimate their costs, businesses can make informed decisions about how to finance their operations and investments. This knowledge allows them to optimize their capital structure and minimize their overall cost of capital (Peterson & Fabozzi, 2002).

Did You Understand?

1. What are the three methods for calculating the cost of capital?
2. What factors determine the cost of capital?
3. What are the sources of capital and how are their costs estimated?

Answer 1: The three methods for calculating the cost of capital are the Dividend Growth Model (DGM), the Capital Asset Pricing Model (CAPM), and the Weighted Average Cost of Capital (WACC).

Answer 2: The cost of capital is determined by the risk associated with the investment project, the prevailing interest rates, and the company's own cost of borrowing.

Answer 3: The sources of capital include equity financing, debt financing, and retained earnings. The cost of equity is estimated using methods like the dividend discount model or the capital asset pricing model, while the cost of debt is determined by factors such as the interest rate on borrowed funds and associated fees.

10.3. CASH FLOW ESTIMATION

Learning Objectives

- To learn and understand different techniques for forecasting cash flows including:
  - Incremental cash flows;
  - Pro forma financial statements;
  - Sensitivity analysis.

Cash flows play a crucial role in capital budgeting. When making investment decisions, it is important to carefully consider the timing and amount of cash inflows and outflows associated with a project. This involves estimating future cash flows and discounting them to determine their present value. By analyzing cash flows, companies can assess the profitability and feasibility of potential investments. It is essential to accurately forecast cash flows, as any errors can lead to incorrect investment decisions and financial losses. Therefore, a thorough understanding of cash flows and the ability to accurately project them is vital in capital budgeting (Peterson & Fabozzi, 2002).

One common mistake in cash flow estimation is failing to consider all relevant costs and revenues. It is important to include both direct and indirect costs, as well as any potential savings or additional revenues that may result from the project. By considering all factors, businesses can get a more accurate picture of the true cash flows associated with the investment.

Another mistake is not accounting for the timing of cash flows. Cash inflows and outflows may not occur evenly throughout the life of a project. It is important to consider when these cash flows will occur and adjust for the time value of money. This can be done by discounting future cash flows to their present value, using an appropriate discount rate.

Additionally, it is important to consider any potential risks or uncertainties that may impact cash flows. This could include changes in market conditions, regulatory changes, or unexpected events. By conducting a thorough analysis of potential risks, businesses can better estimate the likelihood and impact of these factors on cash flows.

10.3.1. Techniques for Forecasting Cash Flows

There are various techniques for forecasting cash flows, which include incremental cash flows, pro forma financial statements, and sensitivity analysis. These techniques are used to estimate the potential cash inflows and outflows associated with a capital investment project.

1. **Incremental Cash Flows:** Incremental cash flows focus on the additional cash flows that result from the implementation of a specific project. For example, if a company is considering investing in a new product line, the incremental cash flows would include the additional revenues generated by the product line, as well as any additional costs incurred.

The formula for calculating incremental cash flows is as follows:

Incremental Cash Flows = Cash Flows with Investment – Cash Flows without Investment

To better understand how this formula works, let's consider a hypothetical example. Suppose a company is considering investing in a new manufacturing facility. The estimated cash flows with the investment are projected to be $500,000 per year. However, if the company decides not to invest, the cash flows are expected to be $300,000 per year.

Using the incremental cash flows formula, we can calculate the potential financial gain from the investment:

Incremental Cash Flows = $500,000 – $300,000

Incremental Cash Flows = $200,000

In this example, the incremental cash flows amount to $200,000 per year. This indicates that by investing in the new manufacturing facility, the company could potentially generate an additional $200,000 in cash flows compared to not making the investment.

By analyzing the incremental cash flows, businesses can make informed decisions about whether to proceed with investment projects. This formula provides a clear and concise way to evaluate the financial impact of potential investments, helping businesses make sound financial decisions (Baker & English, 2011).

2. **Pro Forma Financial Statements:** Pro forma financial statements are another technique used to forecast cash flows. These statements are hypothetical financial statements that project the financial performance of a company under different scenarios.

To illustrate the concept of a pro forma financial statement, let's consider a hypothetical example. Imagine a small retail business that wants to open a new store. The business owner needs to determine if the new store will be profitable and if they can secure the necessary financing.

The owner starts by preparing a pro forma income statement. They estimate the revenue that the new store will generate based on market research and projections. They also estimate the cost of goods sold, operating expenses, and taxes. By subtracting the expenses from the revenue, they can calculate the projected net income for the new store.

Next, the owner prepares a pro forma balance sheet. They estimate the assets that will be required to open the new store, such as inventory, equipment, and fixtures.

They also estimate the liabilities, such as loans or credit lines that will be used to finance the store. By subtracting the liabilities from the assets, they can calculate the projected equity for the new store.

Finally, the owner prepares a pro forma cash flow statement. They estimate the cash inflows and outflows that will occur as a result of opening the new store. This includes cash from sales, payments to suppliers, operating expenses, loan repayments, and any other cash transactions. By subtracting the cash outflows from the cash inflows, they can calculate the projected net cash flow for the new store (Figure 10.3).

Centerfield Sporting Goods Pro Forma Income Statement for the period ending 31 December 2020		
Sales		520,000
Cost of sales		
Materials (leather, plastic)	170,000	
Labour	250,000	
Total cost of sales		420,000
Gross profit		100,000
Operating expenses		
Office salaries	40,000	
	20,000	
Insurance	12,000	
Home office lease	10,000	
Marketing, advertising	4,000	
Repair and maintenance	4,000	
Total operating expenses		90,000
Net income		10,000

Figure 10.3. *An illustration of a pro forma financial statement.*

Source: Pro Forma Financial Statements; QuickBooks Australia (2023).

With these pro forma financial statements, the business owner can assess the financial viability of opening the new store. They can determine if the projected net income, equity, and cash flow are sufficient to cover expenses and generate a profit. This information can then be used to make informed decisions about financing options and overall business strategy (Peterson & Fabozzi, 2002).

3. **Sensitivity Analysis:** It is used to assess the impact of changes in key variables on cash flows. This analysis provides insight into how sensitive cash flows are to variations in these variables.

To illustrate this concept, let's consider a hypothetical example.

Suppose a company is evaluating the construction of a new manufacturing facility. The key variables in this scenario include the initial investment cost, the expected sales volume, and the variable costs associated with production. By conducting a sensitivity analysis, the company can determine how changes in these variables would affect its cash flows.

For instance, let's say the initial investment cost for the facility is $10 million. By increasing this cost by 10%, the company can explore the potential impact on its cash flows. Similarly, by adjusting the expected sales volume or the variable costs, the company can assess the sensitivity of its cash flows to these changes.

Through sensitivity analysis, the company can gain a better understanding of the risks and uncertainties associated with its investment decision. By considering different scenarios and their potential outcomes, the company can make more informed decisions and develop strategies to mitigate potential risks.

Overall, these techniques provide valuable insights into the potential cash flows associated with a capital investment project. By using incremental cash flows, pro forma financial statements, and sensitivity analysis, companies can make more informed decisions and accurately assess the financial viability of their investment options.

Did You Understand?

1. What is the formula for calculating incremental cash flows?
2. How can sensitivity analysis be used to assess the impact of changes in key variables on cash flows?

Answer 1: The formula for calculating incremental cash flows is:

Incremental Cash Flows = Cash Flows with Investment – Cash Flows without Investment.

Answer 2: Sensitivity analysis is used to assess the impact of changes in key variables on cash flows by exploring different scenarios and their potential outcomes. By adjusting variables such as initial investment cost, expected sales volume, and variable costs, companies can determine how sensitive their cash flows are to these changes and develop strategies to mitigate potential risks.

10.4. CAPITAL BUDGETING TECHNIQUES

Learning Objectives

- To learning and understand the following capital budgeting techniques:
  - Payback period;
  - Net present value (NPV);
  - The internal rate of return (IRR);
  - Profitability index.

Capital budgeting techniques are used by businesses to evaluate potential investment opportunities. These techniques help businesses determine whether a proposed investment is worth pursuing and if it will generate a positive return on investment. Some these techniques are discussed below.

10.4.1. Payback Period

Payback period is a financial metric that calculates the length of time required for an investment to recoup its initial cost. It is a simple tool used to assess the profitability and risk of an investment.

To illustrate this concept, let's consider a hypothetical example.

Suppose Company A is considering investing in a new manufacturing machine. The cost of the machine is $100,000, and it is expected to generate an annual cash flow of $20,000.

Using the payback period formula, we can determine how long it will take for Company A to recover its initial investment.

Payback Period = Initial Investment / Annual Cash Flow

In this case, the payback period would be:

Payback Period = $100,000 / $20,000 = 5 years

Therefore, it would take Company A approximately 5 years to recoup the $100,000 investment through the annual cash flow of $20,000.

By analyzing the payback period, Company A can assess the feasibility and profitability of the investment. A shorter payback period indicates a quicker return on investment and lower risk, while a longer payback period implies a slower return and higher risk.

Keyword

Financial Metric – It is a quantifiable measure used to assess the financial performance of a company. It provides valuable insights into the company's profitability, efficiency, and overall financial health.

10.4.2. Net Present Value (NPV)

is a financial metric used to determine the profitability of an investment. It measures the difference between the present value of cash inflows and outflows over a specific time period. By discounting future cash flows to their present value, NPV helps investors assess the value of an investment in today's dollars. A positive NPV indicates that the investment is expected to generate more cash inflows than outflows, making it a potentially profitable venture. Conversely, a negative NPV suggests that the investment may not be financially viable. Therefore, calculating the NPV is crucial for making informed investment decisions (Haka, 2006).

The formula can be expressed as follows:

$$NPV = CF1/(1+r)^1 + CF2/(1+r)^2 + CF3/(1+r)^3 + \ldots + CFn/(1+r)^n - \text{Initial Investment}$$

Quick Fact

The payback period, a commonly used capital budgeting technique, is often favored by small businesses due to its simplicity. However, it does not take into account the time value of money.

where; 'NPV' is the net present value; 'CF' is the expected cash flow for each period (1, 2, 3, ..., n); 'r' is the discount rate; 'n' is the number of periods; and 'initial investment' is the initial amount invested.

To illustrate this concept, let's consider a hypothetical example.

Imagine that you are a business owner considering the purchase of a new machine for your manufacturing plant. The machine costs $50,000 and is expected to generate cash inflows of $10,000 per year for the next five years. Additionally, the machine will require maintenance expenses of $2,000 per year.

To calculate the NPV, we need to discount the future cash flows to their present value. Let's assume a discount rate of 10%.

Year 1: Cash inflow = $10,000, Cash outflow = $2,000

Present value of Year 1 cash flow = $10,000 / (1 + 0.10) = $9,090.91

Present value of Year 1 cash outflow = $2,000 / (1 + 0.10) = $1,818.18

Net cash flow in Year 1 = $9,090.91 – $1,818.18 = $7,272.73

Similarly, we can calculate the net cash flows for Years 2 to 5 and discount them to their present values. Once we have the present values of all cash inflows and outflows, we can sum them up to find the net present value.

In this example, let's assume the net present value of the investment is $5,000. A positive NPV indicates that the investment is profitable, while a negative NPV suggests otherwise. Therefore, in this case, the purchase of the new machine would be considered a profitable investment.

By using the concept of net present value, businesses can make informed decisions about potential investments. It allows them to assess the financial viability of projects and determine their potential for generating positive returns.

10.4.3. The Internal Rate of Return (IRR)

The internal rate of return (IRR) is a financial metric used to assess the profitability of an investment. It represents the annualized rate of return that an investor can expect to earn from the investment over its lifespan. The IRR is calculated by determining the discount rate that results in a net present value (NPV) of zero for the investment's cash flows. In other words, it is the rate at which the present value of the investment's cash inflows equals the present value of its cash outflows. The IRR is often used to compare different investment opportunities and determine which one offers the highest potential return. A higher IRR indicates a more attractive investment, as it represents a higher rate of return. However, it is important to note that the IRR does not take into account the size or timing of cash flows, and it assumes that all cash flows are reinvested at the IRR. Therefore, it should be used in conjunction with other financial metrics to make informed investment decisions.

To calculate IRR, you need to know the initial investment amount and the expected cash flows over the investment period. The cash flows can be positive or negative, and they can occur at different time intervals. By discounting each cash flow back to its present value and summing them up, you can determine the IRR.

The IRR formula is a complex calculation that takes into account the initial investment, cash inflows, and the discount rate. The formula can be expressed as follows:

$$IRR = (C1 / (1+r)^1) + (C2 / (1+r)^2) + (C3 / (1+r)^3) + \ldots + (Cn / (1+r)^n) - \text{Initial Investment}$$

where; 'IRR' is the internal rate of return; 'C1, C2, C3, ..., Cn' are the cash inflows for each period; 'r' is the discount rate; 'n' is the number of periods; and 'Initial Investment' is the initial outlay of cash.

Let's consider a hypothetical example to illustrate the concept. Suppose you are considering investing $10,000 in a project that will generate cash flows over a five-year period. In year one, you expect to receive $2,000, in year two $3,000, in year three $4,000, in year four $2,000, and in year five $1,000. To calculate the IRR, you discount each cash flow back to its present value using a trial and error method until the NPV becomes zero. In this case, the IRR would be approximately 15%.

IRR is an important tool for investors and businesses to assess the potential profitability of an investment. It helps in comparing different investment opportunities and determining which ones are more attractive. A higher IRR indicates a higher return on investment, making the investment more desirable. However, IRR has its limitations and should be used in conjunction with other financial metrics for a comprehensive analysis of an investment.

10.4.4. Profitability Index

The profitability index is a useful tool for evaluating the potential profitability of an investment project. It is calculated by dividing the present value of future cash flows by the initial investment cost. A profitability index greater than 1 indicates that the project is expected to generate positive returns, while a value less than 1 suggests that the project may not be profitable.

To illustrate this concept, let's consider a hypothetical example. Company XYZ is considering investing in a new manufacturing facility. The initial investment cost is $1 million, and the project is expected to generate cash flows of $200,000 per year for the next five years. To calculate the profitability index, we need to discount these cash flows to their present value.

Assuming a discount rate of 10%, we can calculate the present value of the cash flows as follows:

Year 1: $\$200{,}000 / (1 + 0.10) = \$181{,}818.18$

Year 2: $\$200{,}000 / (1 + 0.10)^2 = \$165{,}289.26$

Year 3: $\$200{,}000 / (1 + 0.10)^3 = \$150{,}263.87$

Year 4: $\$200{,}000 / (1 + 0.10)^4 = \$136{,}603.52$

Year 5: $\$200{,}000 / (1 + 0.10)^5 = \$124{,}184.11$

Next, we sum up the present values of the cash flows:

$181,818.18 + $165,289.26 + $150,263.87 + $136,603.52 + $124,184.11 = $758,158.94

Finally, we divide the present value of the cash flows by the initial investment cost:

$758,158.94 / $1,000,000 = 0.758

In this hypothetical example, the profitability index is 0.758, which is less than 1. This suggests that the investment project may not be profitable. However, it's important to consider other factors, such as the company's financial situation and risk tolerance, before making a final decision.

By using the profitability index, businesses can make informed decisions about potential investments. It provides a quantitative measure of the expected profitability of a project, helping businesses assess the viability of their investment decisions.

Did You Understand?

1. What is the payback period and how is it calculated?
2. What is the net present value (NPV) and how is it calculated?

Answer 1: The payback period is the length of time required for an investment to recoup its initial cost. It is calculated by dividing the initial investment by the annual cash flow.

Answer 2: The net present value is a financial metric used to determine the profitability of an investment. It is calculated by discounting future cash flows to their present value and subtracting the initial investment.

10.5. RISK ANALYSIS IN CAPITAL BUDGETING

Learning Objectives

- To learn and understand the following techniques used to analyze and manage risks associated with capital budgeting:
  - Sensitivity analysis;
  - Scenario analysis;
  - Monte Carlo simulation.

Risk analysis plays a crucial role in capital budgeting decisions. It helps organizations evaluate the potential risks associated with investment projects and make informed decisions. By considering the various risks involved, companies can assess the likelihood of success and determine whether the potential returns outweigh the risks.

One important aspect of risk analysis is identifying and analyzing specific risks. This involves examining factors that could negatively impact the project, such as market volatility, changes in government regulations, or technological advancements. By understanding these risks, companies can develop strategies to mitigate them and increase the chances of project success (Haka, 2006).

Another key component of risk analysis is estimating the probability of risks occurring and their potential impact. This requires a thorough analysis of historical data, industry trends, and expert opinions. By quantifying the risks, companies can prioritize them and allocate resources accordingly.

Furthermore, risk analysis helps in determining the appropriate discount rate for calculating the project's net present value (NPV). The discount rate reflects the riskiness of the project and is used to discount future cash flows. By accurately assessing the risks, companies can assign an appropriate discount rate and make more accurate NPV calculations.

In addition, risk analysis enables organizations to compare different investment projects and select the ones that offer the best risk-return trade-off. By evaluating the risks associated with each project, companies can identify the ones with the highest potential returns and the lowest level of risk. This helps in making optimal investment decisions and maximizing shareholder value.

10.5.1. Techniques to Analyze and Manage Risks Associated with Capital Budgeting

Capital budgeting involves making decisions about long-term investments in assets that will generate cash flows over an extended period. As with any investment, there are risks involved that need to be analyzed and managed effectively. The following are some techniques that can be used to analyze and manage these risks.

1. **Sensitivity Analysis:** One technique to analyze risks is sensitivity analysis. This involves examining how changes in key variables, such as sales volume or cost of production, will impact the project's profitability. By varying these variables and observing the resulting changes in the project's net present value (NPV) or internal rate of return (IRR), managers can gain insights into the project's sensitivity to different factors. This information can then be used to make more informed decisions about the project's viability and potential risks.

To illustrate this technique, let's consider an example. Imagine a company is considering investing in a new manufacturing facility. The project's profitability is dependent on various factors, such as the initial investment, production costs, and the selling price of the manufactured goods.

To conduct a sensitivity analysis, managers can identify the key variables that are most likely to affect the project's profitability. In this case, these variables could include the initial investment amount, the cost of raw materials, labor costs, and the selling price of the goods.

Next, managers can assign different values to these variables and observe the resulting changes in the project's profitability. For instance, they can analyze how a 10% increase or decrease in the initial investment would impact the project's net present value (NPV) or internal rate of return (IRR). Similarly, they can examine the effects of changes in raw material costs or labor expenses.

By conducting sensitivity analysis, managers can identify the variables that have the most significant impact on the project's profitability. This allows them to prioritize their risk management efforts and focus on mitigating risks associated with these critical variables. For example, if changes in raw material costs have a substantial impact on profitability, managers can explore strategies to hedge against price fluctuations or seek alternative suppliers.

Furthermore, sensitivity analysis can help managers evaluate the robustness of their capital budgeting decisions. By examining how changes in variables affect the project's profitability, managers can assess the project's sensitivity to different market conditions and potential risks. This information can guide them in making informed decisions and developing contingency plans to address potential challenges (Haka, 2006).

2. **Scenario Analysis:** Another technique is scenario analysis. This involves constructing different scenarios based on different assumptions about future events and their potential impact on the project. By considering a range of possible scenarios, managers can assess the project's vulnerability to different risks and develop contingency plans to mitigate them. For example, if the project

is highly sensitive to changes in interest rates, managers can develop strategies to hedge against interest rate fluctuations.

To illustrate the use of scenario analysis, let's consider an example. Imagine a company is considering investing in a new manufacturing facility. The initial cost of the facility is $10 million, and it is expected to generate annual cash flows of $2 million for the next 10 years.

However, there are several risks associated with this investment. For example, there may be changes in the market demand for the company's products, which could affect the cash flows generated by the facility. Additionally, there could be changes in the cost of raw materials or labor, which could impact the profitability of the project.

To analyze these risks using scenario analysis, the company could consider different scenarios that reflect potential changes in market demand, raw material costs, and labor costs. For example, they could analyze a scenario where market demand decreases by 20%, raw material costs increase by 10%, and labor costs increase by 5%.

By examining the potential impact of these scenarios on the cash flows generated by the facility, the company can assess the level of risk associated with the investment. They can also develop contingency plans or alternative strategies to mitigate these risks. For example, if the analysis shows that the investment becomes unprofitable under certain scenarios, the company may decide to delay or abandon the project.

3. **Monte Carlo simulation:** It is another useful technique for analyzing risks. This involves using computer models to generate a large number of random scenarios based on probability distributions of key variables. By simulating the project's cash flows under different scenarios, managers can estimate the probability of achieving certain financial outcomes and assess the project's risk profile. This information can then be used to make more informed decisions about the project's feasibility and potential risks.

To illustrate the application of the Monte Carlo simulation, let's consider an example. Suppose a company is considering investing in a new manufacturing facility. The decision-makers want to assess the risks associated with this investment before making a final decision.

First, they identify the key variables that could impact the project's financial performance, such as the initial investment cost, operating costs, sales volume, and selling price. They then assign probability distributions to these variables based on historical data, expert opinions, or market research.

Next, they use the Monte Carlo simulation to generate a large number of scenarios, each representing a different combination of values for the variables. By running the simulation multiple times, they can obtain a range of possible outcomes and their associated probabilities (Haka, 2006).

The decision-makers can then analyze these outcomes to assess the risks associated with the investment. They can identify the scenarios with the highest and lowest returns, as well as the most likely outcome. This information can help them make a more informed decision and develop strategies to manage the identified risks.

Once risks have been analyzed, they

need to be managed effectively. One technique for managing risks is diversification. By investing in a portfolio of projects with different risk profiles, managers can reduce the overall risk of the capital budgeting process. This is because the risks associated with individual projects are likely to offset each other, resulting in a more stable and predictable cash flow stream.

Another technique is risk sharing. This involves transferring some of the project's risks to external parties, such as insurance companies or suppliers. For example, managers can purchase insurance policies to protect against the risk of equipment failure or supply disruptions. By sharing risks with external parties, managers can reduce the potential financial impact of these risks and improve the project's overall risk-return profile (Haka, 2006).

Did You Understand?

1. What are the techniques used to analyze and manage risks associated with capital budgeting?
2. How can managers effectively analyze and manage risks using these techniques?

Answer 1:

- Sensitivity analysis;
- Scenario analysis;
- Monte Carlo simulation.

Answer 2:

- Sensitivity analysis involves examining how changes in key variables impact the project's profitability, allowing managers to prioritize risk management efforts.
- Scenario analysis involves constructing different scenarios based on assumptions about future events, helping managers assess the project's vulnerability to risks and develop contingency plans.
- Monte Carlo simulation involves generating random scenarios to estimate the probability of achieving certain financial outcomes, enabling managers to make informed decisions and manage risks effectively.

10.6. CAPITAL RATIONING

Learning Objectives

- To learn and understand the concept of capital rationing.

Capital rationing refers to the process of allocating limited financial resources among various investment projects. In simpler terms, it involves making decisions about which projects to invest in when there is a constraint on the availability of funds (Bierman & Smidt, 2012).

The concept of capital rationing arises when a company has more investment opportunities than it has funds to invest. This can occur due to various reasons, such as limited access to external financing, a desire to maintain a certain debt-to-equity ratio, or a need to prioritize certain projects over others.

When faced with capital rationing, companies must carefully evaluate and select the projects that offer the highest return on investment. This requires analyzing the potential profitability, risks, and expected cash flows of each project. By doing so, companies can determine which projects align with their strategic goals and provide the most value.

Capital rationing also involves setting a maximum limit on the total amount of funds that can be allocated to investments. This limit helps companies prioritize projects and avoid overextending their financial resources. By establishing a capital budget, companies can ensure that they make the most efficient use of their available funds.

To illustrate this concept, let's consider a hypothetical scenario. Company XYZ has a total capital budget of $1 million and is evaluating three potential investment projects: Project A, Project B, and Project C. Each project requires a different amount of capital investment and is expected to generate varying returns.

Project A requires an investment of $400,000 and is estimated to generate a return of $200,000 per year for the next five years. Project B requires a larger investment of $600,000 but is projected to yield a higher return of $300,000 annually for the next five years. Lastly, Project C demands the largest investment of $800,000 but promises the highest return of $400,000 per year for the next five years.

Given the limited capital budget, Company XYZ must carefully consider the potential returns and risks associated with each project to make an informed decision.

One method for allocating resources is the profitability index, which calculates the ratio of the present value of expected cash flows to the initial investment. By comparing the profitability index of each project, Company XYZ can determine which project offers the highest return per dollar invested.

Another method for allocating limited resources is the payback period, which measures the time it takes for an investment to recoup its initial cost. Company XYZ can compare the payback periods of each project and prioritize those with shorter payback periods, as they provide a quicker return on investment.

Additionally, Company XYZ may consider the risk associated with each project. If Project A has a lower risk profile compared to Project B and Project C, it may be more favorable to allocate a larger portion of the capital budget to Project A, ensuring a more stable return on investment.

10.7. REAL OPTIONS ANALYSIS

Learning Objectives

- To learn and understand the concept of real options analysis.

Real options analysis is particularly useful in evaluating investments that have uncertainty and flexibility. It recognizes that investments are not static decisions made at a single point in time, but rather dynamic processes that can be adjusted based on changing circumstances and new information. By considering the value of embedded options, investors can make more informed decisions and better manage risk.

One key concept in real options analysis is the idea that options have value. Traditional investment valuation methods, such as discounted cash flow analysis, often fail to capture the full value of flexibility and uncertainty in investment decisions. Real options analysis aims to address this limitation by explicitly considering the value of embedded options (Bierman & Smidt, 2012).

There are several types of embedded options that can be evaluated using real options analysis. The option to expand allows investors to increase their investment if certain conditions are met, such as increased demand or improved market conditions. This option can be valuable if there is a high likelihood of future growth.

The option to defer allows investors to delay their investment decision until more information becomes available. This can be useful in situations where there is uncertainty about future market conditions or technological advancements. By deferring the investment, investors can gather more information and make a more informed decision.

According to Cooremans (2009) views, the option to abandon allows investors to exit an investment if it is not performing as expected. This option can be valuable in situations where there is a high risk of failure or if market conditions change significantly. By having the option to abandon, investors can limit their losses and avoid sunk costs.

The option to switch allows investors to switch to an alternative investment if it becomes more attractive. This option can be valuable in situations where there are multiple investment opportunities with varying levels of risk and return. By having the option to switch, investors can take advantage of changing market conditions and make the most profitable investment decision.

Real options analysis involves estimating the value of these embedded options using various quantitative and qualitative techniques. These techniques can include decision trees, Monte Carlo simulations, and real options pricing models. By incorporating these techniques into the investment evaluation process, investors can better understand the potential value and risks associated with their investment decisions.

Remember

Real options analysis recognizes that investment decisions often involve flexibility. By considering the value of future options to expand, abandon, or delay a project, decision-makers can make more informed choices.

To illustrate the application of real options analysis, imagine a company, XYZ Inc., that is considering investing in a new product line. This investment would require a substantial amount of capital, and there is uncertainty regarding the demand and profitability of the new product. However, there are also potential opportunities for expansion and growth in the future.

Using traditional investment valuation methods, such as discounted cash flow analysis, XYZ Inc. may determine that the investment does not meet the required return on investment threshold. However, this approach fails to consider the potential value of the embedded options associated with the investment.

By applying real options analysis, XYZ Inc. can evaluate the value of the embedded options and make a more informed decision. Real options analysis recognizes that the investment in the new product line provides XYZ Inc. with the flexibility to adapt and respond to changing market conditions. It allows the company to delay, expand, or abandon the investment based on future developments.

For example, if XYZ Inc. invests in the new product line and the demand exceeds expectations, the company can expand production and capture additional market share. This expansion option has value because it allows XYZ Inc. to generate additional profits. On the other hand, if the demand is lower than anticipated, the company can choose to delay or abandon the investment, minimizing potential losses.

Real options analysis also considers the potential for future growth opportunities. For instance, if XYZ Inc. successfully enters the market with the new product line, it may gain a competitive advantage and open doors for further expansion. This growth option has value as it allows the company to capitalize on future opportunities and increase its overall value.

By evaluating these embedded options, real options analysis provides XYZ Inc. with a more comprehensive understanding of the potential value of the investment. It enables the company to make better-informed decisions by considering the flexibility and potential future opportunities associated with the investment.

10.8. DECISION TREES

Learning Objectives

- To learn and understand the concept of decision trees.

Decision trees offer a visual depiction of decision-making processes. They are a useful tool in analyzing complex investment decisions because they provide a structured framework to evaluate various possible outcomes and their associated probabilities. By mapping out the decision tree, investors can gain a better understanding of the potential risks and rewards of their investment choices (Bierman & Smidt, 2012) (Figure 10.4).

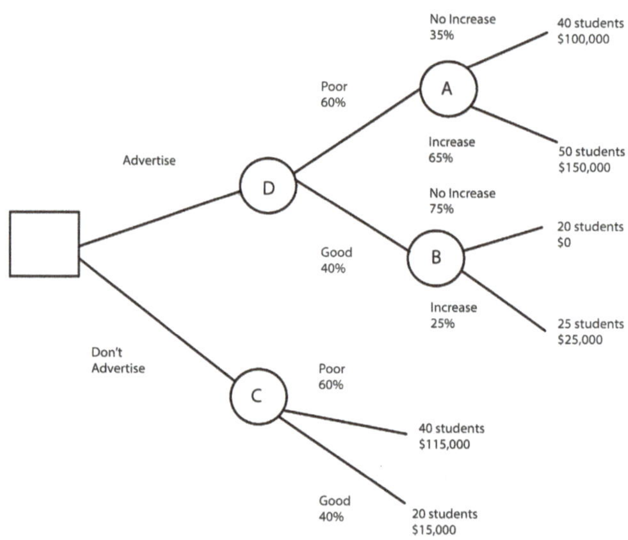

Figure 10.4. *A decision tree illustration.*

Source: Decision Trees (n.d.).

Now, let's consider a hypothetical example to illustrate the application of decision trees in investment analysis. Imagine a company, XYZ Corporation, is considering whether to invest in a new product line. The decision tree will help them evaluate the potential outcomes and probabilities associated with this investment.

The first step in constructing the decision tree is to identify the key decision points and the possible outcomes at each point. In this case, the initial decision point is whether to invest in the new product line or not. The possible outcomes are successful market penetration, moderate market penetration, or market failure.

Next, we assign probabilities to each outcome based on historical data, market research, and expert opinions. Let's assume there is a 40% chance of successful market penetration, a 50% chance of moderate market penetration, and a 10% chance of market failure.

Once the decision points and probabilities are determined, we can proceed to calculate the expected values associated with each outcome. The expected value is the sum of the product of each outcome's probability and its corresponding payoff. For instance, if successful market penetration yields a profit of $500,000, moderate market penetration yields a profit of $200,000, and market failure results in a loss of $300,000, the expected value can be calculated as follows:

$$\text{Expected value} = (0.4 \times \$500{,}000) + (0.5 \times \$200{,}000) + (0.1 \times -\$300{,}000) = \$200{,}000$$

The expected value represents the average outcome of the investment decision. In this case, the expected value is $200,000. However, it is important to note that the expected value alone does not provide a complete picture of the investment's risk and potential return.

To further evaluate the investment decision, we can calculate the decision tree's utility value. The utility value incorporates the investor's risk tolerance and preferences. By assigning utility values to each outcome, we can assess the investor's satisfaction or dissatisfaction with the potential outcomes.

For example, let's assume that the investor assigns a utility value of 0.8 to successful market penetration, 0.6 to moderate market penetration, and 0.2 to market failure. We can then calculate the utility value of the decision tree as follows:

$$\text{Utility value} = (0.4 \times 0.8) + (0.5 \times 0.6) + (0.1 \times 0.2) = 0.62$$

The utility value indicates the overall desirability of the investment decision. In this case, the utility value is 0.62, suggesting that the investor would be reasonably satisfied with the potential outcomes.

By using decision trees, investors can gain valuable insights into the risks and rewards associated with complex investment decisions. The visual representation allows for a clearer understanding of the decision-making process and facilitates the evaluation of various possible outcomes and their probabilities. Additionally, incorporating utility values enables investors to consider their risk tolerance and preferences when assessing the desirability of the decision (Cooremans, 2009).

Did You Understand?

1. What is capital rationing?
2. What are some methods for allocating resources during capital rationing?
3. What are the main types of embedded options that can be evaluated using real options analysis?
4. How can real options analysis help investors make more informed decisions and better manage risk?
5. How do decision trees assist investors in evaluating complex investment decisions?

Answer 1: Capital rationing refers to the process of allocating limited financial resources among investment projects when there is a constraint on the availability of funds.

Answer 2: Some methods for allocating resources during capital rationing include using the profitability index to determine the return per dollar invested and using the payback period to prioritize investments with shorter payback periods. Companies may also consider the risk associated with each project when making allocation decisions.

Answer 3: The main types of embedded options that can be evaluated using real options analysis are the option to expand, the option to defer, the option to abandon, and the option to switch.

Answer 4: Real options analysis recognizes that investments are dynamic processes that can be adjusted based on changing circumstances and new information. By considering the value of embedded options, investors can make more informed decisions and better manage risk.

Answer 5: Decision trees provide a visual depiction of decision-making processes and offer a structured framework to evaluate various possible outcomes and their associated probabilities. By mapping out the decision tree, investors can gain a better understanding of the potential risks and rewards of their investment choices.

CASE STUDY

- **Introduction:** This case study aims to analyze the capital budgeting and decision-making process of POWERCHINA, a leading global engineering and construction company. The company operates in various sectors, including power generation, transmission, and distribution, as well as infrastructure development. The case study will focus on a specific project undertaken by POWERCHINA and evaluate the decision-making process behind it.
- **Background:** POWERCHINA was approached by a government agency to construct a hydropower plant in a remote region. The project involved building a dam, power generation facilities, and transmission lines. The estimated cost of the project was $1 billion, with a projected lifespan of 30 years. The government agency offered to provide a loan at a 5% interest rate to finance the project. POWERCHINA had to evaluate the financial viability of the project and decide whether to proceed.
- **Capital Budgeting Analysis:** To assess the financial feasibility of the project, POWERCHINA conducted a capital budgeting analysis. The analysis involved estimating the project's cash inflows and outflows over its lifespan and calculating various financial metrics.
- **Cash Inflows:** The primary source of cash inflows for the project was the revenue generated from selling electricity. POWERCHINA estimated the annual revenue based on the projected electricity generation capacity of the hydropower plant and the prevailing electricity prices. Other potential sources of cash inflows included government subsidies and carbon credits.
- **Cash Outflows:** The major cash outflows for the project included construction costs, operating expenses, and maintenance costs. POWERCHINA estimated these costs based on industry benchmarks and historical data from similar projects.
- **Financial Metrics:** To evaluate the financial viability of the project, POWERCHINA calculated several financial metrics, including net present value (NPV), internal rate of return (IRR), and payback period. NPV measures the project's profitability by calculating the present value of its cash inflows and outflows. IRR represents the project's rate of return, while the payback period indicates the time required to recover the initial investment.
- **Decision Analysis:** Based on the capital budgeting analysis, POWERCHINA determined that the project had a positive NPV, indicating its profitability. The IRR was higher than the government's cost of capital, suggesting a favorable return on investment. Additionally, the payback period was within an acceptable range. Considering these factors, POWERCHINA decided to proceed with the project.
- **Conclusion:** This case study highlights the importance of capital budgeting and decision analysis in assessing the financial viability of projects. By conducting a thorough analysis of cash inflows, outflows, and financial metrics, POWERCHINA was able to make an informed decision regarding the hydropower plant project. The company's decision to proceed was based on the positive NPV, favorable IRR, and acceptable payback period. This case study demonstrates the significance of financial analysis in guiding investment decisions and ensuring the long-term success of projects.

SUMMARY

Chapter 10 discusses capital budgeting as the process of planning and managing long-term investments in a business. It involves assessing potential projects, determining their viability, and allocating financial resources accordingly. One method commonly used in capital budgeting is the Payback Period, which calculates the time required for an investment to recover its initial cost. Another method is the Net Present Value (NPV) analysis, which discounts future cash flows to their present value and subtracts the initial investment. The Internal Rate of Return (IRR) calculates the discount rate at which the NPV becomes zero. Sensitivity analysis assesses the impact of changes in key variables on the profitability of an investment. Risk analysis evaluates potential risks associated with an investment, such as market risk, technological risk, and financial risk. To mitigate these risks, organizations can employ strategies like diversification and using risk-adjusted discount rates. The time value of money is a fundamental concept in finance that recognizes the idea that money available in the present is worth more than the same amount of money in the future. Discounting future cash flows to their present value is a common practice in financial analysis, allowing investors to compare different investment opportunities and assess their profitability.

The cost of capital is an important factor to consider when making investment decisions. It is the rate of return that must be earned on an investment project to satisfy the expectations of investors and lenders. The cost of capital is determined by factors such as the risk associated with the investment project, prevailing interest rates, and the company's own cost of borrowing. The riskier the investment project, the higher the cost of capital will be. When interest rates are high, the cost of capital will also be high. The company's own cost of borrowing also affects the cost of capital. There are several methods for calculating the cost of capital, including the Dividend Growth Model (DGM), Capital Asset Pricing Model (CAPM), and Weighted Average Cost of Capital (WACC). Each method has its own strengths and weaknesses. The DGM calculates the cost of equity by estimating future dividends and discounting them back to the present value. The CAPM takes into account the risk-free rate of return, expected market return, and the beta of the company's stock. The WACC calculates the overall cost of capital by considering the proportion of debt and equity in the company's capital structure. It is important for businesses to understand the different sources of capital, such as equity financing, debt financing, and retained earnings, and how to estimate their costs. The cost of equity can be estimated using methods like the dividend discount model or the CAPM, while the cost of debt is determined by factors such as interest rates and fees. By understanding these sources of capital and their costs, businesses can make informed decisions about financing their operations and investments.

Cash flow estimation is crucial in capital budgeting as it helps in making informed investment decisions. It involves estimating future cash flows and discounting them to determine their present value. Accurate forecasting of cash flows is essential to assess the profitability and feasibility of potential investments. Mistakes in cash flow estimation include not considering all relevant costs and revenues, not accounting for the timing of cash flows, and not assessing potential risks or uncertainties. Techniques for forecasting cash flows include incremental cash flows, pro forma financial statements, and sensitivity analysis. Incremental cash flows focus on the additional cash flows resulting from a specific project. Pro forma financial statements are hypothetical statements that project the financial performance of a company under different scenarios. Sensitivity analysis assesses the impact of changes in key variables on cash flows. These techniques provide valuable insights into the potential cash flows associated with a capital investment project, helping businesses make informed decisions and accurately assess the financial viability of their investment options.

Capital budgeting techniques are used by businesses to evaluate investment opportunities and determine their profitability and feasibility. One such technique is the payback period, which calculates the time required for an investment to recoup its initial cost. The net present value (NPV) is another technique that measures the difference between the present value of cash inflows and outflows over a specific time period. A positive NPV indicates a profitable investment. The internal rate of return (IRR) is a metric that represents the annualized rate of return from an investment and is used to compare different investment opportunities. The profitability index is a tool that evaluates the potential profitability of an investment project by dividing the present value of future cash flows by the initial investment cost. A value greater than 1 indicates a profitable project. These techniques help businesses make informed investment decisions by assessing the financial viability and potential returns of projects.

Risk analysis is an important part of capital budgeting decisions as it helps organizations evaluate potential risks and make informed choices. It involves identifying and analyzing specific risks, estimating their probability and impact, and determining the appropriate discount rate for calculating net present value (NPV). Risk analysis also helps in comparing different investment projects and selecting the ones with the best risk-return trade-off. Techniques such as sensitivity analysis, scenario analysis, and Monte Carlo simulation can be used to analyze and manage risks. Diversification and risk sharing are effective strategies for managing risks in capital budgeting.

Capital rationing refers to the process of allocating limited financial resources among different investment projects when there is a constraint on the availability of funds. Companies must carefully evaluate and select projects that offer the highest return on investment. This can be done by analyzing potential profitability, risks, and expected cash flows. Setting a maximum limit on the total amount of funds that can be allocated to investments helps companies prioritize projects and avoid overextending their financial resources. Real options analysis is a method used to evaluate investments that have uncertainty and flexibility. It recognizes that investments are dynamic processes that can be adjusted based on changing circumstances and new information. Real options analysis considers the value of embedded options, such as the option to expand, defer, abandon, or switch investments. By estimating the value of these options, investors can make more informed decisions and better manage risk. Decision trees are a visual tool used to analyze complex investment decisions. They provide a structured framework to evaluate various possible outcomes and their associated probabilities. Decision trees help investors understand the potential risks and rewards of their investment choices by mapping out the decision-making process.

MULTIPLE CHOICE QUESTIONS

1. **What is capital budgeting?**
   a. The process of planning and managing short-term investments in a business.
   b. The process of planning and managing long-term investments in a business.
   c. The process of allocating financial resources for daily operations in a business.
   d. The process of determining the profitability of an investment in a business.
2. **Which method in capital budgeting calculates the time required for an investment to recover the initial investment?**
   a. Payback Period.
   b. Net Present Value (NPV) analysis.
   c. Internal Rate of Return (IRR).
   d. Sensitivity analysis.
3. **What is one of the main reasons why accurate estimation of cash flows is important in capital budgeting?**
   a. To determine the profitability and feasibility of potential investments
   b. To analyze potential risks and uncertainties
   c. To assess the timing and amount of cash inflows and outflows
   d. To evaluate the financial impact of potential investments
4. **What is one common mistake in cash flow estimation?**
   a. Failing to consider all relevant costs and revenues
   b. Not accounting for the timing of cash flows
   c. Ignoring potential risks and uncertainties
   d. Overestimating future cash flows
5. **What technique is used to estimate the additional cash flows resulting from a specific project?**
   a. Pro forma financial statements
   b. Sensitivity analysis
   c. Incremental cash flows
   d. Payback period
6. **What financial metric calculates the length of time required for an investment to recoup its initial cost?**
   a. Net present value (NPV)
   b. Internal rate of return (IRR)
   c. Payback period
   d. Profitability index

7. What financial metric is used to determine the profitability of an investment by measuring the difference between the present value of cash inflows and outflows?

a. Net present value (NPV)

b. Internal rate of return (IRR)

c. Payback period

d. Profitability index

8. What is one important aspect of risk analysis in capital budgeting?

a. Identifying and analyzing specific risks

b. Calculating net present value

c. Allocating resources accordingly

d. Comparing investment projects

9. What is one technique used to analyze risks in capital budgeting?

a. Sensitivity analysis

b. Payback period

c. Real options analysis

d. Decision trees

10. What is one method for allocating limited resources in capital rationing?

a. Profitability index

b. Monte Carlo simulation

c. Risk sharing

d. Real options analysis

11. What is one key concept in real options analysis?

a. Options have value

b. Payback period

c. Sensitivity analysis

d. Monte Carlo simulation

12. What is one benefit of using decision trees in investment analysis?

a. Provides a structured framework

b. Calculates net present value

c. Estimates the probability of risks

d. Determines the appropriate discount rate

Answers to Multiple Choice Questions

1. (b); 2. (a); 3. (a); 4. (a); 5. (c); 6. (c); 7. (a); 8. (a); 9. (a); 10. (a); 11. (a); 12. (a)

REFERENCES

1. Baker, H. K., & English, P., (2011). Capital budgeting: An overview. *Capital Budgeting Valuation: Financial Analysis for Todays Investment Projects*, 1–16.
2. Bennouna, K., Meredith, G. G., & Marchant, T., (2010). Improved capital budgeting decision making: Evidence from Canada. *Management Decision*, *48*(2), 225–247.
3. Bierman, Jr. H., & Smidt, S., (2012). *The Capital Budgeting Decision: Economic Analysis of Investment Projects*. Routledge.
4. Cooremans, C., (2009). *The Role of Formal Capital Budgeting Analysis in Corporate Investment Decision-Making: A Literature Review*. In ECEEE Summer Study.
5. *Decision Trees*, (n.d.). Default. https://kfknowledgebank.kaplan.co.uk/decision-trees- (accessed on 04 April 2024).
6. Haka, S. F., (2006). A review of the literature on capital budgeting and investment appraisal: Past, present, and future musings. *Handbooks of Management Accounting Research*, *2*, 697–728.
7. MoneyUncle. (2022). *Power of Compounding in Stock Market*. https://www.linkedin.com/pulse/power-compounding-stock-market-askmoneyuncle/ (accessed on 04 April 2024).
8. Nordqvist, C., (2024). *What is the Time Value of Money? Definition and Examples*. Market Business News. https://marketbusinessnews.com/financial-glossary/time-value-of-money/ (accessed on 04 April 2024).
9. Peterson, P. P., & Fabozzi, F. J., (2002). *Capital Budgeting: Theory and Practice* (Vol. 10). John Wiley & Sons.
10. *Pro Forma Financial Statements*, (2023). QuickBooks Australia. https://quickbooks.intuit.com/au/blog/running-a-business/pro-forma-financial-statements/ (accessed on 04 April 2

Index

FSC
www.fsc.org
MIX
Papier | Fördert
gute Waldnutzung
FSC® C083411

Kolibri 360 GmbH
Ferdinand-Jühlke-Straße 7
99095 Erfurt, Deutschland
produktsicherheit@kolibri360.de